Exile to Sweet Dixie

The Story of Euphemia Goldsborough, Confederate Nurse and Smuggler

by E. F. Conklin

Thomas Publications
Gettysburg, PA 17325

*This book is dedicated to my mother and father
who gave me a life of unconditional love.*

ɞ   ɞ   ɞ

*This work is also dedicated with affection to
Elizabeth Crim
the granddaughter of Euphemia Goldsborough
and Betsy Stagner
the great grand-daughter
and to all subsequent generations
of these three remarkable women.*

"...I fear I am <u>implicated most seriously</u> in the <u>attempted</u> escape of prisoner. A letter <u>directed</u> was found on his person and probably I shall go to "Sweet Dixie" sooner than you however I am not one <u>bit afraid</u> & <u>defy</u> the whole <u>Yankee Nation send me where they will</u>. I am <u>able</u> & <u>willing</u> to <u>suffer hardships</u> & <u>loss</u> for <u>myself</u> for the sake of a <u>country</u> & <u>people that I love</u>..." [1]

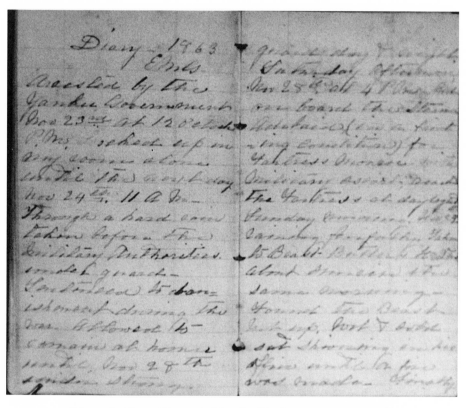

Pheme's diary, "Arrested by the Yankee government..."

Table of Contents

Preface

This book, which offers the highlights of the personal life and war experiences of Euphemia Mary Goldsborough, is based on the Goldsborough collection. Researching the collection has been both an honor and a responsibility; a delight and a nightmare. Pheme's phonetic spelling, the incomplete Confederate records available, and the propensity of Southerners to go by their middle names, made verification and research of the individuals sharing her experiences quite a challenge.

I first came across the Goldsborough collection when I was researching *Women at Gettysburg-1863* and included Euphemia in that volume. I knew then that she needed an entire book to cover the material so lovingly preserved by her descendants. There are a few war era women well known to history who have a great deal of information compiled on their lives in publications or in museums or archives. We all know their names; they are in our history books and our encyclopedias. However, in two decades of researching women in the Civil War, I have never come across a collection of this size or content concerning an extraordinary, yet almost unknown, woman of the war. Hopefully, there are others out there; if so, they would certainly be an important addition to the growing base of information now coming to light on women's war service.

The Goldsborough collection is an extensive one. It includes furniture, household goods, clothing and personal items, jewelry, quilts, diaries, documents, letters, manuscripts, flags, photographs, prints, Confederate bonds and currency, a journal, newspapers, notices, broadsides, tickets, invitations, cards, art work, maps, passes, appointments, poetry, and war mementos such as hair from Stonewall Jackson's horse and Confederate uniform buttons and emblems. Unfortunately, some of the written items have been stolen, but the transcripts are still available. Most of the collection's items pertain to Civil War era history and this book contains the research on those selected items. They are organized into several chapters and appendices for clarity.

The heart of the collection is two leather bound volumes. Originally there had been three, but the third was one of the items stolen. In these volumes are the autographs of over a hundred men with whom Pheme was in contact during her time as a nurse to Confederate wounded at Gettysburg. These volumes also served as a diary which she commenced when she was arrested and exiled in November 1863 and cover subsequent years to 1868. The intermingled text is separated into two chapters: "The Hospital Books" and "The Diaries."

There are a number of other Gettysburg related items which are also shown in this book. In my years as a Licensed Battlefield Guide at Gettysburg, I had never seen a Confederate nurse's pass for that field. The Goldsborough collection has two, plus the glass she used to quench the thirst of the wounded. Also included are letters exchanged between Pheme and her former Gettysburg patients imprisoned in the North.

This is a piece of the Confederate experience of the War Between the States, "one little thread in the warp of the great movement." It is a story of one woman's personal courage and endurance and her commitment to Southern Independence. Additional text on the events and environment that influenced that experience are seen through Southern eyes. To perceive Euphemia Goldsborough's story, it can be viewed no other way.

On a personal note, Pheme was with me during a number of private tragedies and losses. Researching her story provided, in part, the strength I needed to face my own life's duties and struggles. It is hard to let her go. But go she must; her story very much deserves to be heard. I sincerely hope I have done her justice.

Acknowledgments

There are a number of individuals who contributed their time and energy to my search for the identity of the people in this book. After exhausting every source of which I knew, I turned to those listed below and they responded quickly and generously.

First and foremost is DeAnne Blanton, Military Archivist at the National Archives in Washington, DC. DeAnne located the sources for a number of seemingly impossible identifications. It is my good fortune to count such a knowledgeable person as a friend. Colonel Robert Driver, historian of Confederate Rockbridge County, was very generous in sharing his extensive research. He identified veterans in Pheme's diary from the barest of details. Jill McGown of the Leyburn Library, Washington and Lee University, provided maps, letters, and the manuscripts to identify the elusive Mohler clan. Daniel Hartzler, acknowledged expert on Confederate Maryland troops, verified some of the names and units. Alice Williams from the Historical Society of Rockbridge County spent two days helping me go through the genealogy of Rockbridge's families. Louise Arnold-Friend, of the United States Military History Institute, took on the gruesome task of finding out who some of these individuals could not have been. Also Robert Trout, researcher and writer on the Confederate cavalry, for his assistance.

There was assistance given in other ways. Kathie Tennery, friend, colleague, and font of information, pointed me in the direction of Rockbridge researchers, including Winifred Hadsel, for help in locating sites. Randy Herrell of Alabama, an admirer of Pheme's, loaned General Lee's photograph inscribed to her for inclusion in this book. Marie Melchiori, friend, colleague, and researcher extraordinaire, located and copied Pheme's complete Provost Marshal file. Any researcher blessed with Marie's help is lucky indeed. Danielle Nelson, former ranger at City Point, identified the name of the Confederate truce boat. David Johnson, librarian at the Casemate Museum, donated the photo of Fort Monroe and explained the logistics of Pheme's arrival, stay, and departure.

Thanks also to my friend, Susan Hanson, for all the help on that memorable frozen research trip to Rockbridge County and the hours spent proofing. Thanks to Marge Estilow for her time and help proofing the manuscript. My appreciation goes to the staff at C. Burr Artz, Frederick County's library for their ready and generous help to find obscure historical details and provide resources.

This is an opportunity to gratefully acknowledge the staff at Thomas Publications not only for their work and input, but for their support and interest in women's history. Research on women's service and experiences during the war would be of little use if it were not shared through publication.

But none of the above would have been called upon if the Goldsborough collection had not been preserved with due honor by Mrs. Elizabeth Crim, Pheme's granddaughter. Spending time with Miss Elizabeth was a delight. The opportunity to meet and know her was possibly the best part of this project. It is through her generosity that Pheme's story is remembered and her service recognized. Mrs. Betsy Stagner, Pheme's great granddaughter, was very much part of this effort. She is a gracious hostess and an enthusiastic supporter; adding greatly to the pleasure of the work on this book. Mrs. Stagner has obviously inherited the Goldsborough commitment to family and life's other real values. I am personally and professionally indebted to both ladies. They have provided a gift to all who cherish Confederate history.

And lastly, but forever, my gratitude to my husband and son, who adopted Pheme into the family and lived with her the last four years. But above all, for standing by me during those years, as the strong and loving men they are, through some of the darkest days of my life.

Psalm 26

Judge me, O Lord; for I have walked in mine integrity; I have trusted also in the Lord; therefore I shall not slide.

Examine me, O Lord, and prove me; try my reins and my heart.

For thy loving kindness is before mine eyes: and I have walked in thy truth.

I have not sat with vain persons, neither will I go in with dissemblers.

I have hated the congregation of evil doers; and will not sit with the wicked.

I will wash mine hands in innocency: so will I compass thine altar, O Lord:

That I may publish with the voice of Thanksgiving, and tell all of thy wondrous works.

Lord, I have loved the habitation of thy house, and the place where thine honor dwelleth.

Gather not my soul with sinners, nor my life with bloody men;

In whose hands is mischief, and their right hand is full of bribes.

But as for me, I will walk in mine integrity: redeem me, and be merciful unto me.

My foot standeth in an even place: in the congregations will I bless the Lord.

The Life and Times of Euphemia Goldsborough

The Times

"Oh, Liberty! how many crimes are committed in the name!"[1]

From its inception, the United States did not enjoy a harmonious spirit among its people. Sectional agendas of protective tariffs and measures to limit growth, diverse cultural backgrounds and values, and the ethical question of slavery protected by the Constitution precluded a lasting union. The Federal government could not and did not serve the interests of all its citizens.

It has been said that the seeds of civil wars grow at home in the hearts of men where outrage upon outrage blossoms into an anger that does not look back. In those stirring and terrible times preceding our Civil War, there was no realistic retreat from passions created by unforgivable acts and unforgiving reactions. The growing chasm between the people that led to secession could no longer be bridged by tolerance and compromise for the common good. The election of Lincoln was more an excuse than a reason for disunion. The reasons had been supplied long before 1860.

There are a variety of reasons for civil wars and for our country one of the most emotional, then and now, is that of slavery. It is interesting to note that the abolition movement in Maryland began as early as 1789. The American Colonization Society, which was funded by state constitutional law, expended over a quarter of a million dollars in manumissions. "In no State of the Union had emancipation as rapidly progressed as in Maryland...."[2] By 1860 there were 87,188 slaves in Maryland, slightly less than 13% of the total population which included about the same number of free blacks. "Maryland did all this with limited means, and with no parade or ostentation of humanity, and her whole people approved the legislation."[3]

The citizens of Maryland resented the activities of the Northern abolition movement and saw such events as the Nat Turner Rebellion and John Brown's Raid as the consequence of the "madness of fanaticism."

> *In fact, public sentiment was in favor of the gradual extinction of slavery in the state, but in consequence of the violent denunciation and improper interference of Northern abolitionists, a reaction had taken place, not in public sentiment, but in public policy.[4]*
>
> *The objects of the abolitionists were destructive and negative. They simply proposed to destroy an institution...which would ruin the agricultural system of the South...Compensating advantages they had none to offer...If let alone, Maryland, we repeat, would in time have become a free State, but the interference of the abolitionists on the North prevented that result.[5]*

These expressed feelings of nineteenth century Marylanders may have been similar to those experienced by Pheme, an independent minded young woman, and her family. In a letter in the Provost Marshal section of this volume, Pheme strongly derides the "emancipation man." It would seem that Pheme found only the tactics and aggression offensive, for indeed, the Goldsboroughs owned no slaves. The 1860 census lists one white servant in the Goldsborough home [Ann Wilson] and, ironically, Pheme's only surviving child would bear the same name.

&a.   &a.   &a.

There can be little understanding of Pheme's experiences and feelings if her environment is not explored. The risks involved in her service to the Confederacy while a resident of Baltimore cannot be appreciated unless one is acquainted with some of the events and activities of that city both before and during the war. The increasingly oppressive state of military occupation, the Unionist's control of civic and public entities, the physical assaults, and wholesale arrests of Southern sympathizers made daily life exceedingly dangerous. Pheme and her family, who no doubt wholeheartedly supported her efforts for the South, were among many who would pay the penalty for adhering to their beliefs. Whether the Goldsborough family were from the start devoted sympathizers of Southern Independence is not known. It would be easy to accept that many citizens of Baltimore, indeed of the state of Maryland, were thrust into that position of sympathy merely because the actions that were enforced by the Federal government and its military were so outrageous.

The following is by no means a thorough compilation of events in Baltimore's war time history. The events chosen are to illustrate those that would have affected anyone with leanings towards the South, especially the Goldsborough family, and specifically Pheme herself. These events emphasize the risk that she took in her smuggling activities and may also explain the sentiments revealed in a letter from March 1863 when Pheme wrote of the Yankees: "I just hate the very air they breathe and would like to kill every one I see."

Baltimore was a disturbing place to live in the 1850s, which was the decade in which the Goldsborough family moved into the city. The Know Nothing Society politicized as the American Party had a stranglehold on the city through its officials and the elections held that decade were marked by riots and murder. The Know Nothing Society viewed both foreigners and Catholics as "undesirables" along with anyone not in sympathy with their doctrine. Naturalized citizens and others were driven from the polls unable to cast their votes. Elections were "a mockery of elective franchise...it became manifest that no free or fair expression of the popular will...would be permitted by the bands of armed and lawless ruffians who took and maintained possession of the polls."[6] At noon on one mayoral election day, the opposing candidate withdrew his name from the ballot on the grounds that "any persistent attempts to vote upon the part of my friends can only be attended with loss of life and the general disorder of [the] city."[7]

The police, all Know Nothings, "made no effort to protect citizens...but remained unconcerned spectators of the violence to which they were subjected."[8] This extended to taking over important industries, driving "undesirables" from employment, ignoring the rights of property owners, outrages perpetuated on innocent citizens, robberies on public highways, savage assaults, murders in the streets and in the homes. All of this was overseen by a system of "recognized violence and despotic ruffianism" infamous for a lack of arrests and release of those few arrested, and "no official vigilance to protect the citizens."[9]

A bipartisan "City Reform Association" was finally organized that petitioned the state legislature in 1860 for help which came in the passage of reform bills. The police bill, the election law, and the jury law manifested in the removal of judges, the election of 1859 declared null and void, and new appointments for police officials. "It is impossible to overrate the change that the organization of an efficient police force wrought in the condition of the city...",[10] when a new election brought in a reform mayor and city council. The internal chaos that rocked the city for years was ended; however, it was but a taste of the harsh military rule Baltimore would endure during the war.

Many Southerners, including those in Maryland, believed that the North wanted war. Peace overtures were rejected and Lincoln's attempt to relieve Fort Sumter was seen as "a feint and a trick to tempt the Confederates into striking the first blow, so that the demagogues might kindle the passions of the North, by talking of insult and outrage to the flag of the Union."[11] The armed soldiers, responding to Lincoln's call for 75,000 volunteers and moving through Baltimore "ostensibly" to protect the capital were seen by Marylanders as hostile invaders, the movement a pretense, with the real intention of securing Maryland in the North. However, on April 18, 1861 the first lot of six hundred soldiers, though met by an angry mob, passed safely through the city.

The next day, April 19, two thousand more Union soldiers arrived in Baltimore to be greeted at the train station by another angry mob that would resist their passage through the city. Even with the mayor personally walking with the troops and the city police risking their lives while forced into the position of violent confrontation with the very citizens they were sworn to protect, the agitation was so great on both sides that violence was inevitable. Four soldiers and twelve civilians died that day. This violence "was a sudden outbreak of indignation, on the part of the people, at the presence and passage of Northern troops, destined, as they believed, to an unconstitutional, and wicked, and uncalled for war upon their brethren."[12]

Maryland's governor called out the militia and the mayor requested that Washington send no more troops through Baltimore until emotions cooled down. But that very night they learned that more regiments were on the road "loud in their threats of vengeance and resolved to fight their way through to Washington" while the city was filled with hundreds of citizens just as determined to resist. The same night both state and city officials agreed to order the railroad bridges into the city burned to prevent certain bloodshed as they were "inflexibly determined to resist all attempts to force the city into secession or into acts of hostility to the Federal government..."[13] Also in April, a special session of the state legislature was called when it declared it had no legal authority to consider secession, but Maryland's efforts to remain neutral were doomed.

Troops were rerouted through Annapolis to Washington and things settled down to the point where a large body of Union soldiers, again escorted by the mayor and a large police presence, passed through the city without incident on May 8. Regardless, on the night of May

13, Major General Benjamin Butler took possession of Federal Hill, an eminence that overlooked the city, thus commencing the military occupation of Baltimore which remained throughout the war. Fort McHenry's batteries would soon turn on the city and a number of other forts were afterward constructed that would encircle the city. Baltimore would eventually be beset with numerous and huge Union general hospitals, Union camps, and barricades.

With the huge guns of Federal Hill turned on Baltimore, Butler issued an order forbidding transportation of supplies to the South, assemblies of any kind, and the display of any Secession flags or banners. All state military officers were to report to him. Although Butler was "rebuked and recalled" for his "unauthorized" occupation of the city, he was merely moved over to command Fort Monroe. Major General George Cadwalader replaced him.

In April, May, and again in June 1861, the state legislature met in Annapolis and denounced the lawless and aggressive policy of which the state was victim and the unconstitutional acts of the administration and its agents. In truth, protest was all they could do. Any armed resistance would not only result in failure but in "certain destruction."

When Lincoln suspended the writ of habeas corpus the wholesale arrests began. All police commissioners were arrested, including Marshal Kane whom Pheme would meet years later in Richmond, the mayor, members of the House of Delegates, Congress, state senators, and newspaper editors. All were held with no charge. The Baltimore police system served as an arm of the provost marshal and its positions were filled by the same "Know Nothings" that had held sway in the 1850s. Long before the state legislature's September 1861 meeting, plans were made for the arrest and quiet transportation of its Southern members. Major General Nathaniel Banks, who replaced Cadwalader for a short time, was given this task and gave his instructions: "It has become necessary that any meeting of the Legislature, at any place or time, shall be prevented...The arrests should be made while they are in session...Any resistance will be forcibly suppressed, whatever the consequences...."[14]

"As to Maryland, we have put the iron heel upon her," crowed one Federal congressman, "and will crush out her borders."[15]

While units were formed within the state for service in the Union Army, thousands of Maryland's Southerners made their way into Confederate lines to serve with the South. "The women of Maryland sent their sons, their husbands, and their lovers to die for the Confederacy. Twenty thousand of the men of Maryland went across the border to the aid of the South...They went to the aid of a free people fighting for the right to govern themselves in safety and in honor."[16] This was done in great secrecy; not only the men but their families were endangered by following the Southern star. Early in the war, one group of men marched out of the city in a mock funeral and, when well out of danger, removed their arms which were concealed in the coffin and slipped away to the South.

The Confederate victory at the first battle of Manassas (July 21, 1861) brought great satisfaction to Baltimore Southerners. Confederate colors were displayed much to the anger of Major General John A. Dix, who had replaced Banks and had forbidden any display of Confederate colors. Information listing the Confederate dead in the newspapers was ordered suspended because it had a "tendency to dignify the Southern rebellion." One Baltimore woman wrote: "When the news came that my brother was killed, it was two weeks before it could be confirmed. Then we had to hire a provost guard to get his body. We were forbidden to hold a funeral, because he was the first Maryland soldier to be brought home, and the authorities feared a demonstration; so we women had to take him in a furniture van to Greenmount [Cemetery], where he was buried without a monument or marked grave."[17]

The Maryland election in November 1861 for governor and other state officials was a repeat of the "shameless mockery" endured during the 1850s. Not only were the polls protected from the "pollution" of the Southern vote, interpreted as anyone opposing the Union candidate, but hundreds more citizens were arrested. In December, the new state officials offered praise and passed resolutions in support of Union activities. New governor Augustus Bradford expressed utmost devotion to the Union and fawned over Lincoln's government, although the newly elected did chide the Federal government for "useless and wicked agitation of the slavery question." Slavery was to be abolished in the District of Columbia in April 1862 and many Maryland slaves, some of whom were owned by Unionists, ran off to the capital.

During the 1861-62 session the Treason Bill was passed. Its provisions listed a myriad of "treasonable" acts and the varying subsequent punishment, including death. Although this stringent bill would be little used, the citizens of Maryland did not know that. The content of the bill made an impression on Pheme. She cut it out from the newspaper in its entirety and kept it in her journal.

By 1862 the Southern citizens of Maryland had no power, no rights, and no voice. The battle at Front Royal [May 23, 1862] was the first time Marylanders in opposing armies crossed swords and it resulted in the capture of a Maryland Union regiment. There was great tension for several days in Baltimore at this news and a number of Southern sympathizers were "set upon and badly beaten." Command of the Middle Department[18] went from Dix to Major General John E. Wool in June 1862. Wool would prove to be unpopular with both the Union and Southern camps in Baltimore.

During the summer of 1862, and until the entrance of Confederate forces under Lee, in September, Maryland was undisturbed from without. Within she presented a state of affairs which the Consolidationists might contemplate with satisfaction, as the fruition of their highest hopes. Though she had offered no resistance to Federal power she was treated as a conquered province, without a single state right, or a single Constitutional guarantee remaining. Her legislature and the municipal authorities of Baltimore were still in confinement, untried, and their places filled with the creatures of military power. There was not even the pretense of necessity, military or other, to palliate these proceedings; on the contrary, with insolent mockery, the "loyalty" of her people was praised in reports of secretaries and a proclamation of the president, and the protection of the Constitution promised, as the reward of their fidelity.

Yet, in the face of these pledges, the people were none the less subjected to oppression and outrage. Arrests were made, imprisonments prolonged, right of trial denied, confiscations made, commerce interdicted, and slaves carried off. Free speech and a free press were things of the past. Property of all kinds was openly seized and appropriated by the agents of the Federal government or its armed marauders, who dispensed with the superfluity of judicial proceedings by pronouncing its condemnation themselves. Houses [including the Goldsborough's] were invaded and ransacked by night and by day; private papers seized; and men and even women torn from the bosoms of their families and hurried away to imprisonment or exile. A minister of the gospel was arrested and imprisoned for refusing to allow a flag to be displayed from his church. Even infants in the nurses' arms, were arrested for wearing knots of red ribbon, which the "loyalists" were pleased to regard as a "disloyal" color. As to the conduct of a certain faction of the "loyal" citizens, the spies and delators, we pass it over in silence for [the] very shame. Nor can we enter into the details of the insults, wrongs, and outrages that were daily and hourly committed upon the people of this State, for the remembrance still rouses indignation too hot for the calmness of impartial history.[19]

From eighty year old Gertrude Winder, mother of Major General William H. Winder, to six year old Annie Lamb, females of all ages and positions were arrested.

In July 1862 Lincoln called for 300,000 troops. Maryland filled her quota with four infantry regiments and a battery of light artillery. The draft was instituted to fill any shortfall. Funding for the bounty and equipage of these men was passed by the state legislature only after physical assaults and the subsequent resignations of those who were against it. Also, at this time, the city council required all city employees to take the oath. It was suggested that this requirement be extended to all citizens of Baltimore but General Wool rejected the idea on the grounds that it would send thousands of men "to swell the army of Jefferson Davis."

On September 5, 1862 General Robert E. Lee and the Army of Northern Virginia crossed the Potomac. There was an explosion of excitement in Baltimore with rumors of an attack on the city. This brought out Union men organizing in militia groups and another period of "violent assaults" on Southern sympathizers. After the battle of Sharpsburg on September 17, 1862, a number of Baltimore's Southern women, including Pheme, went to Frederick, Maryland to nurse Confederate wounded. They may have accompanied the large number of volunteer surgeons who came to Frederick to help out with the appalling number of wounded.

In October when the Confederates burned a commercial ship from New York, Federal gunboats began to actively cruise the Chesapeake and captured spies, mail, and valuables on their way south. Two or three gunboats a week with goods going to Confederate lines were captured. It was ordered for all "coastwise traders to obtain official permits at custom house in Baltimore on penalty of confiscation of the goods, and fines and imprisonment."[20] In August 1862 all persons leaving the city by Patuxent, Potomac, and West River boats were ordered to obtain permits and take the oath.

War activity bustled in Baltimore. Locust Point would receive up to sixty vessels a day whose cargoes were immediately forwarded to Washington, D.C. in railroad cars numbering up to four hundred. Baltimore became an important and busy center for the Union war effort and it severely affected commercial trade. An embargo was put on the commerce of Baltimore and long term bank loans were unavailable due to the unrest.

On November 26, 1862 all Maryland state prisoners at Fort Warren were released and those from Baltimore received a sympathetic welcome from their friends in the city. Some merely passed through

Baltimore on their way south to join the Confederacy. Pheme would meet a number of them in Richmond during her exile.

A petition had been organized by Baltimore's Union citizens to remove Wool on the allegation "that his rule was not sufficiently strict." Whether or not this was the impetus, Wool was replaced by Major General Robert E. Schenck on December 22, 1862. With this new commander and his agent, the "pestilential" Lt. Colonel Fish, the screws were tightened unmercifully.

> *While the armies were thus honorably contending on fields of battle, General Schenck and his congenial provost-marshal, William S. Fish, found a safer sphere of distinction in tyrannizing over the unarmed inhabitants of Baltimore. Fish, who had been lieutenant-colonel in the 1st Connecticut Cavalry, was a brutal ruffian and debauchee, and from his accession to office on January 21, 1863, every imaginable insult and outrage were heaped upon the people, until the time when his career found its proper close in the Albany penitentiary. [See Appendix 4] His earliest exploits were upon the churches.[21]*

Churches and later all public buildings were required to display Union flags; anyone who did not comply or removed a flag was arrested.

Orders went out to music dealers and publishers in Baltimore that publication or sale of Secession music (which was broadly interpreted) was forbidden and all such were confiscated along with the copper plates of various pieces. All these businessmen were required to take the oath. All photographers were prohibited from selling images of Southern military and political leaders. The wearing of the colors red and white was strictly forbidden. Homes were routinely invaded and ransacked in search for forbidden "traitorous" items and, in Colonel Fish's case, confiscated and at times sold for personal gain.

When Lee invaded Maryland en route to Pennsylvania in June 1863 excitement flamed across the state. Free people of color were leaving the western sections of Maryland and flooding into Baltimore for fear of being captured. Lincoln called for another 100,000 men, one tenth of that number required from Maryland. In Baltimore all business was abandoned and the hopes of Southerners rose. Entrenchments were constructed by impressed blacks and Southern sympathizers at approaches to the city and barricades were set up. The city's barriers of resistance to keep hostiles out also kept the citizens in. On June 29 when the city was believed to be in real danger, organizations of citizens were called out by a general alarm to man the barricades. Schenck declared martial law in the city and county of Baltimore and all counties on the western shore of Maryland. This was never removed.

Schenck was noted for his prolific orders. A series of them were issued at the time of the Gettysburg campaign including, in part, the following: [On June 30] "'Until further orders, no person will be permitted to leave the city of Baltimore without a pass properly signed by the provost marshal, and anyone attempting to violate this order shall be promptly arrested and brought before the provost marshal for examination...[On July 1] Until further orders the citizens of Baltimore city and county are prohibited keeping arms in their possession unless enrolled as volunteer companies for the defense of their homes.' In squads of three or four, they [the military] acted in concert with the police diligently searching the dwellings of persons supposed to be 'disloyal' for guns."[22] The Goldsborough home was searched, but no guns were found.

Another order on July 1 stated that, "...the writer of any such interrupted letter [going to or from the South] living within this department will be arrested and sent beyond the lines...."[23] On July 3 Schenck ordered every business and home to fly the Union flag. "In consequence of this order, nearly everyone complied with the request, and those who failed to comply were marked, and afterwards paid the penalty."[24]

"The news of the tremendous battle of Gettysburg produced a great excitement in Baltimore, the hopes of the Southern sympathizers being blasted by Lee's retreat, while the feelings of the Unionists were much elated. The streets and newspaper offices were constantly thronged by crowds of people eagerly seeking the latest intelligence, and the knowledge of Lee's check had a great effect upon the celebration of the Fourth of July."[25]

Wounded Union and Confederate officers and men flooded into Baltimore. Schenck's order on July 10 stated:

No rebel officer or soldier can be received or entertained in any private house, or in any place other than the hospital to which he is regularly assigned...No person not thoroughly loyal will be permitted, under any circumstances, to visit or have access to any military hospital...no passes, under any circumstances, will be granted to visit Ft. McHenry.[26]

A large number of the surgeons of Baltimore were dispatched to the battle-field of Gettysburg, and the sanitary and Christian commission went to the same place...Many ladies and gentlemen of Baltimore also went in search of friends and relations wounded in the battle, or to act as nurses in the hospitals...the railroads having suspended travel, many loads [of stores] were sent to Gettysburg by wagons.[27]

Dozens of Baltimore women left for Gettysburg to nurse Confederate wounded and Pheme made that journey about this time. How this was managed is unknown. The requirement of taking the oath to obtain a pass to leave the city limits would have precluded any visibility or use of regular travel routes. On July 21 when the order requiring "passes for people coming to or leaving the city" was revoked, Pheme was already gone.

The November 1863 election was of great political importance in Maryland. It included five seats in Congress which the Radical Republicans were determined to win and the important state and county offices were up. The election was not run by state laws, but by military laws. The Provost Marshal was ordered to arrest any voter "they might consider disloyal" and the election judges were ordered to demand an oath of allegiance under penalty of arrest if they did not comply.

This was too much even for the Union governor of Maryland who issued a lengthy proclamation to be printed in the newspapers to commit the upcoming election to be held under state guidelines that omitted any requirements of oaths and arrests. Before the proclamation appeared in print, Schenck issued written orders to all newspapers forbidding its publication until the day of the election when it would be too late. When it was then published, it contained an appendage from Schenck explaining that the military's disregard of Bradford's proclamation was pretty much done for everyone's own good:

> *The explanation of General Schenck's will possibly appear somewhat lame and inconsistent, but this whole business was tainted with falsehood and inconsistency from beginning to end. Governor Bradford was in a false position when, professing to represent a free and sovereign state, he yet upheld an administration whose policy it was to crush out all state freedom and independence.*
>
> *General Schenck was in a position equally false when professing to regard the constitution and laws, and be solicitous for the general good, in act he trampled on the former, and saw no way of securing the general good, but by the triumph of a faction who would sustain him in any wrong he might please to perpetuate. As inconsistent were the 'Union' people, who, while clamoring that they were the immense majority—were, in fact, the State—could never devise measures stringent enough to prevent the minority from meeting, speaking, writing, voting, or in any way manifesting their insignificance.*[28]

Schenck was elected into Congress from Ohio and resigned from the military on December 5, the day after Pheme set foot on Virginia soil as an exile. Brigadier General Henry H. Lockwood then took command of the Middle Department. Except for her concerns about family and friends at home, Pheme was no longer affected by Federal rule. She was a free citizen of the Confederate States of America and would remain so until the end of the war.

The Goldsborough coat of arms.

The Life

"The glory of a race well run
of earnest duty, nobly done."[1]

The Goldsborough genealogy has been traced back over forty generations to Hugo de Goldesburgh who had been granted land in Yorkshire, Great Britain. The first Goldsborough to be born in North America was Nicholas Goldsborough III, circa 1690. He was Pheme's great, great, grandfather.

Euphemia Mary Goldsborough was born June 5, 1836 to Martin and Ann Hayward Goldsborough at "Boston" in Talbot County, Maryland. Boston still stands today and is privately owned. During the 1850s the Goldsborough family moved to 49 Courtland Street, on the northeast corner of Mulberry, in Baltimore. There were eight children, seven daughters and one son listed in the 1860 census. By the time of the war, however, only seven children are noted as residents. Pheme was the third eldest. Mona, Pheme's biographer, was the youngest. Mr. Martin Goldsborough, listed as a "general agent" in the census, was a dealer in farm machinery and stock.

During part of the 1850s Pheme was in Tallahassee, Florida where her uncle, Richard Hayward, lived. She attended a girls' school there, probably the Leon Female Academy, and one report card from the 1850s survived. She was proficient in all subjects then considered important for the education of young ladies, including French, algebra, drawing, and spelling. Pheme's one weak subject was "Whispering" in which she consistently received the same hieroglyphic mark, implying "that the Pupil has not whispered."

Despite her inclination to speak in a normal tone of voice, Pheme developed into an intelligent and very well educated woman. The knowledge she displayed in her poetic allusions is remarkable. She was also a talented artist in both design and application, to which some of the surviving pieces in her collection attest. She no doubt enjoyed the social and cultural activities of her day and was apparently quite popular. There is a family story about her having had a number of beaus, some of whom had the bad timing to visit simultaneously. Pheme sent the Goldsborough servant down to tell the gentlemen "Miss Effie begs to be excused." Euphemia was referred to both as Pheme and as Miss Effie.

As the 1850s drew to a close, Pheme would have been in her early twenties. Whether or not she was caught up in Baltimore's political chaos of that decade is not known, but during the 1860s she

"Boston," Pheme's birthplace in Talbot County, Maryland.

The Courtland Street house, taken earlier this century just before demolition. The Goldsborough home is on the corner displaying the smaller flag from the second story window.

was very much in the thick of things. The Goldsboroughs were devoted Southern sympathizers, especially Pheme, who utilized all the strengths she possessed to serve the Confederacy and its people. Her service evolved into smuggling mail, clothing, medical supplies, and food to the South and into the prisons in the Baltimore area. She helped escaped prisoners return South and later engaged her energies as nurse to wounded Confederate prisoners.

Pheme "was one of the central and most active figures in the late war, so far as Maryland was interested. She devoted her youth to the Southern Cause, and was almost unequaled in her successful efforts in sending supplies, and sometimes arms, to the officers and men of the Maryland line. Into every Federal prison in the United States where Confederate soldiers were confined went articles of comfort, both of food and raiment [sic], to the suffering prisoners, while she worked day and night to procure funds to further that purpose."[2]

The collection has a ticket to a tableaux for Tuesday, October 21, 1862 at 8 o'clock, admission 50 cents. The papers confiscated from her home in November 1863 included what appears to be a script for a tableaux containing a list of "actor's" names which were no doubt of great interest to the Union authorities. [See Provost Marshal file]

Maryland was a microcosm of the country torn asunder—suspended in an iron grip between two sides, both of whom viewed the citizens of the state with suspicion. The North saw her as one of the arenas of rebellion; the South by 1862 saw her as lost to the Union. With the repressive and arbitrary military rule in Baltimore, the risks were great. With everything to lose, commitment must have been strong indeed to adhere to Southern beliefs.

Although neither Pheme's father nor brother served in the Confederate army, many of her friends did. Maryland men enlisted in the Southern army at the cost of losing their families and homes. A nurse in Richmond commented on the hard position in which these Confederate soldiers were placed. She wrote of prejudice against Marylanders and the difficulties faced by Maryland soldiers who usually remained privates and did not rise up the ranks:

> *Luxuries received from other states for their soldiers, which though trifling in themselves were so gratifying to their recipients could not come to them; the furlough, that El Dorado to the sick soldier, was the gold which could not be grasped, for there was no home that could be reached. Even letters, those electric conductors from heart to heart, came sparingly after long detention, often telling them of loss of the beloved at home, months after the grave had closed upon them.*[3]

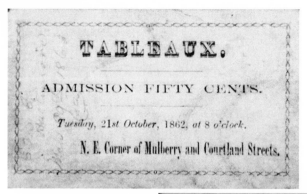

"God! bless you my dear dear friends, keep you from harm & bring you safely back home & friends when all is over. I will see you in the morning as you go. Truely Pheme."

In turn, the Maryland women must have suffered terrible anxiety when their men went South, for the men could well have stepped into oblivion. The homes of known Confederate soldiers in Baltimore were watched carefully, contact by letter or in person, though uncommon, were grounds for arrest, imprisonment, and possible exile. "Throughout the South there were the wayside hospitals, the ladies' kitchens, the meetings in churches and town halls; but Maryland could have none of these. All service rendered by Maryland's Confederate women was done in secrecy and at great risk to themselves and their families."[4]

The Goldsborough home was a refuge for any Confederate soldier. Mona wrote of:

...Maryland boys who came and stayed with us in the face of all danger. Rebel boys home to see family and sweethearts found plenty of their rebel friends here ready to hide them away for weeks at a time and take chances of discovery and all the punishment the government saw fit to deal out to us. There are some living today who can recall just such cases as I describe. If the old Courtland house could speak it could tell some curi-

ous tales of refugees from Fort Delaware and Camp Chase; of the Baltimore boys who wore the grey and slipped home sometimes the underground route, as blockade running was called; of piles and piles of clothes stacked up to be sent down South as soon as the opportunity presented itself; of hundreds and hundreds of letters destined to be sent to the Army by the Confederate blockade runners....

Pheme began nursing in September 1862. "After the Battle of Antietam, Miss Goldsborough went at once to Frederick City [Maryland] where the wounded had been conveyed and gave the Confederate soldiers assigned to her ward unremitting care."[5]

Pheme may have traveled with the group of Baltimoreans who went to Frederick and its environs to help with the wounded. This brief mention above of Pheme's work at Frederick that appeared in her obituary some thirty years later is the only information come to light about her nursing after Antietam.

— GETTYSBURG

The collection has a great deal more about her service at Gettysburg. Traveling from her home to Gettysburg and obtaining leave to nurse Confederate prisoners would have been fraught with obstacles, yet it was accomplished by a large number of Southern women from Baltimore. Though the journey must have been an interesting part of the whole experience, neither Pheme nor Mona wrote about it. However, a wounded Confederate prisoner housed at the Pennsylvania College hospital did, relating details about the journey and the women's hostile reception from Union authorities.

He summarized what he had been told by his Baltimore nurses and offered it up as a declaration to the women's perseverance:

...For weeks, they had been preparing for the entry of Lee into Maryland,—into Baltimore, and comforts, clothing, delicacies of every description, they had hoarded up, hoping soon to be able to distribute them, with their own fair hands, among the men who were fighting for the cause they loved; and when the dreadful news of our repulse reached them, their first thought was to visit our hospitals and supply our wants. What if passports to leave the city on the railroad were denied to all except those who would take 'the oath'; did they not take their carriages and ride through the country? What if the bridges were guarded, did they not ford or ferry the stream? and when the hotel keepers in Gettysburg were ordered not to receive them in

their houses; did they not go to the houses of private citizens,
stay in barns and outhouses, or remain with us day and night
in the hospital, reclining in a chair or resting on the floor in a
room of the building we vacated for them, when sleep would
overcome them? What if large trunks full of comforts for us
were seized on their arrival; did they not go back to Baltimore
and return with dresses that had pockets as large as haver-
sacks and almost numberless? And, finally, when every plan to
thwart them had failed, and the yankees hoped by personal
hardships inflicted upon them, and by insults directly given, to
drive them away; did they not tell the yankees to their faces
they had come prepared to bear insults and wrongs for the men
they loved? Or as I heard one put it in very strong language
(speaking to an officer who had the politeness to apologize for a
false accusation made against her, which caused her arrest) 'I
want no apology, we came here expecting and prepared for this,
we can bear it for the cause; to us contact with such as you is
synonymous with insult, there is the door.[6]

It is not known when Pheme left Baltimore, if she was one of the
women who turned back home to replenish confiscated supplies, or
when she arrived at Gettysburg. It is known that she was on the
field by July 18 as her pass to nurse at the College Hospital bears
that date. And thanks to Mona's manuscript we know with whom
she had traveled:

When the guns at Gettysburg had ceased to volley and thun-
der many of the ladies of Baltimore offered their services to
nurse in the hospitals there. Among these ladies, Miss
Euphemia Goldsborough, who was one of the most active spir-
its of the Southern Cause in Baltimore, hurried with Miss
McCrea and Mrs. Dubois Eagerton and many others to the scene
where they were assigned to duty as hospital nurses and to
other departments of usefulness.[7]

Baltimore women were noted as nurses at the Confederate hos-
pitals located at Black Horse Tavern, the Pennsylvania College, the
Seminary, the Plank farm, in the fields, in tents, barns, and in town.
Most of the women were unidentified. Confederate Surgeon
Simon Baruch was at Francis Bream's Black Horse Tavern and wrote:
"Two young women belonging to a historic Maryland family came to
the hospital under the chaperone of an elderly English nurse and
remained with us, occupying garret rooms, until the hospital closed.
They administered to the wounded, prepared the food and dress-

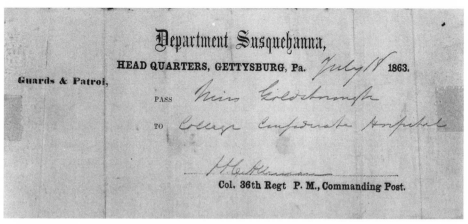

Department Susquehanna,

HEAD QUARTERS, GETTYSBURG, Pa. *July 8* 1863.

Guards & Patrol,

PASS *Miss Goldsborough*

TO *College Confederate Hospital*

Col. 36th Regt P. M., Commanding Post.

Pass to the Confederate College hospital.

ings, and read the burial service over those who succumbed. Their services were inestimable."[8] "...three grand, Christian women from Baltimore..."[9] were noted at the Plank farm.

Some were identified. In addition to Pheme, McCrea, and Eagerton, the names of Mrs. Banks, Miss Maggie Branson, Mrs. J. Harman Brown, Miss Duvall, Miss Dora Hoffman, Miss Howard, Miss Annie Long, Miss Matilda Saunders, Mrs. Warrington and her daughter can be found in narratives about the aftermath of the battle:

> *...Mrs. Brown being assigned to the desperately wounded, who were, for the most part, kept under tents or in barns, while Miss Saunders was set to nursing in the town of Gettysburg. Mrs. Brown, setting out in the early morning, trudged through the fields under an almost incessant rain, wet up to the knees, nursing and caring for the wounded and dying until late at night, when she returned to her hired room in a farm house.[10]*

At least three of these women were at the Pennsylvania College hospital: Pheme, "Hettie" McCrea, and Maggie Branson [See Appendix 2]. This building, which still stands as part of the Gettysburg College campus, was a large four story structure, containing Confederate wounded variously estimated from six to nine hundred. In 1863 it was located just outside the town limits.

The wounded Confederates at the College Hospital were in a sorry state. A prisoner there wrote of conditions and what the arrival of the ladies from Baltimore meant to him:

> *...In this hospital, there were six hundred of our wounded men, and about five of our surgeons remained with them.... As a consequence of the small number of surgeons left with us, our men*

*in the hospital suffered much. Unless it was a case of amputa-
tion needed immediately or the stopping hemorrhage, they had
not time to attend to any one. Thus for the first two weeks there
were no nurses, no medicines, no kinds of food proper for men
in our condition...and for men who were reduced to mere skel-
etons from severe wounds and loss of blood, the floor was a
hard bed with only a blanket on it.... Day after day passed by
with no difference, the same hard floor, the same hard crack-
ers, the same want of attention, and it had its effect on the men,
as is always the case. We each day became weaker and weaker.*

*...And in that hospital,—those weary days,—those restless
nights, ah, mothers, sisters, wives, at home, your presence was
the sunshine needed in those gloomy hours, it was the heart
yearning for you, that showed itself on quivering lips and moistened eyes. Yet we were not wholly forsaken. One day as I was
waiting, I heard a lady's voice, it was sweet music to my ears.
A few moments afterwards, two ladies from Baltimore came
into our room. To speak a few kind words, to ask us what was
our principal wants, to promise to come soon again...next day,
more came and then more, until every hospital had two or more
of 'our angels', as we used to call them, doing their works of
mercy. And what they did, and what they told us, and what
they passed through for us, what tongue can tell?...the ladies of
Baltimore were preeminently the persons, to whom we were indebted for everything that made our situation bearable.*[11]

"Miss Goldsborough was first put to work in the College Hospital. The North was a new field for active operations and the fight at
Gettysburg found the people of the town unprepared for the emergency thrust upon them by the 'Rebels.' The College was...bare of all
necessary comforts."[12]

If the term "necessary comforts" encompassed medical supplies,
food, clothing, and bedding, it was an accurate one. The needs that
the medical personnel strived to meet were overwhelming. Addi-
tionally, the patients and caregivers were plagued by the unwelcome
presence of "gawkers." "Thousands of citizens from all parts of the
North flocked to Gettysburg to see a battlefield and get a view of the
terrible rebels,"[13] wrote one wounded Confederate at this site. Some
were described as "hypocritical New England preachers, and fanati-
cal men and women who were astounded that many Rebels actually
believed in their cause and could even read and write."[14] The Confederates subjected to these individuals soon learned that requests
for money or food would quickly send them away.

The doctors and nurses at the College Hospital did the best they could with what they had. Pheme's willingness to give assistance in any capacity would employ her in an extraordinary service.

While the confusion was greatest and heros [sic] were lying without pillows on the bare floor of the ward legless and armless, waiting for their time to come for attention, Miss Goldsborough found it her privilege to support, in his last moments, the gallant Col. [Waller Tazewell] Patton, a Virginian [7th VA], whose bravery has since been the theme of many tongues.

The surgeons in charge decided that it was imperative to place Col. Patton in practically a sitting posture to prevent suffocation. Being shot through the lungs, and unconscious, it was impossible to save his life unless he could be propped up, and there was absolutely nothing to be had to prop him with. Seeing the difficulty, Miss Goldsborough decided to offer herself as the necessary agent. Accordingly she seated herself on the bare floor, feet extended, the surgeons tenderly placed the dying officer against her back and secured him there. She sat there, still as a wooden image never daring to move lest the slightest motion should bring on a hemmorrage [sic] and death insue [sic].

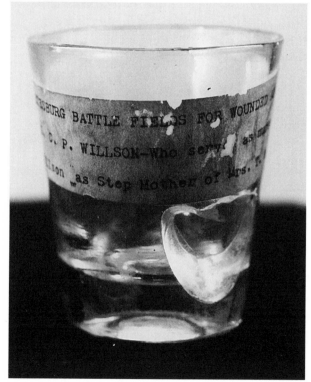

The glass Pheme used while a nurse at Gettysburg.

I have heard her describe the numbness that stole over her as she sat the night through, holding up the fast dying officer. It was said by a veteran afterwards, that of all touching sights in his memory, the recollection of that picture would stand before him. 'Midnight, a brave soldier, for whom the last taps were sounding, a young frail woman sitting by the light of a flickering candle supporting the dying hero of many hard fought battles, surrounded by the dead and dying and some 'grown old in wars.'

All efforts to save Col. Patton were futile, he died soon afterwards....[15]

Patton died on July 21. The Richmond *Daily Enquirer* listed Colonel Patton's obituary on August 31 and noted that he had been "nursed by a Baltimore lady with as much tenderness as if she had been his sister." In view of her later contact with Patton's family in Richmond, this "Baltimore lady" may have been Pheme.

Lack of clothing for the Confederate wounded was a major problem:

One of the most villainous acts of our keepers, while at the College Hospital—besides the insults offered the ladies—was this; when our men were brought to the building, all of them being wounded, were more or less covered with blood and dirt, and the ladies from Baltimore made arrangements with a sympathizer, who lived near, to have all the washing done that would be needed at the hospital, and they would pay for it. As soon as the yankees found out this was being done, they stopped it, making many of the men who were unable to obtain a change of under-clothing, lie for weeks in clothing covered with a mass of putrid blood. After our friends came, the majority of us got at least a part of a change of clothing....[16]

One Gettysburg household had four women from Baltimore staying with them for a few days:

They were very delightful ladies and were well supplied with money. They spent the whole day out on the field in the hospitals where the Confederate wounded were. We did not suspect their intentions at first, but when they tried to buy up men's civilian clothes, and even women's clothing, we began to understand what they were about. As soon as my father learned what their real mission was, he insisted that my mother must send them away...the ladies begged very earnestly to be allowed to stay, saying that they were much pleased with their accommodations...Mother was sorry to send them away as they were willing to pay well for every attention. They even offered to increase the amount, but father was relentless....[17]

Clothing may have been procured with the intent of aiding prisoners to escape, but there was a general and desperate need among the Confederate wounded for clothing. Civilian clothes would have been the only type available. The women from Baltimore would hardly have expected to procure Confederate uniforms. The women's clothing could very well have been for the nurses. When Pheme returned home from Gettysburg she had nothing left of her clothes except those on her back.

Want of clothing was still present at Camp Letterman, the general hospital site at Gettysburg where all the wounded were eventually moved. Pheme did her part to secure what she could:

> *An amusing incident occured [sic] while in Camp [Letterman] Hospital...[there] was a great need of suitable clothing and, for some reason known only to men in authority, it was against the rules to provide them with new boots and clothes, but Miss Goldsborough was determined that one at least whose needs were especially great should not be sent to a northern or western prison destitute as he was. She feigned an excuse to go into town, secured a permit and started off in an army ambulance that was going there that morning. After securing the longed for treasures and what articles she could find, she happened upon a friendly spirit.... They tied the boots securely under the immense hoop-skirt Miss Goldsborough rejoiced in and all the other traps that could be fastened on and then started off bravely to camp. But on reaching the official place to meet the ambulance, to [her] dismay, there stood the dreaded Yankee officer instead of just a teamster. [When] the officer officiously insisted upon assisting her to get in the ambulance her fears of detection were something appalling. She was sure the boots would bump against the side of the ambulance as soon as she attempted to get in it. However, she made a desperate effort and got in safely. Neither of the boots dropped down or bumped against each other. The camp was reached safely. The officious Yankee assisted her out and she reached her tent in safety. Then, when the opportunity presented itself, she smuggled the effects to the rejoiced 'Reb' and went on her way tending the wounded and dying.*[18]

Camp Letterman was established on July 20 about one mile east of the town of Gettysburg on the York Pike. Pheme's pass to nurse at this site was dated July 21. There had been over 60 hospital sites serving both armies on and around the battlefield. These had been evacuated and over 16,000 of the wounded were sent either to permanent military hospitals in the North or to prisons; over 4,000 were moved to Camp Letterman:

This location was a good one.... At that time, it was on high, mostly well-drained ground, in a large grove, which provided both shade and free movement of fresh air...the camp area was drained and the tents were pitched...The railroad was only thirty rods away, which permitted litters to be walked to the cars. A good spring on the property, along with several wells that were late dug, provided a neverending supply of clean, fresh water.... After a while, the general hospital, became the very model of a clean, efficient, and well-run medical facility, the first of its kind actually on a battlefield anywhere.... At its peak, the hospital had more than four hundred hospital tents, set up in six double rows, about ten feet apart. Each tent held up to ten patients.... Every medical officer had charge of from forty to seventy patients, which totalled 1,600 on August 30....[19]

Camp Letterman would close in November. Of Pheme's experience there, Mona wrote: "There were one hundred men assigned to Miss Goldsborough's ward, fifty Federal and fifty Confederate soldiers, some officers and some private soldiers.... Her entire time

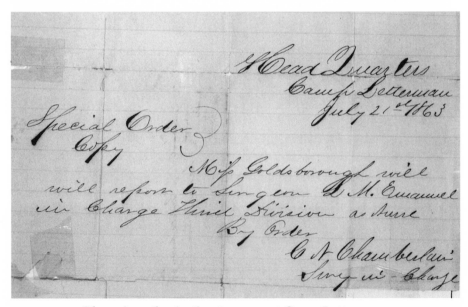

Pheme's authorization to nurse at Camp Letterman.

was passed, nursing day and night except such time as sleep was absolutely desired...." The ward Pheme was assigned to most likely consisted of ten tents. Mona further wrote:

> *The U.S. soldiers were placed there to insure her discharge of duty without treason to the government. Miss Goldsborough recognized the importance of showing no partiallity [sic], and many of both armies owed their lives to her good nursing, common sense and justice, while she gladly forgot party spirit for the time and saw the necessity of sacrificing self to the good of the Southern wounded, and discharged her obligations to the many in order to secure the care of wounded, dying soldiers of the Confederate Army. She remained there nine weeks, working incessantly, forgetting the world and self, living only to comfort and support the suffering and dying.*

A Union nurse, Sophronia Bucklin, served at Camp Letterman. She listed her daily duties there, which must have been similar to Pheme's:

> *The first round in the morning was to give the stimulants, and to attend to the distribution of the extra diet. After the thorough organization of the plan had been completed, we were not called up to dress wounds, unless by special request, wound dressers being assigned to each section of the ward; but for a time, that duty had come next after the distribution of the extra diet. Beef tea was passed three times a day, stimulants three times, and extra diet three times—making nine visits which each woman nurse made a day to each of* [the men under her care]. *This was done besides washing the faces and combing the hair of those who were still unable to perform these services for themselves, preparing the extra drinks ordered by the surgeons, and seeing that the bedding and clothing of every man was kept clean by the men nurses.*[20]

Bucklin also commented on the lack of food, the rain and mud, and the "uncovered wells...dug on the verge of the timber," which at night were "a great terror."[21]

While at Camp Letterman Pheme received and wrote letters to her former Confederate patients who were then in prisons. On September 3 she wrote to Lt. Anderson J. Peeler, of Co. I, 5th Florida at Johnson's Island. "Probably you will be somewhat surprised to hear we are all still in Camp—& so far have all kept well, except for an occasional Headache or Heartache, I scarcely know which." [See Provost Marshal file] While Lt. Peeler had been at Camp Letterman he penned a moving letter in Pheme's "Hospital Books." In it he expressed "for myself and my wounded and sick comrades the heart-felt gratitude we feel for your kindness to us here and at the College Hospital...many whose fevered brows you have bathed and to whose wants you have ministered with such indefatigable attention will long treasure in their hearts and memory your name and kind deeds with a feeling of sacred friendship...." Another Floridian wrote, "Be assured, Miss G, that you will never be forgotten, for your kindness has deeply stamped your image on our hearts and indelibly written your name on the tablets of our memory...words are not sufficient to express our feelings...." Other patients echoed these sentiments.

Pheme, like most nurses who stay at one site for a length of time, had a special patient—Sam Watson from Texas. In the first "Hospital Book" Pheme wrote: "Samuel Watson, Co. E, 5th Texas Reg Lost his right arm. One of the most attractive boys I ever saw. Very ill but little hope of his recovery but hope for the best. [September] 8th Better today, decidedly (illegible) poor fellow [September] 9th much better today, strong hope of his recovery." In the second book, Pheme wrote: "Sam H. Watson, Washington, Tex Sacred Died Sept. 13th, sundown, Sunday afternoon 1863. Buried in Grave No. 3, commencing at the right, 8th section. My poor lost darling. Would to God I could have died to save you but all is over. Worldly sufferings are ended. If tears or love could have availed I had not been left to weep by his graveside." Pheme left Gettysburg immediately after she buried Sam Watson.

Mona wrote of Pheme's arrival home in Baltimore:

> She returned to us the most delapidated [sic] young girl that tongue or pen could describe. During the nine weeks of camp life and hard work at nursing she had worn out all supplies taken there and sent to her by her family and the traveling garments she wore up to Gettysburg, were things of the past. The hornets had built a nest in her bonnet and so it was necessary for her to return to Baltimore in her nurse's attire.
>
> We did not know her at first. It was the 13th of September, 1863, a warm afternoon.[22] Our mother was lying down taking an afternoon nap as usual, the writer sitting near her. Suddenly a vague consciousness of another presence was felt and looking up a figure standing in the doorway explained the sensation. At first we scarcely knew her, so worn and changed, so utterly exhausted with the sights of the battlefield and death bed scenes in the hospitals. The awful sights of those days, the anguish and suffering, witnessing the operations in the hospitals where legs and arms were sawed off like those of cats and

dogs and where blood poured in streams from the operating tables, where she stood beside the poor boys in grey and heard their last messages and prayers. Little wonder to us of mature years that the life and youth in this frail woman's body was almost exhausted, for in truth she was never the same joyous girl again. Such things leave red letter marks that time never effaces.

We mingled our tears with hers as we listened to descriptions of the closing scenes of young lives sacrificed to duty and honor and country. Some were mere boys in years but brave and 'counting it gain' to die in such a cause while far away from home and friends with only a stranger's hand to close eyes that would never again behold the dear home faces or respond to other eyes that would watch in vain for the soldier's return.

On September 22, Pheme wrote Sam Watson's mother a heartbreaking letter informing her of her son's death. [See Personal Collection]

Pheme resumed her smuggling activities. She was able to send and receive letters and boxes to prisoners held in West's Buildings hospital and Ft. McHenry. She corresponded with Confederates in Northern prisons and made efforts to aid escaped prisoners. On November 23, the day of the night she would be arrested, she wrote to Colonel Rawley White Martin of the 53rd Virginia. A former patient at Gettysburg, he was, at that time, held at Ft. McHenry on his way to Point Lookout:

I cannot tell but this <u>may be the last</u> letter Col. M you will [illegible] be troubled to decipher from me as I fear I am <u>implicated most seriously</u> in the <u>attempted</u> escape of a prisoner. A letter <u>directed</u> was found on his person and probably I shall go to 'Sweet Dixie' sooner than you however I am not one <u>bit afraid</u> & <u>defy</u> the whole <u>Yankee Nation send me where they will</u>. I am <u>able</u> & <u>willing</u> to <u>suffer hardships</u> & <u>loss</u> for <u>myself</u> for the sake of a <u>country</u> & <u>people that I love</u>. But probably it will all <u>blow over</u> & my friends may be <u>unnecessarily alarmed</u>.... [See Provost Marshal file]

It did not blow over.

— ARREST ————————————

"On the 23rd of November," Mona wrote, "at midnight Col. Fish, who was then in charge of this department sent three officers and a number of guards to arrest Miss Goldsborough for treason. The soldiers surrounded the house...[which was in] a neighborhood well known and popular as a residence locality." Mona further described what happened:

The Yankees filed into the house and took up formidable attitudes, while some stood guard outside. They had enuf [sic] powder and shot along to kill a company, but the idea in those days was to over-power whereever [sic] they could. This was not such an easy matter as they sometimes found out to their loss. Southern women are not cowards and some of the besieged [family] were [not] frightened, though of course excited, for the arrest was made at a serious time. There were hampers packed and waiting to be smuggled into Fort McHenry that very night, and it was almost impossible to get them unpacked and hustled out of sight without attracting the attention of the guards. The family was large however, seven daughters, all with their wits about them and a father and mother especially on the alert. The unpacking was accomplished while the searching party was upstairs looking all over the house, in bureau drawers, in old closets, wardrobes, and every empty and occupied room being looked over for evidence of treason; this little pleasantness, had been vouchsafed before, when the Yankees reported finding a wagon load of guns secreted. In reality, not a gun had been in our house for the past twenty years, at least.

A detective made the arrest first, and then after asking Miss Goldsborough if she had nursed at Gettysburg and she had told him 'yes' he put his hand on her shoulder and said, 'You are my prisoner, consider yourself under arrest.' Then my Lord Cardinal called in his gallant officers and guards with their little swords and guns and all rushed upstairs and spread over the house like the darkness that spread over Egypt.

Before leaving the hall where all this took place one very knightly officer told the guard that if Miss Goldsborough attempted to move to shoot her down. She quietly remarked 'I'm not coward enough to run.' After an hour spent in ramsacking [sic] desks for papers, they departed, actually telling us they were tired and sleepy; but only the officers left, and the guards locked up the prisoner in a cold room, and took position on the outside of the door. They had strict orders not to allow any members of her family to speak to her, but they did. Each one as he went on duty said if we would not tell the next guard he would let us see and speak to our sister and one kind hearted soldier, when he found she was in a room with no fire, and the weather bitterly cold, even went so far as to assist us in getting a stove into the room, and each guard kept up the fire as he came on duty during the time she was locked in that particular *room. We can say now, after the lapse of so many years, as we said then, that the private soldiers were very kind and full of sympathy; it was the higher class of officers who acted in the South like beasts. At least in our experience it was always so.*

The news of the arrest spread on the wings of the wind. Friends and strangers in sympathy with the South full of interest and genuine feeling. There were no idle curiosity seekers abroad in these war times. About eleven o'clock the following morning a detective came to escort Miss Goldsborough before the great Col. Fish of pestilential memory. She said unless he brought a carriage he would have to see Col. Fish alone as she had no intention of walking through the public streets with him to Col. Fish's office. He insisted and she steadfastly refused so he had to go and bring a carriage though as a matter of course he could have forced her to go on foot.

Our father was greatly grieved but he accompanied his daughter to the Provost Office and there heard them pronounce the sentence of banishment for the war. She was given permission to carry two trunks and just exactly $225 in federal money, not another cent and was told if she tried to come back before the close of the war she would be tried for her life and shot as a spy.

Pheme wrote in her diary: "Through a hard rain taken before the Military Authorities under guard. Sentenced to banishment during the war. Allowed to remain at home until Nov. 28th under strong guard day & night. Saturday Afternoon, Nov. 28th at 4 PM put on board the Steamer Adelaid (in a fainting condition) for Fortress Monroe with military escort."

Mona described November 28, the day Pheme left their home, not knowing when she would see her family again:

She left the house about three o'clock in the afternoon. The streets, doorsteps, windows and every available spot was packed with an eager sympathetic crowd to see her leave under such painful circumstances. Not a sound disturbed the peace! All seemed to feel it a funeral instead of a military banishment. She faced the crowd bravely but fell forward like a dead woman as soon as she was seated in the carriage. She was determined to show no signs of fear or distress before any possible enemy in that dense crowd, so she threw off our father's assisting arm and with erect head passed down the steps to the carriage alone, followed by the gentlemen and friends of our family, and the high official who was there to see his orders carried out.

Pheme wrote: "Reached the Fortress [Monroe] at daylight Sunday morning Nov 29th, raining fearfully. Taken to Beast Butler's HdQtrs about sunrise the same morning. Found the Beast not up. Wet & cold sat shivering in his office until a fire was made. Finally he came (this 2 headed monster) I was turned over into his hand by the guard and evidence handed in. Strong enough: the beast said to cost me my head 'under any other Government than the mild & glorious stars and stripes' Again banished for the war with orders that if I attempted to return, to be shot. But what was sentence of death & banishment at the hands of these cruel tyrants that I hated..."

Mona wrote: "No sympathy was shown this heroic Southern girl by Gen. Butler. No regard for her tender age or youth, but he sternly demanded to know what she had been sent to him for. Her reply was 'For feeding the hungry and clothing the naked.' She refused to reply to another question or a shaft of bitterness, but calmly awaited his decision. Though subjected to the most rigorous search personally [she was, in fact, strip searched], and her trunks upset in [sic] the floor and examined, she nevertheless carried through to Richmond certain dispatches and delivered them safely at headquarters. This, in the face of a Northern prison—even death itself—she ventured and accomplished." The dispatches were hidden in the secret compartment of a lap desk borrowed from a cousin.

Pheme was initially put in a "damp, cold cellar" but "Belonging to an old colonial family, she was widely known and friends and some relatives used every effort to secure official influence, and succeeded in getting her removed..."[23] Pheme was moved to the Hygeia Hotel which sat right outside Fort Monroe. She shared a room with other female prisoners.

Pheme was put on board the truce boat *New York* on the night of December 2 and reached City Point the evening of the next day.

There "a French Frigate of War was recognized lying near them. Soon a boat was launched and manned. An officer descended and took his seat then and the seaman rowed rapidly to the Exchange boat, pulled up and the officer came on deck. Bowing and smiling he said he called to pay his respects to the Miss Confederate whom he was told was on board. He was dressed in full uniform, low cut shoes and silk stockings, evidently arrayed to make a call of ceremony. Miss Goldsborough was presented, the officer paid her all the compliments his limited command of language allowed, placed his hand over his heart, bowed and returned to his ship."[24]

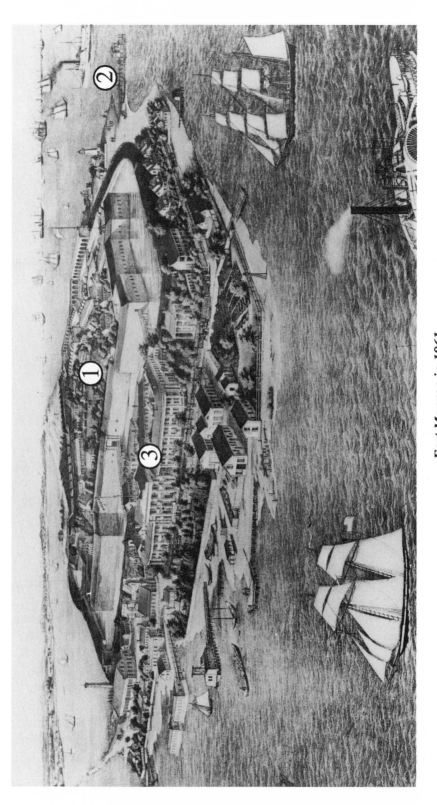

Fort Monroe in 1861.

1. The fort. 2. The engineer's wharf where Pheme arrived and departed. 3. The Hygeia Hotel.

(Courtesy of the Casemate Museum)

The lap desk taken by Pheme to Richmond when exiled. Note the opened door of the secret compartment situated under the drawers.

Pheme recorded in her diary: "When I awoke in the morning of Dec. 4th our [Confederate truce] Boat had arrived and with a light & bounding heart I bid goodby to Yankee rule & tyranny. And for the first time found myself seated on our <u>little Boat</u> with the Starry Cross, the flag of the free waving over me."

— *Exile* ———————————————

Pheme arrived in Richmond on December 4, 1863 feeling "truly that I was alone 'a stranger in a strange land,'" but her efforts on behalf of the Confederate soldier had touched many lives. By the next day groups of friends, Marylanders in the Confederate army, former patients, and other exiles, came to pay their respects. "Upon arriving in Richmond, Miss Goldsborough was welcomed right royally, feasted—not as they could have done before the war—but generously and proudly. Many doors were opened to her and many hearts.... The Southern people welcomed her royally to the Confederacy and to their homes...and many life-long friendships were formed.... The Maryland Line sent a formal invitation to Richmond for her to dine with them in camp and from far and near came letters from the wives and mothers of officers and men who had been nursed at Gettysburg."[25] Pheme later accepted invitations to visit the homes of the Houston brothers and that of Colonel Martin. The family of Colonel Patton "sought her out, having heard of her efforts to save his life, and insisted that she should make her home with them during the war. Though appreciated, this kind invitation was not accepted."[26] Pheme appeared to have made the decision to stand on her own as best she could. Both during and after the war she exhibited neither desire nor inclination for reward or recognition for her service.

At this point in time Richmond had the dubious distinction of being the most expensive city in the Confederacy in which to live. Costs for necessities had increased ten to fifteen times what they had been in 1860 and there were shortages even at those inflated prices. Morale was low, housing was scarce, and the citizens faced a lean winter. Pheme stayed at the Spotswood Hotel for four days, then moved to a boarding house. She received an appointment at the Commissary General's office, passed the board and started her position there on the first day of 1864. "Mr. [President Jefferson] Davis instructed General [Lucius B.] Northrope [Commissary General of the Confederacy] to offer Miss Goldsborough a position in the Treasury Department, which was filled to overflowing. When informed there was no vacant position for Miss Goldsborough he said, 'Well, then make one!'...On one occasion when the Maryland troops were in Richmond and were passing through the streets, Miss Goldsborough was recognized in the crowds of Department Ladies, who were eagerly watching the troops. The word passed rapidly along the line and Maryland's bravest sons paid tribute to her, exiled daughter, and while cheering, the entire regiment passed her with hats off—a compliment to her personally."[27]

In January 1864 as Pheme moved to another boarding house, the city was in a state of excitement over the arrival of Brig. Gen. John Hunt Morgan, who had recently escaped from an Ohio prison. February brought the news of the great tunnel escape from Libby Prison and the details of Colonel Ulrich Dahlgren's cavalry raid. Dahlgren's orders to torch the city and assassinate Confederate officials produced outrage in both citizen and political arenas, darkening the tone of the war to a new low. In March thousands of Richmond citizens stood at Rockett's Landing to greet six hundred released prisoners of war, some of whom were Pheme's former Gettysburg patients. With the end of April came the sad news of the death of Joseph Davis, Jefferson Davis' four year old son.

On May 9, 1864 Pheme wrote that there were "Battles raging all around. Sounds of cannon ringing in my ears day and night. <u>Days of sorrow</u> with our bravest & best being brought back to us dying & dead." Those cannon heralded the battles of the Wilderness [May 5-7, 1864], and those of the Spotsylvania Campaign [May 7-20, 1864] which included Yellow Tavern [May 11, 1864] just six miles outside of the Confederate capital. Yellow Tavern claimed the life of the popular Maj. Gen. J.E.B. Stuart. Richmond churches remained opened daily for prayer.

June brought the horrific battle of Cold Harbor [June 3, 1864] and the commencement of the Petersburg Campaign [June 1864 to May 1865]. Commanding Maj. Gen. Jubal Early was sent into the Shenandoah Valley that had been raped, pillaged, and burned by Maj. Gen. David Hunter. Early chased Hunter back up the valley and proceeded onto his Washington Raid [June 27 to August 7, 1864]. As the valley was temporarily safe, Pheme left Richmond on July 18 in the company of Captain Andrew Houston, another former patient, to travel west to his home in Rockbridge County. Pheme wrote, "His family, God bless them, I can never forget for their kindness to the <u>homeless</u> exile."

Pheme returned to Richmond in mid-September to a city under siege. Although ill herself, she worked at the "Department in the morning, Hospital in the afternoon until entirely broken down." In November came the news of Lincoln's reelection and any lingering hopes of an equitable peace were lost. Pheme moved to another boarding house, one step ahead of rising costs, and received an appointment in the Treasury Department. Harsh weather settled on the Confederate capital and the armies that surrounded it. Flour went for $800 a barrel. Cold, hungry, and desperate, Richmond braced itself for another bleak winter.[28]

In the early days of the harsh January of 1865, Pheme took the Danville and Richmond train to Pittsylvania County for a visit with Col. Rawley White Martin and his family. Colonel Martin had been exchanged in June 1864. Pheme wrote: "Found his mother & sisters sweet and lovely & kind and God will reward them, for their kindness to the weary wanderer." On her return to Richmond six weeks later she caught the train at Danville and wrote, "Meeting all the refugees from Columbia S C—old and young pushing & <u>rushing</u> 'fleeing from wrath to same.'"

By February plans were being made for evacuation of the capital. Pheme wrote: "A month of weariness, hard work at the office, doubts for the success of our beloved Cause, the safety of our Capital, headaches and heartaches." Lee had made overtures of peace to Grant but was rebuffed. Sheridan ruled the valley, having destroyed railroads, bridges, and locks on the James River.

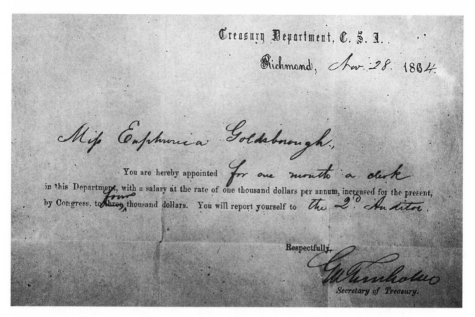

Treasury Department, C. S. A.

Richmond, *Nov. 28.* 1864.

Miss *Euphemia Goldsborough,*

You are hereby appointed *for one month* a *clerk* in this Department, with a salary at the rate of one thousand dollars per annum, increased for the present, by Congress, to *four* thousand dollars. You will report yourself to *the 2d. Auditor.*

Respectfully,

G. Trenholm

Secretary of Treasury.

One of Pheme's appointments to work at the Treasury Department.

Pheme recorded in her diary: "March 22nd. Our prisoners from Johnson's Island returned. Brave Soldiers and gentlemen. How my heart warmed toward all of their kind. Thursday, March 23rd Had a perfect reception at my office, of officers & friends I had known on the bloody field of Gettysburg, when it had been my happy privilege to nurse and attend them."

Three days later Pheme left Richmond with Capt. Thomas Houston for his home in Rockbridge County. Surrounded by hostiles, the only outlet was south to Danville, then back north to Lynchburg and west to Rockbridge. Pheme wrote:

I left Richmond in company with Capt. T. D. Houston to visit his dear home again, little dreaming the terrible fate of our glorious Capital in a week's time. Met Capt. [Robert] McCulloch at Danville...reached Lynchburg that night, found the canal boat not running. Left Lynchburg Tuesday morning March 28, in an Ambulance & pair of condemned mules to journey over the mountains a distance of 40 miles (with Capts Houston & McCulloch) which we were two days accomplishing. The first night stopped in the mountains at the house of a Stranger & asked for lodgings. With true Virginia (All honor to the brave old state) hospitality we were received by the owner...Early next morning we started, reach-

The Confederate Treasury Department was housed in the old U.S. Customs building in Richmond. It was one of the buildings that survived the war. Note the ruins in the foreground. (Courtesy Virginia State Library)

ing the home of Capt. McCulloch about 4 pm where we were most cordially greeted, he having returned from an imprisonment of two years.

It was in Rockbridge County just over the mountains from Appomattox County that Pheme learned of the fall of Richmond and the surrender of Lee:

> *In deep sorrow and humiliation I must record the evacuation of our much loved City Richmond April 2nd 1865. April 5th I came to Dr Houstons and here the news of General Lee's Surrender Sunday April 9th reached us on Monday afternoon April 10th. I could not believe it at first, but in a few hours our weary, worn, crushed, and bleeding soldiers began to come, returning through the mountains. Our army disbanded, their muskets stacked, our people scattered to the four winds. Oh! days, & weeks of agony & fears. With no word of comfort of hope or of home.*

The surrender affected many Southerners with the same despondent shock. Diaries of Southern women record the end of life as they knew it with profound grief. Mary Chesnut of South Carolina wrote: "We are shut in here—turned with our faces to a dead wall. No mails. A letter is sometimes brought by a man on horseback, traveling through the wilderness made by Sherman. All RR's destroyed—bridges gone. We are cut off from the world—to eat out our own hearts."[29] A Confederate veteran stated, "...when all else was gone, when life was paralyzed, when hope was dead...to the physical suffering, the mental torment, was added the crucifixion of the soul."[30]

In June 1865 Martin Goldsborough came to Rockbridge County to bring his daughter home. They arrived in Baltimore on July 2, 1865.

— Postwar

The War for Southern Independence was lost and Southern bereavement would last for generations. The entire region would suffer economically, politically, socially, and culturally well into the twentieth century. Southerners picked up the pieces of their lives and worked to rebuild their shattered world. Organizations came to life in Baltimore to help support the destitute Confederates. Pheme was no doubt involved in these efforts.

In an address at a reunion of the Association of the Maryland Line held in Baltimore, Captain Frances W. Dawson praised Marylanders for their service to the Confederacy and the people of the South:

> When all else failed—when the banner of the South was furled forever—you came forward to alleviate our grief in showing us that you were as true in defeat as in triumph, and that, for you, failure abated not a jot the merit, or the justice of the freedom for which we fought, nor lessened by a particle your interest in us, or your care for us. It seemed, indeed that in our poverty, in the ashes of our homes and confronting a problem which was then insoluble and is not solved yet, we were dearer to you than in the pomp and pride of a struggle, which—if right were might—must have had the consummation we wished.

Captain Dawson enumerated a few of the groups that assisted the people of the South, "in their sorest need, without wounding their pride or insulting their poverty." The Baltimore Agricultural Aid Society, formed immediately after Appomattox, supplied stock, farming tools, and seed, along with $80,000. Martin Goldsborough was almost certainly involved with this project. In 1866 the Southern Relief Association was organized and held a fair which raised almost $165,000 for distribution. In 1867 the Maryland legislature appropriated $100,000 "for the relief of the destitute people in the States wasted by civil war." An additional $20,000 was privately donated. The money was used to buy provisions for distribution to people in the lower South who were suffering from the want of food. In 1867 the Ladies Depository was formed for the purpose of obtaining needle and "fancy work" for the impoverished women of the South to earn a living.

Captain Dawson finished his address with two passages from a letter by General Lee on receipt of a gift of clothing. Lee wrote:

I beg that you will express to them my grateful thanks for this mark of kindness, which I shall value most highly in remembrance of their munificent bounty bestowed on thousands of destitute women and children by the 'Association for the Relief of Southern Sufferers,' the fruits of which shall live long after those who have received it have mouldered into dust.... I am fully aware of the many and repeated acts of sympathy and relief bestowed by the generous citizens of Baltimore upon the people of the South, acts which will always be remembered, <u>but which can never be repaid, and which will forever stand at monuments of their Christian charity and kindness</u>. I know, too, that by their munificence they have brought loss and suffering on themselves, for which I trust God will reward them.

On June 29, 1874, Pheme married Charles Perry Willson in Cambridge, Maryland. A former resident of Frederick, Maryland, Sgt. Maj. Charles Willson had served in Co. G, 7th Virginia Cavalry, Laurel Brigade. Although this unit fought at Gettysburg, Charles was not with it; he was on furlough recuperating from a gunshot wound to the right thigh received early in the Gettysburg Campaign. Pheme was 38 when she married. Her hair, which had shown streaks of gray shortly after her arrest, was almost completely white on her wedding day.

Charles was a man with a delightful sense of humor. An example of this was the marriage contract he offered Pheme [See Personal Collection]. He was the widower of a close friend of Pheme's and with her marriage, Pheme became stepmother to five children. She would give Charles three more; Martin, Sam, and Ann.

They removed to Summit Point, Jefferson County, West Virginia, where their hospitality was soon acknowledged and will be long remembered. Twenty years ago it was a real privilege to meet there in winter and all gather round the blazing fire, when host and hostess and many guests would recall their war experiences. Sometimes the guests would be snowed in and we would have a house party for days of the bachelor veterans of the war and there we would sit for hour after hour in the old southern home, the soldiers with their favorite dogs that followed them everywhere, stretched at full length before the huge fire of logs that burned away only to be replaced while first one battle scene and then another was repeated by some who were in the fight. This would go on for days and never get tiresome.[31]

Charles and Pheme's wedding photos.

Martin Willson, one of Pheme and Charles' two sons.

Ann Willson, Pheme's only surviving child.

In Summit Point, the Willsons farmed, ran a mercantile establishment and a boarding house. Their home still stands today, as does the Episcopal Church of the Holy Spirit, a small stone chapel built largely due to Pheme's effort. "Mrs. Willson devoted the same energy to church work that she had given to the Confederate cause."[32] She had raised about a third of the construction funds, even requesting a donation from the Queen of England. The little church has two stained glass windows; one for Martin and Ann Goldsborough, Pheme's parents, and one for Martin and Sam, Pheme's sons, who died in the same week in November 1880.

Pheme buried her boys in one of the first family plots at Green Hill Cemetery in Berryville, Virginia. In 1893 Charles died. He was buried on the same small knoll, according to his wishes, where he "could see the sun rise." On March 10, three years later, Pheme died of cancer.

In 1896 this earnest, active, self-sacrificing Southern lady with the spirit of Joan of Arc quietly joined the great army of martyrs and laid down the cross in the shadow of the Rock and was laid to rest in Virginia, the State she dearly loved, near the little town of Berryville in Clark [sic] County, beside her husband and children. Her death closed another historical page in the annals of Maryland's brave, patriotic women.

Acknowledged as a genius with pronounced intellect, she was urged to write reminiscences of the war for Southern History—but falling into ill health she never complied with the wishes of her many friends.

And so a varied life has closed and shut up the treasure house of a brilliant memory. Like many for whom she risked her life and liberty, she has passed—fully prepared tho' untrumpeted [sic] to a glorious reward. Thus with tears for her loss, regret for her sorrows, we lay with reverence the laurel wreath upon her grave.[33]

Ninety-nine years later, almost to the day, in March 1995, another wreath was laid in reverence on Pheme's Berryville grave. It was during a private ceremony preceding her induction in Annapolis into the Maryland Women's Hall of Fame. Euphemia Mary Goldsborough Willson was the first Confederate woman to be so recognized. Maryland finally honored her courageous daughter.

Charles and Pheme's house in Summit Point, WV, as it looks today.

The Episcopal Church of the Holy Spirit in Summit Point, WV.

Taken at the wreath laying ceremony in March 1995 at Pheme's grave in Green Hill Cemetery, Berryville, Virginia. The woman is Stephanie Wortz, interpreter at GNMP, who portrayed Pheme as one of the women who served at Gettysburg.

Pheme was inducted into the Maryland Women's Hall of Fame. At the ceremony are (l to r): Gov. Parris Glendening; Stuart Crim, Pheme's great grandson; Betsy Stagner, great granddaughter; and Phyllis Trickett, chairperson of the Maryland Commission for Women. Seated is Mrs. Elizabeth Crim, Pheme's granddaughter.

The Monument to Maryland's Confederate Women was unveiled in 1918.
The pedestal reads: "To the Confederate Women of Maryland 1861-1865.
The brave at home. In difficulty and danger, regardless of self, they fed the
hungry, clothed the needy, nursed the wounded, and comforted the dying."
It is located at Charles and University in Baltimore. (Courtesy Museum of the Confederacy)

The Hospital Books

Pennsylvania College Hospital and Camp Letterman, Gettysburg, 1863

"...in the hour of suffering during 'Our College days'..." [1]

The Hospital Books kept by Euphemia Goldsborough recorded some of the men she met at the Pennsylvania College Hospital and at Camp Letterman while serving as nurse to the wounded Confederate prisoners. Entries include autographs, letters, and poems in gratitude for her nursing service and friendship. They were not recorded in sequence of time or place. Most are in pencil; some are in pen. Obvious by the penmanship, most men signed their own names. However, in a few instances two or as many as five names would be in the same hand; presumably those soldiers were unable to pen their own names. Understandably, some were extremely difficult to decipher in reflection of the situation in which they were written. The transcription includes the punctuation or the lack thereof, spelling, and abbreviations. Following each entry is information pertaining to that individual.

Excluding the duplicates, the anonymous, and the unidentified, there are 114 individuals represented by the entries. [See Appendix 1 for alphabetical listing by state] They include two Federal military personnel, two civilian doctors, four Confederate surgeons, and two Confederate chaplains. Of the remaining 104 Confederate soldiers, five died, two took the oath, and, as the only happy note, one [J. W. Watson of the 3rd North Carolina] escaped. The bulk of the soldiers, 56 in number, were paroled and/or exchanged within a few months of their capture, many of whom were unable to continue service in the army. The remaining 40 were destined for imprisonment, most transferred to either Point Lookout, Johnson's Island, or Fort Delaware. Three of the men imprisoned at Fort Delaware would suffer as members of the Immortal Six Hundred. The men recorded in Pheme's books were among the thousands who eventually left Gettysburg and were processed through Baltimore. During this huge influx the city's residents were arrested for speaking to, saluting, or otherwise showing sympathy to the wounded prisoners. Almost all of Pheme's former patients were taken to the West's Buildings in Baltimore which were six converted warehouses along Union Dock on Pratt Street. The West's Buildings served as a hospital and was rated very poorly by those confined there. No sympathetic visitors were allowed. These prisoners were then either returned South on parole and/or exchanged, sent to Fort McHenry for temporary confinement, or transferred to the prisons of the North.

A unique bond was forged between the female nurses and their sick or wounded patients during the Civil War. The physical health of a patient was only part of the concern for the nurses; mental, emotional, and spiritual well-being were also important. The close human connection between nurse and patient was often deep and lasting and sometimes extended to their respective families. Many nurses' photos had a "pride of place" in soldier's homes; correspondence was sometimes continued for decades, and respects were paid by personal visits after the war. One soldier put it succinctly in a letter of gratitude to his nurse: "There are kind deeds received which a <u>man</u> cannot ever forget, more especially when they are done by one who does not expect any rewards for them, but the satisfaction of having helped humanity."[2]

The texts from both "The Hospital Books" and "The Diaries" are contained in these two leather bound volumes. The third volume was stolen from the descendant's home in the late 1980s.

For the Confederate women of Maryland or of any other state held in Union control, the price of "having helped humanity" was at the cost of great personal risk. Outside of the Confederacy the commitment of Southern women to aid the Confederate soldier was nowhere stronger than in Baltimore. An example is drawn from the letters between two nurses at Gettysburg, Hettie McCrea and Maggie Branson, and Thomas Houston, their former patient and later prisoner at Johnson's Island. [See Appendix 2] The women journeyed to Gettysburg a full year after the battle, located Thomas' brother's grave, identified the corpse, and had it removed to a family plot in Greenmount Cemetery, Baltimore. "...I cannot say to you...what I wish, " Houston wrote. "The tongue finds no speech warm enough for the heart...Henceforth, your names, in one family, will be sacred and household words...."[3]

At Gettysburg the Confederate prisoners were aware of the risks taken and abuse endured by the Southern women who came to that field to nurse them. The men who placed their names in Pheme's books had suffered battle wounds and were far away from home and loved ones. It was these few friends like Pheme to whom they looked for human kindness and care. Pheme corresponded with these men after Gettysburg, renewed acquaintance with some during her exile in Richmond, and became fast friends with a few for many years after the war.

The pall of imminent imprisonment added to the soldier's lot at Gettysburg. "I am too sad at the thought of leaving this place made pleasant by the smiles and cheering words and kind friends to go to some dungeon where tyranny and oppression reigns supreme," wrote William Bailey of the 5th Florida, who was fated as one of the Immortal Six Hundred, and would die in captivity. Imprisonment for the men in the following pages at Point Lookout, Johnson's Island, and Fort Delaware was a degrading and dehumanizing experience. Inadequate food distribution was excused as justified in retaliation for Andersonville. Hunger, want, disease, brutality, and murder were much the fabric of Confederate experience in prisons, along with the desperate hope for release. In 1863 officials of both governments postured over issues effecting exchange, while human stockpiles swelled the prisons' rolls. "Rumors, that never came to anything, of an immediate general release, were every day occurrences...we were kept on the rack by alternate hope and disappointment."[4]

To list the prisons' statistics of size, length of operation, number of inmates, etc. would be to sanitize the suffering and anguish. To understand what the men in Pheme's books were facing at Gettysburg as their wounds healed well enough to be transported, only the prisoners' own experiences can provide. There is no attempt at objectivity here; the subjects' narratives are immersed in misery and hardship.

The Prisons

"You don't have to die to go to hell."

— WEST'S BUILDINGS ———

Henry Shepherd, Co. D, 43rd North Carolina, was not listed in the "Hospital Books," but nonetheless had a similar fate. Wounded by a bullet passing through his right knee on Culp's Hill, he was captured on July 3. He was removed to a general hospital in Frederick, Maryland for a month, where he "was under the charge of the regular army surgeons, at whose hands I received excellent and skillful treatment."[5] He was then transferred to West's Buildings and it is in his recollections that we are given the picture of what the wounded Confederates experienced once they left the hospitals at Gettysburg. It is reasonable to assume that Pheme's patients endured much the same trials. Like Shepherd, Thomas Houston and Robert McCulloch, two men whose names were listed in Pheme's books, were sent to Johnson's Island via West's Buildings. Subsequent to their release, Houston and McCulloch played an important part in Effie's diaries. Shepherd wrote:

> *On the 14th of August I was taken to Baltimore. Upon arriving, I was forced to march with a number of fellow prisoners from Camden Station to the office of the Provost Marshal, then situated at the Gilmor House, directly facing the Battle Monument. The weather was intensely hot, and my limb was bleeding from the still unhealed wound. After an exhausting delay I was finally removed in an ambulance to the 'West Hospital' at the end of Concord street, looking out upon Union Dock and the wharves at that time occupied by the Old Bay Line or Baltimore Steam Packet Company.*
>
> *The West Building was originally a warehouse intended for the storage of cotton, now transformed into a hospital by the Federal government. It had not a single element of adaption for the purpose to which it was applied.*
>
> *The immense structure was dark, gloomy, without adequate ventilation, devoid of sanitary or hygienic appliances or conveniences, and pervaded at all times by the pestilential exhalations which arose from the neighboring docks. During the seven weeks of my sojourn here, I rarely tasted a glass of cold water, but drank, in the broiling heat of the dog days, the warm, impure draught that flowed from the hydrant adjoining the ward*

in which I lay. My food was mush and molasses with hard bread, served three times a day.

When I reached the West Building, I was destitute of clothing, for such as I had worn was nearly reduced to fragments, the surgeons have mutilated it seriously while treating my wound at Gettysburg. My friends made every effort to furnish me with a fresh supply but without avail. The articles of wearing apparel designed for me were appropriated by the authorities in charge, and the letter which accompanied them was taken unread from my hands. Moreover, my friends and relatives, of whom I had not a few in Baltimore, were rigorously denied all access to me; if they endeavored to communicate with me, their letters were intercepted; and if they strove to minister to my relief in any form, their supplies were turned back at the gate of the hospital, or confiscated to the use of the wardens and nurses.[6] ...Not one of those who would gladly have ministered to my needs, was ever allowed to cross the threshold, or in any form to communicate with me.[7]

On one occasion a party of Baltimore ladies who were anxious to contribute to the well being of the Confederate prisoners in the West Building, were driven from the sidewalk by a volley of decayed eggs hurled at them by the hospital guards. I was present when this incident occurred, and hearing the uproar, limped from my bunk to the window, just in time to see the group of ladies assailed by the eggs retreating up Concord street in order to escape these missiles. They were soon out of range, and their visit to the hospital was never repeated, at least during my sojourn within its walls.[8]

A word here in reference to the methods of treatment, medical and surgical, which prevailed in West Hospital...The surgeons of that time seemed to be timorous in the application of their own agency, and the carnival of horrors which was revealed on more than one occasion in the operating room, might have engaged the loftiest power of tragic portrayal displayed by the author of 'The Inferno.' The gangrene was cut from my wound as a butcher would cut a chop or a steak in the Lexington market; it may have been providential that I was delivered from the anaesthetic blundering then in vogue, and 'recovered in spite of my physician.' Consideration originating in sensibility, or even in humanity, found no place in West Hospital. To illustrate concretely, a soldier, severely wounded, was brought into the overcrowded ward in which I lay. There was no bunk or resting place at his disposal, but one of the stewards recog-

nizing the exigency, soon found a ghastly remedy. 'Why,' he said, pointing to a dying man in his cot, 'that old fellow over there will soon be dead, and as soon as he is gone, we'll put this man in his bed.' And so the living soldier was at once consigned to the uncleansed berth of his predecessor.[9]

...I endured my seven weeks torture from thirst and hunger in the cavernous recesses of West Hospital...[10] I remained in West Hospital until September 29th, 1863.[11]

— JOHNSON'S ISLAND ———

Henry Shepherd was transferred to Johnson's Island along with other men in Pheme's "Hospital Books." In fact, he was placed in the same block with Thomas Dix Houston and Robert McCulloch. Shepherd was also released with Houston and McCulloch in March 1865 and was almost certainly part of the group whose arrival in Richmond was described in her diary.

Prisoners who traveled from West's Buildings to Johnson's Island went by the Northern Central Railway from Calvert Station through Pittsburgh to Sandusky, Ohio. Shepherd's narrative described his prison experience in Block No. 11, Johnson's Island:

This [Johnson's Island], one of the most celebrated of the Federal prisons, is situated about three miles from Sandusky, near the mouth of its harbor...On every side, Lake Erie and the harbor encompassed it effectually. Nature had made it an ideal prison. There was but a single hope of escape, and that was by means of the dense ice which enveloped the island during the greater part of the winter season. I once saw 1,500 Federal soldiers march in perfect security from Sandusky to Johnson's Island, a distance of three miles, across a firmly frozen harbor. This was in January, 1864. The area of the island was estimated at eight acres....

During the summer months, when the lake was free from ice, a sloop of war lay constantly off the Island, with her guns trained upon the barracks. Yet, notwithstanding, there were a few successful attempts to escape. I knew personally at least two of those who scaled the high wall and made their way across the frozen harbor under cover of the friendly darkness...Those who failed, as by far the greater number did (for I can recall not more than three or four successful attempts in all), were subjected to the most degrading punishments in the form of servile labor, scarcely adapted to the status of convicts.[12]

The island prison was intended for the confinement of Confederate officers only, of whom there were nearly three thousand immured within its walls during the period of my residence. The greater part of these had been captured at Gettysburg and Port Hudson.[13]

During the earlier months of my life on the Island, a sutler's shop afforded extra supplies for those who were fortunate enough to have control of small amounts of United States currency. This happier element, however, included but a limited proportion of the three thousand, so that, for a greater part, relentless and gnawing hunger was the chronic and normal state. But even this merciful tempering of the wind to the shorn lambs of implacable appetite, was destined soon to become a mere memory; for suddenly and without warning, the sutler and his mitigating supplies passed away upon the ground of retaliation for alleged cruelties inflicted upon Federal prisoners in the hands of the Confederate government. Then began the grim and remorseless struggle with starvation until I was released on parole....

With the disappearance of the sutler's stores and the exclusion of every form of food provided by friends in the North or at the South, there came the period of supreme suffering by all alike. Boxes sent prisoners were seized, and their contents appropriated. Thus began, and for six months continued, a fierce and unrelenting conflict to maintain life upon the minimum of rations furnished from day to day by the Federal commissariat. To subsist upon this or die of gradual starvation, was the inevitable alternative. To illustrate the extreme lengths to which the exclusion of supplies other than the official rations was carried, an uncle of mine in North Carolina...forwarded to me, by flag of truce, a box of his finest hams...The contents were appropriated by the commandant of the Island, and the empty box carefully delivered to me at my quarters. The rations upon which life was maintained for the latter months of my imprisonment were distributed every day at noon, and were as follows: To each prisoner one-half loaf of hard bread, and a piece of salt pork, in size not sufficient for an ordinary meal. In taste the latter was almost nauseating, but it was devoured because there was no choice other than to eat it, or endure the tortures of prolonged starvation. Stimulants such as tea and coffee were rigidly interdicted. For months I did not taste either, not even on the memorable first of January, 1864, when the thermometer fell to 22 degrees below zero, and my feet were frozen.

*Vegetable food was almost unknown, and as a natural re-
sult, death from such diseases, as scurvy, carried more than
one Confederate to a grave in the island cemetery just outside
the prison walls. I never shall forget the sense of gratitude
with which I secured, by some lucky chance, a raw turnip, and
in an advanced state of physical exhaustion, eagerly devoured
it as I supported myself by holding on to the steps of my bar-
rack. No language of which I am capable is adequate to por-
tray the agonies of immitigable hunger. The rations which were
distributed at noon each day, were expected to sustain life until
the noon of the day following. During this interval, many of us
became so crazed by hunger that the prescribed allowance of
pork and bread was devoured ravenously as soon as received.
For six or seven months I subsisted upon one meal in 24 hours,
and that was composed of food so coarse and unpalatable as to
appeal only to a stomach which was eating out its own life. So
terrible at times were the pangs of appetite, that some of the
prisoners who were fortunate enough to secure the kindly services of a rat-terrier, were glad to appropriate the animals which
were thus captured, cooking and eating them to allay the fierce
agony of unabating hunger. Although I frequently saw the rats
pursued and caught, I never tasted their flesh when cooked, for
I was so painfully affected by nausea, as to be rendered inca-
pable of retaining the ordinary prison fare.*

*The winters in the latitude of Johnson's Island was doubly
severe to men born and raised in the Southern states. Moreover,
the prisoners possessed neither clothing nor blankets intended
for such weather as we experienced. During the winter of 1863-
64, I was confined in one room with seventy other Confederates.
The building was not ceiled, but simply weather-boarded. It
afforded most inadequate protection against the cold or snow,
which at times beat in upon my bunk with pitiless severity. The
room was provided with one antiquated stove to preserve 70
men from intense suffering when the thermometer stood and
fifteen and twenty degrees below zero. The fuel given us was
insufficient, and in our desperation, we burned every available
chair or box, and even parts of our bunks found their way into
the stove. During this time of horrors, some of us maintained
life by forming a circle and dancing with the energy of despair.*

*The sick and wounded in the prison hospital had no especial
provision made for their comfort. They received the prescribed
rations, and were cared for in their helplessness, as in their dying
hours, by other prisoners detailed as nurses. To this duty I was*

once assigned and ministered to my comrades as faithfully as I was able from the standpoint of youth and lack of training.

The mails from the South were received only at long and agonizing intervals. I did not hear a word from my home until at least four months after my capture. The official regulations prescribed 28 lines as the extreme limit allowed for a letter forwarded to prisoners of war. When some loving and devoted wife or mother exceeded this limit, the letter was retained by the commandant, and the empty envelope, marked 'from your wife,' 'your mother,' or 'your child,' was placed in the hands of the prisoner. During my confinement at Johnson's Island, I succeeded in communicating with ex-President Pierce [through relatives]...I addressed a letter to the former President, in the hope that he might exert some salutary influence which would induce the authorities to ameliorate our unhappy condition.

I received a most kind and cordial letter from Mr. Pierce, who declared, "You could not entertain a more mistaken opinion than to suppose that I have the slightest power for good with this government."[14]

— POINT LOOKOUT —————

First Sergeant N. F. Harman of Georgia described this site:

I was landed at the Federal prison of Point Lookout, MD. After searching us and taking our money, knives, and other articles, we were placed inside the prison. All of our blankets were kept by officers, but later we were each allowed one blanket. We had no barracks. Our shelter was canvas tents of the bell style. In each tent fifteen to twenty men were placed. The floors of these tents were of damp earth; no planks or straw for dryness. Our beds were on this dirt floor. Two of us slept together—one blanket on the ground, one to cover with.

The wind had a clean sweep from one side of the Chesapeake Bay. We never had any wood or coal for fires nor any fireplaces.

...The prison was in a square inclosure with a plank wall eighteen feet high. About three feet from the top was a platform for the guards to walk on. These guards were negroes from the plantations, mainly from North and South Carolina. About twenty-five feet from the walls and next to the tents was a ditch known as the 'dead line.' If a prisoner crossed it, he was immediately shot.

At night there was a patrol of two negro soldiers inside the prison for each division, and these divisions, thirteen in number, had each a thousand men in them. This night patrol was to keep watch on the prisoners. Every one had to be in his tent when 'taps' was sounded and all lights had to be put out, and talking was not permitted. I knew of the negro patrols calling men out of their tents and chasing them up and down the streets until they were exhausted....

One night one of these patrols shot into a tent and killed two men. When the officer came rushing in to see what was the matter, the negro said he shot into the tent to make the prisoners stop talking. The fact was, all the men in this tent were asleep; but nothing was ever done to this negro patrol for the murder of two men who were asleep when shot.

It was a common thing for these negro guards and the negro patrols to amuse themselves by calling the prisoners out and forcing them to amuse them in many ways. The officers did not seem to care, but allowed such humiliation.

Now as to our rations. At 7 a.m. we were marched into a cook house, holding some five hundred plates. On each plate was a piece of pork about one-sixth of a pound. As each man came in he took his stand at a plate until the five hundred men each had a plate, then at signal each man took his meat and we were marched out. At 9 a.m. the bread wagon entered the prison, and each one was given one-half loaf of bread. At noon we were again marched in to the cook room and got a pint of so-called soup, but it was little more than salt water. No beans or peas or grease of any kind appeared in this soup. Once a week we received a mackerel or piece of codfish, uncooked in place of meat. This we had to eat raw and salty, as we had no means to cook it or to soak it. We had no means of kindling fires. Our supply of water was from six wells with pumps. Of these, only one well could be used for drinking purposes. This well was in my division, No. 5. If the water from the other wells was allowed to stand even one night, a thick green scum formed, as if copperas was in it, and the water was unfit to drink. The death rate was heavy.[15]

— FORT DELAWARE ————

W. H. Moon, Co. I, 13th Alabama, was captured along with many others of Archer's Brigade on July 1. He described the conditions at Fort Delaware:

We arrived at Fort Delaware about the 5th of July, and were put into newly built barracks consisting of long rows of buildings. The material was all rough and the planks nailed on vertically with strips to cover the openings between....

At the time of our arrival there was much rain, and the island, being formed by the drifting of mud between the two channels at the mouth of the Delaware River, soon became a bog where the men had to pass. After the whole place had become a veritable bog, the authorities had plank walks built, which made the passageway better. For three or four months we were supplied with plenty of bread and meat; but as the winter approached our allowance was cut to about half, which was wholly inadequate to supply sufficient nourishment to keep the men from starving and freezing when the cold winter set in. Through the long winter months the men sat in groups upon their bunks or stood leaning against the walls on the sunny side of the buildings, wrapped in their old blankets, conversation generally being about the many good things they had to eat at their homes in Dixie. The winter was so cold that the ice in the river by the ebb and flow of the tide drifted in great icebergs, so that when the tide was at low ebb, it looked like a vast plain covered with stacks of ice, no water being visible.

A division contained four hundred men and two heaters. Around these crowds would gather in compact mass several deep, so that no one else could get near enough to receive the benefit of the heat. The houses being very open, in cold weather the heat could be felt but a short distance even from a red-hot stove. The prisoners were allowed one suit of clothes, a cheap overcoat, and one inferior blanket to each man. These, with the one heater to two hundred men, were the only protection against the bitter cold winds that swept across the Delaware River and up the bay....

Those who crowded around the stove continually were dubbed stove rats. On very cold days those who spent most of their time on their bunks trying to keep warm would get down in the passway between the bunks, form in column of one or two with as many in the rear as wished to participate, and charge the 'stove rats.' The hindmost would push those in front until the stove was cleared. The rear ones of this column would take their turn at the stove. These charges and countercharges would on very cold days sometimes continue for several hours....

In February we were moved into the old barracks south of where we had been staying. These were formerly occupied by commissioned officers, who had been moved to other parts. When we entered these new quarters, the bunks and floors were covered with snow, which we had to clear out before starting up our little heaters. The next morning from our division four corpses were taken, frozen stiff. For four months, during the coldest of the winter, very few of the eight or nine thousand prisoners at Fort Delaware had sufficient food to satisfy their hunger at any time. The Yanks said they were retaliating on us for the way their men were being treated at Andersonville, Ga....

Quite a number of the older men who required more food to sustain life became very much emaciated, and succumbed to the cold, being found on their bunks in the morning frozen to death. How any survived the ordeal through which we had to pass that winter seems strange to me now. Early every morning we would get down from our bunks and trot around to warm up and get some feeling in our feet, which were benumbed with cold till they felt more like clogs to the legs than feet.

The prevailing diseases were small pox in winter and measles and diarrhea in summer. From these diseases hundreds died and were buried on the Jersey shore [Finns Point-now a National cemetery]. The manner of burial was to dig a ditch six feet wide and six feet deep, put in three boxes containing corpses one on top of the other, then extend the ditch, using the dirt to cover the boxes.[16]

Fort Delaware provided the officers who made up the Immortal Six Hundred; a group chosen for another retaliation. When repeated requests were disregarded to stop the shelling of Charleston civilians unable to leave that city, 600 Union officers were taken from Andersonville and placed in the same city quarter as the civilians. The Union authorities having been duly notified, requested the same number of Confederate officers from Fort Delaware for placement on Morris Island in the line of fire from Confederate forts. In mid-August the Six Hundred began a hellish eighteen-day voyage, confined and packed into a lightless hold, awash with bodily fluids. The men spent six weeks in a stockade pen under the shells of artillery duels and were then moved to Fort Pulaski. As the Union authorities had learned that Union prisoners at Andersonville received only cornmeal and sorghum for rations, it was decided to place the Six Hundred on the like. As there was no sorghum available, the prisoners existed on ten ounces of cornmeal, the worms therein, and the flesh of the cats who freely roamed the prison. Neither clothing or blankets were issued, nor were boxes from friends allowed.

The retaliatory expedition south terminated on the 4th day of March, 1865...we were taken aboard the steamer...We were landed at Fort Delaware in due time. The prisoners at the fort had largely increased in numbers during our absence. They were in comparatively good health, and the contrast between their appearance and that of the emaciated, haggard, and ragged survivors of the 600 was most marked. The photographs of sick soldiers, after their return from Confederate prisons, taken by the United States Sanitary Commission, and industriously and widely distributed for the purpose of firing the Northern heart, would have brought a blush of shame to the Northern cheek, if they could have seen a photograph of the group of Confederate prisoners, taken on our return to Fort Delaware.[17]

Fort Delaware, which had been described as "the lower most Hells of human Hells," was seen differently by the tortured eyes of the Immortal Six Hundred. The above narrator [Col. Abram Fulkerson, 63rd Tennessee] wrote on his return to the prison: "Our party greatly enjoyed the superior accommodations and privileges of the Delaware prison...." Apparently Col. Fulkerson had discovered a lower human Hell.

Signatures [Book I]

E. M. Goldsborough
General Hospital
Gettysburg, Penn
Aug. 4th

Samuel Watson
Co. E 5th Texas Reg
Lost his right arm. One of the most attractive boys I ever saw. Very ill but little hope of his recovery but hope for the best 8th Better today, decidedly [illegible] poor fellow 9th much better today, strong hope of his recovery

Samuel Watson, Co. E, 5th Texas, suffered amputation and died on September 13. [See lamentation of Watson's death in Book II, page 70, and T. J. Sneed's letter page 78; also Pheme's letter to Mrs. Watson in the Personal Collection section, page 130].

Sergeant Wm R Elam
Co H 18th Va Regt
Spring Mills
Appomattox Cty
Virginia

Sergeant William Robert Elam, Co. H, 18th Virginia, was shot in the right thigh, transferred to West's Buildings, paroled and exchanged at City Point 9/63, and admitted into a Richmond hospital.

Samuel T. Reynolds
Mecklenburg, Va.
Co. E, 14th Va. Reg
"3"

Samuel T. Reynolds, Co. E, 14th Virginia, was a musician. He was wounded, transferred to West's Buildings, paroled and exchanged at City Point 9/63, admitted into a Richmond hospital and furloughed.

Corpl. C. L. Parker
Richmond, Va
Co. I, 1st Va Reg

Corporal Calvin Lee Parker, Co. I, 1st Virginia, had his left leg amputated, was transferred to West's Buildings, paroled and exchanged at City Point 11/63, admitted into a Richmond hospital, and joined the Invalid Corps.

Wm. H. Gaskins
OS Co. K, 8th Va.
Fauquier, Va.

Orderly Sergeant William H. Gaskins, Co. K, 8th Virginia was "wounded and captured", and died at Camp Letterman November 5, 1863 of "obstinate diarrhea."

J. B. Burroughs Co. D
2nd Va Cavalry

James B. Burroughs, Co. D, 2nd Virginia Cavalry, was gunshot in the left hip, transferred to West's Buildings, paroled and exchanged at City Point 11/63, admitted into a Richmond hospital, and declared "unfit for service."

C. F. Burroughs Co. D
2nd Va Cavalry

Christopher Frank Burroughs, Co. D, 2nd Virginia Cavalry, was left as a nurse, transferred to Ft. McHenry, then Point Lookout in 9/63, from where he was discharged 11/1/64. He died November 11, 1864 and was buried at Hilton Head, South Carolina.

A. A. Ross 1st S.C.
Cavalry Co. H

A. A. Ross, Co. H, 1st South Carolina Cavalry, was wounded in the legs, transferred to West's Buildings, paroled and exchanged at City Point 9/63.

J. R. Dunlap Co. C *Jeff Davis Legion Miss*	John R. Dunlap, Co. C, Jeff Davis Legion (cavalry under Hampton) lost his right leg, was transferred to West's Buildings, paroled and exchanged at City Point 10/63.
J. H. Hamilton *2nd Sergeant Co. H* *7th Tennessee Reg* *Nashville, Tenn*	Sergeant John H. Hamilton, Co. H, 7th Tennessee, was gunshot in the knee, transferred to West's Buildings, paroled and exchanged at City Point 9/63.
Tent No. 1 *Sergt. Francis M. Woods* *Co. G, 5th Fla Vol* *Mosley Hall* *Madison County,* *Florida*	Sergeant Francis Marion Woods, Co. G, 5th Florida, suffered grapeshot through both thighs, was transferred to West's Buildings, paroled and exchanged at City Point 9/63.
A. J. Loyd *32nd Co I N C*	Andrew J. Loyd, Co. C, 32nd North Carolina, had both thighs gunshot, was transferred to West's Buildings, paroled and exchanged at City Point 11/63, and admitted into a Richmond hospital.
I. H. Mason *30 N C Co F*	Israel H. Mason, Co. F, 30th North Carolina, was wounded on 7/1 and died 7/16/63.
D. Walkins *14th N C Reg Co E*	David Walkins, Co. E, 14th North Carolina, suffered amputation of the right arm, was transferred to West's Buildings, paroled and exchanged at City Point 9/63.
J W Watson *Com I 3rd N C*	J. W. Watson, Co. I, 3rd North Carolina, was slightly wounded, taken prisoner, escaped, and returned to his regiment.
Wm C Brown *Co A 18th Reg Va Vols*	William Clay Brown, Co. A, 18th Virginia, was gunshot in the left leg, transferred to West's Buildings, paroled and exchanged at City Point 9/63.

Thomas G Dunbar *Co B 14th Ten Reg*	Thomas G. Dunbar, Co. B, 14th Tennessee, was an ambulance driver. He suffered a gunshot to the foot, was captured 7/3, transferred to West's Buildings where he was paroled and presumably exchanged and returned to his regiment.
T B Rouse *Co F 2nd N C*	T. B. Rouse, Co. F, 2nd North Carolina, had his leg amputated, was transferred to West's Buildings, paroled and exchanged at City Point 11/63 and admitted into a Richmond hospital.
B F Pittman *Co B 2nd Bat N C*	B. F. Pittman, Co. B, 2nd North Carolina Battalion, was wounded in the hip 7/3 and died at Camp Letterman 9/14/63.
William H Beck *Com H 5th Fla Reg*	William H. Beck, Co. H, 5th Florida, was gunshot in the left hip, transferred to West's Buildings, paroled and exchanged at City Point 11/63. He returned to his regiment and surrendered at Appomattox.
T L Gales *Co I 43 N C Regt* *nurse*	T. L. Gales, Co. I, 43rd North Carolina, was left as a nurse, transferred to West's Buildings, paroled and exchanged at City Point 11/63. He continued to nurse until his death 11/64.
J H Griffith nurse *Co B 43rd N C Regt*	Josiah H. Griffith, Co. B, 43rd North Carolina, was left as a nurse, reported for duty as hospital nurse 8/10/63 at Camp Letterman, was transferred to West's Buildings, paroled and exchanged at City Point 11/63.
T A Sparrow nurse *Co A 55 N C Regt*	Thomas A. Sparrow, Co. A, 55th North Carolina, was left as a nurse, transferred to West's Buildings, then Ft. McHenry, then Point Lookout in 9/63. He was paroled and exchanged 9/64 and died 9/25/64.

John Hancock
Co B 2nd N C Bat

John Hancock, Co. B, 2nd North Carolina Battalion, was left as a nurse, transferred to West's Buildings where he was suffering from "debility." From there he was transferred to Ft. McHenry, then to Point Lookout in 1/64. He was paroled and exchanged 11/64.

J H Brown
Co F 5th Texas

J. H. Brown, Co. F, 5th Texas, was gunshot in the right hip, transferred to West's Buildings, paroled and exchanged at City Point 11/63, and admitted into a Richmond hospital.

J F Ford
Co K 5th Texas

J. F. Ford, Co. K, 5th Texas, was wounded in the left hip and thigh, transferred to West's Buildings, paroled and exchanged at City Point 9/63.

Robt. Reddick
21st Regt Miss Vols

Robert H. Reddick, Co. F, 21st Mississippi, was wounded in the head and leg, transferred to West's Buildings, then to Ft. McHenry, then to Point Lookout where he was exchanged 2/65.

Jacob Ganey
Co F 3rd Ga

Jacob Ganey, Co. F, 3rd Georgia, was wounded, transferred to West's Buildings, paroled and exchanged at City Point 9/63.

Sergt J D Wilson
Co F 8th S C Regt

Sergeant Joseph D. Wilson, Co. F, 8th South Carolina, was wounded in the leg, transferred to West's Buildings, paroled and exchanged at City Point 11/63, and admitted into a Richmond hospital.

J W Middleton,
private
Co H 27 Va Regt

Jonathan W. Middleton, Co. H, 27th Virginia, was left as a nurse, transferred to West's Buildings, then to Ft. McHenry where he took the oath.

Britton Parker
2nd Regt Co G S C

Britton Parker, Co. G, 2nd South Carolina, had his right leg amputated, was transferred to West's Buildings, paroled and exchanged at City Point 11/63, admitted into a Richmond hospital and entered the Invalid Corps.

John W. Whitesill *Co B 19th Va*	Sergeant John Wesley Whitesill, Co. B, 19th Virginia, had his left leg amputated, was transferred to West's Buildings, exchanged and entered the Invalid Corps in 8/64.
James Bruchett *Co K 8 Regt Va vol*	James M. Bruchett, Co. K, 8th Virginia, had his left leg amputated, was transferred to West's Buildings, paroled and exchanged at City Point 11/63.
C H Maloney *Co K 18 Va Regt*	Clem H. Maloney, Co. K, 18th Virginia, was wounded in the thigh, transferred to West's Buildings, transferred to Point Lookout, paroled and exchanged at City Point 4/64.
Thomas J Cloud *Co C 3rd Ala*	Thomas J. Cloud, Co. C, 3rd Alabama, was wounded in the right thigh, transferred to West's Buildings, transferred to Point Lookout, paroled and exchanged at City Point 3/64, admitted into a Richmond hospital and furloughed.
Sergt. J. B. Worsham *Co D 24th Virginia Vols*	Sergeant John B. Worsham, Co. D, 24th Virginia, was wounded in the right thigh, transferred to West's Buildings, paroled and exchanged at City Point 8/63, and admitted into a Richmond hospital.
Sergt. J.S. Haltiwanger *Co (H) 3 S C Regt*	Sergeant J. S. Haltiwanger, Co. H, 3rd South Carolina, had his foot amputated, was transferred to West's Buildings, paroled and exchanged at City Point, and admitted into a Richmond hospital 11/63 where his leg was amputated.
J. L. Haltiwanger *Co H 3rd S C Regt*	J. L Haltiwanger, Co. H, 3rd South Carolina, was left as a nurse, transferred to West's Buildings, paroled 11/63 and furloughed until exchanged.
S J Bouknight *Co M 7th S C Regt*	S. J. Bouknight, Co. M, 7th South Carolina, was left as a nurse, transferred to West's Buildings, exchanged, and returned to his regiment.

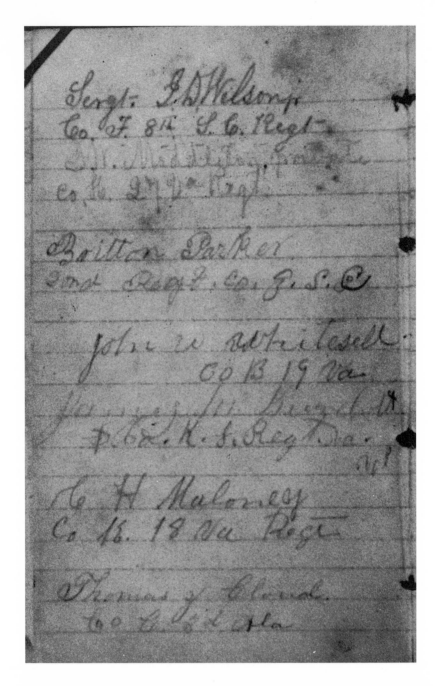

A good example of what most pages look like. This page lists Sergt. J D Wilson Co F 8th SC Regt; J W Middleton private Co H 27 Va Regt; Britton Parker 2nd Regt Co G SC; John W. Whitesill Co B 19th Va; James Bruchett Co K 8 Regt Va vol; C H Maloney Co K 18 Va Regt; and Thomas J Cloud Co C 3rd Ala.

J Hanson Co M *7th S C Regt*	Joseph Hanson, Co. M, 7th South Carolina, had his right leg amputated, was transferred to West's Buildings, paroled and exchanged at City Point 11/63.
A D Grant Co C *8th S C Regt*	Alexander D. Grant, Co. C, 8th South Carolina, lost his left leg, was transferred to West's Buildings, paroled and exchanged at City Point, listed as "permanently disabled."
——— *Camens,* *Villa P O Miss*	[unidentified]
W P Dodds *Co D 17th Reg* *Miss Vol*	William P. Dodds, Co. D, 17th Mississippi, had his left leg amputated, was transferred to West's Buildings, paroled and exchanged at City Point 11/63, admitted into a Richmond hospital, disabled and retired from service.
From West Point, Ky *R H Brushear* *Co H 3rd Ark*	Sergeant Richard H. Brushear, Co. H, 3rd Arkansas, had his leg amputated, was transferred to West's Buildings, paroled and exchanged at City Point 11/63.
T. E. Gaillard *Co I 2nd S C* *Winnsboro So Ca*	Corporal T. E. Gaillard, Co. I, 2nd South Carolina, was wounded in the thigh 7/2 and died 10/12/63.
N. Tshear, Sergt Co H *from West Point Ky* *3rd Ark Regt.*	Sergeant Napoleon N. Tshear, Co. H, 3rd Arkansas, had his right shoulder amputated, was transferred to West's Buildings, paroled and exchanged at City Point 11/63, admitted into a Richmond hospital, and furloughed indefinitely.
J R Gaulding Co F *57 Va Reg*	John R. Gaulding, Co. F, 57th Virginia, was gunshot in the back, transferred to West's Buildings, paroled and exchanged at City Point, and admitted into a Richmond hospital.

E J Davis Co F
3 Georgia Vols

E. J. Davis, Co. F, 3rd Georgia, was wounded in both thighs, transferred to West's Buildings 10/63, then to Point Lookout from where he was paroled 4/64 and exchanged at City Point. He applied to, but was "totally disqualified" for, the Invalid Corps.

E M Day
Moody Battery
La

Edward M. Day, the Moody Battery of the Madison Light Artillery, was wounded in the thigh, transferred to West's Buildings, paroled and exchanged at City Point 11/63, admitted into a Richmond hospital and furloughed.

J W Wells
Co F 17th Miss Vol

John W. Wells, Co. F, 17th Mississippi, was wounded in the hip, transferred to West's Buildings, then Point Lookout where he was paroled 4/64 and taken to City Point.

J M Thompson
Co F 21st Reg Vols

John M. Thompson, Co. F, 21st Mississippi, had his left leg amputated, was transferred to West's Buildings, paroled and exchanged at City Point 11/63, and admitted into a Richmond hospital.

J J Smith
Co E 22 Ga

John J. Smith, Co. E, 22nd Georgia, was gunshot in the abdomen and had his right arm amputated, transferred to West's Buildings, paroled and exchanged at City Point 11/63, and admitted into a Richmond hospital.

C L Parker
Co I 1 Va Vol

This is a duplicate signature. See page 57.

Charlotte N C
Henry J Seavers
Co K 4 N C S Troops

Henry J. Seavers, Co. K, 4th North Carolina, suffered from "debility", was transferred to West's Buildings, then to Ft. McHenry, then in 7/64 to Point Lookout where he was exchanged in 2/65.

W A G Lewis
Co F 26 N C

William A. G. Lewis, Co. F, 26th North Carolina, was captured at Gettysburg suffering from "debility", transferred to West's Buildings in 10/63 where he took the oath 4/30/64 and was released.

Salisbury
W D C Peeler
Co K 4 N C Troops

William D. C. Peeler, Co. K, 4th North Carolina, suffered from "debility", was transferred to West's Buildings, then Ft. McHenry, then in 2/64 to Point Lookout, where was released in 2/65. He was paroled in Salisbury 5/65.

Wesley Liles
Co E 7th N C

Wesley Liles, Co. E, 7th North Carolina, was gunshot in the knee, transferred to West's Buildings, paroled and exchanged at City Point 10/63, admitted into a Richmond hospital, and furloughed.

R W Moore
Co K 17th Miss

Robert W. Moore, Co. K, 17th Mississippi, was "detailed to wait on the wounded in Pa," transferred to West's Buildings, exchanged 10/63, furloughed, never returned to the regiment, and was dropped from the rolls.

R L T Hollingsworth
Co B 3rd S C Regt

Robert L. T. Hollingsworth, Co. B, 3rd South Carolina, was wounded in the right thigh, transferred to West's Buildings, paroled and exchanged at City Point 11/63.

W G Sharpe Co C 13th
Miss Regt

W. G. Sharpe, Co. C, 13th Mississippi, was wounded in both thighs, transferred to West's Buildings, paroled and exchanged at City Point 11/63, and admitted into a Richmond hospital.

R M Hutchins
Co E 53 Ga Regt

Robert Maxwell Hutchins, Co. E, 53rd Georgia, was "detailed as nurse left in Penn," transferred to West's Buildings, then to Ft. McHenry in 12/63. He was transferred to Point Lookout 1/64 and exchanged 2/65.

J A Marsh Co A *2 Regt S C V*	James A. Marsh, Co. A, 2nd South Carolina, was wounded through the hip, thigh, and rectum, transferred to West's Buildings, and was admitted into a Richmond hospital 10/63.
J J Griffith *Co I 50th Geo Regt*	John J. Griffith, Co. I, 50th Georgia, had his right leg amputated, "secondary hemorrhage occurred 20 times during July and August" at Camp Letterman, was transferred to West's Buildings, paroled and exchanged at City Point 11/63, and admitted into a Richmond hospital.
William Adkins *Co H 1st So Ca Cavalry*	William Adkins, Co. H, 1st South Carolina Cavalry, was left as a nurse, transferred to West's Buildings, paroled and exchanged at City Point 11/63.
S B Sturdevant *139 Regt 3rd Div 6 Corps* *Wilkes Barre* *Wyoming Valley*	Assistant Surgeon S. B. Sturdevant, 139th Pennsylvania, was mustered in 2/63, and promoted to surgeon of the 84th Pennsylvania 8/64.
Geo. Mass. Teale *9th NYSM*	George Massingburd Teale, 9th New York State Militia (83rd New York) was a regimental hospital steward and was detached for duty at Gettysburg from July to November 1863.

The following were in a pocket in the back cover.

A printed card:

Capt. R. N. Gardner *5th Reg. Fla. Vols.* *Perry's Brigade* *Tallahassee, Florida*	Capt. Richmond N. Gardner, Co. K, 5th Florida, see entry in Book II, page 69.

A handwritten card:

D. G. White
E. C. White
Bragg's Army
Hardee Division

Colonel David G. White was from Cecil County, Maryland. He served as an officer on General William J. Hardee's staff, adjutant of the 6th Battalion, Arkansas Cavalry and as colonel of the 5th Georgia Cavalry.

The initials of E. C. White do not match any in the Compiled Service Records, but there was a Major E. B. White who was quartermaster on Hardee's staff. Major White was from Maryland.

When Pheme received these cards is unknown.

Written on a folded piece of paper which enclosed a sprig of pine:

Lient. J E Weymouth   [See entry Book II, page 73]
Co E 18th Va Regt

Signatures [Book II]

Miss Goldsborough,
In placing my autograph in your book, I cannot allow the opportunity to pass or at the same time expressing for myself and my wounded and sick comrades the heartfelt gratitude we felt for your kindness to us here and at the College Hospital. Prisoners and 'strangers in a strange land,' many whose fevered brows you have bathed and to whose wants you have ministered with such indefatigable attention will long treasure in their hearts and memory your name and kind deeds with a feeling of sacred friendship.

I hope the fortunes of war may never be such as to throw us together under similar circumstances again but if such should be the case I can only hope that I may meet with one like yourself whose social attractions as a lady and cheering words and kindly sympathy has contributed so my [sic] to beguile the many weary hours of my otherwise almost unendurable situation. For I assure you our 'College days' are the green spot of the days of my captivity. The greatest sacrifice you have made was to have humbled your proud spirit to meeting as social equals and treating with respect those whose conduct in the war have them to be enemies of 'Woman', oppressors of woman, and destitute of manliness and 'true' honor. May the day soon come when this unhappy war shall close with triumph to our arms and cause and when your friends, the 'Florida boys' shall have the pleasure of greeting you in the sunny south, the 'land of flowers' where by every means in their power they will be happy to shew [sic] by acts what they feel at heart—their appreciation of your kind attention.

> *"My native land I turn to you*
> *With blessing and with prayer*
> *Where man is brave and woman too*
> *And free as mountain air."*

Lt. A J Peeler
Perry's Fla Brigade

Lieutenant Anderson J. Peeler, Co. I, 5th Florida, was wounded in the head. He was sent to Johnson's Island where he was paroled and exchanged in 3/65. [See letter Provost Marshal file].

Gen'l. Hospital
Gettysburg, Pa.
Aug. 5th, 1863

Miss Goldsborough,
I would feel that I was wanting in gratitude if I placed my autograph in this little book without returning my thanks for your kindness while wounded and a prisoner I have been. Many have been the lonely and weary moments that you have relieved by your pleasant company and cheering words have frequently caused me to forget my suffering and greatly supplied the place of the absent and loved relatives of whose tender care I have

been deprived. Be assured, Miss G, that you will never be forgotten, for your kindness has deeply stamped your image on our hearts and indelibly written your name on the tablets on our memory. We know not what awaits us in the future, but whether agreeably or disagreeably situated, our minds will often wander in pleasant recollections of the past, rendered so only by the kind attention we received at such hands as yours and by such pleasant association. But those pleasant associations are soon to be severed. It will afford us the greatest pleasure some day to be able to contribute in some manner to your happiness. We can never hope to reward you. But there is a reward awaiting you at the last great day when your page of charity shall be balanced and your good deeds enumerated, and it shall be said to you, "Inasmuch as you have done it to the least of those you have done it unto Me."

But words are not sufficient to express our feelings. I hope that we may soon meet when there will be no military restraint or military authority to "molest us or make us afraid." But in time of peace when the roar of cannon and rattle of musketry shall have ceased, and when the cause for which we have sacrificed so much, and expended so much treasure and spilt so much blood shall have triumphed, and Maryland, your own State, shall be relieved of her own yoke and shall occupy a proud place in the "Southern Confederacy."

> The time has come at last
> When I must say goodbye
> To pleasures of the past
> Which make me heave a sigh.
> So then, Miss G., adieu
> I wrote in this token
> And may our friendship true
> From no cause be broken.

Truly your friend,
R. N. Gardner
Capt. Co "K"
5th Fla. Regt.

Captain Richmond N. Gardner, Co. K, 5th Florida, had his left arm amputated. He was sent to Johnson's Island and exchanged in 3/65.

Sam H. Watson
Washington
Tex

<u>*Sacred*</u>

Died Sept. 13th, sundown, Sunday afternoon 1863. Buried in Grave No. 3 commencing at the right, 8th Section
My poor lost darling. Would to God I could have died to save you but all is over. Worldly sufferings are ended. If tears or love could have availed I had not been left to weep by his graveside.

[See Book I on page 56]

General Hospital
Gettysburg, Pa.
Aug. 4, '63

Miss Goldsborough:
After being so long with us and being thy majestic self in meekness to meet the wants of the wounded while at the College and here— I could not write my autograph without an appreciation of your kindness & benevolence. Such a being is too lovely for earth, and Heaven's reward can only repay thee. I hope we may meet again after the hush of war way down in the south where beautiful rills, streams, and rivers wind their majestic course to the mighty deep.

Where balmest flowers are seen.
In there sweetest fragrance green.

George H. Jones
Capt. Co B
22 Ga. Regt.

Captain George H. Jones, Co. B, 22nd Georgia, was wounded in the loin, transferred to West's Buildings 9/63, and then to Johnson's Island where he was exchanged in 3/65.

Gen'l Hospital
Gettysburg, Pa.
Aug. 6th, 1863

Miss Goldsborough:
In placing my name in your book I desire to thank you for your kindness to my suffering comrades and myself. But I am conscious of my inability to do so in proper style.

Page with Sam Watson's signature and Pheme's comments after his death.

*"All words are idle
Unless the heart could speak"*

*Respy
J. W. Lockert
Lt. Col. 14th Tenn Regt.
P.O. Clarksville, Tenn.*

Colonel James W. Lockert, 14th Tennessee, was wounded in the right leg, transferred to West's Buildings, sent to Johnson's Island and then to Pt. Lookout where he was released in 3/65.

*John H. Daniel
1st Reg Va Infantry
Richmond
Va*

John H. Daniel, Co. A, 1st Virginia, was wounded in the right foot, paroled and exchanged at City Point 9/63.

*General Hospital
Gettysburg, Pa.*

Miss Goldsborough-

May truth *and* affection *which are the materials of a pure and holy love cast in the brightest mould of honor ever cement the union of thy confiding heart with ours in heavenly bondage, and though we may not meet again on earth, may our exit from it be hailed with joy in that bright region of glory by the fair ones whose angelic hands have bathed our wounds and soothed our troubled spirits in this hour of our affliction, is the sincere wish of a Southern Friend-*

*Tom W. Givens
Lt. 8th Fla.
Perry's Brigade
Anderson's Div.
Hill's Corp. [sic]*

August 6, 1863

Lieutenant Thomas Wilkes Givens, Co. K, 8th Florida, was wounded in the left foot, sent to Johnson's Island where he was paroled 2/65 and transferred for exchange.

*Jas. H. Robinson
Lient. Co "K" 9th Va Regt
Portsmouth, Va*

Lieutenant James H. Robinson, Co. K, 9th Virginia, was wounded in the right forearm and right side, transferred to West's Buildings, then to Ft. Delaware where he was exchanged 10/64.

N T Bartley
Lt. Co C 7th
Va Reg
Orange C H
Va

Lieutenant Nathan T. Bartley, Co. C, 7th Virginia. His records do not state if he was wounded. He was transferred to West's Buildings, then Point Lookout, then Ft. Delaware where he was released 6/65.

Jno E Weymouth
Co E 18th Va Regt
address Cartersville Va.

Lieutenant J. E. Weymouth, Co. E, 18th Virginia, was wounded in the mouth and breast. He was sent to Johnson's Island where he was released 6/65.

"Bright be thy dreams of future bliss
May all thy plans succeed."

W J F Ross
St. Maj 2nd Geo Batt
Macon Georgia
(Formerly—Thomasville
Ga.)
Near Gettysburg Pa
August 9th 1863

Sergeant Major William J. F. Ross, Co. C, 2nd Georgia Battalion, was wounded in the right knee and gunshot in the left leg and trunk. He was transferred to West's Buildings, paroled and exchanged at City Point 8/63. [See letter Provost Marshal file].

Julian Betton
Tallahassee
Florida
Orderly Sergeant
Company
M
2nd Florida
Regiment

Well, Miss Pheme, I am no hand for writing poetry or pretty mementos in albums, but I can leave you my name and say that when Genl. Lee again crosses the Potomac I will strike my third blow for Maryland provided God our father, "the God of battles" will have by that time put strength in my wounded limb. For Right and Liberty, Maryland, and Miss Pheme, I will ever fight.

Jule Betton Rebel

Sergeant Julian Betton, Co. M, 2nd Florida, was wounded in the right thigh, transferred to West's Buildings, paroled and exchanged at City Point 9/63, and admitted into a Richmond hospital where he remained about a year and was then furloughed.

Thos W Shine
OS Co (K)
5th Fla Regt
Tallahassee
Fla
Nephew of Maj
Jas T Rhodes
N C

Thomas W. Shine, Co. K, 5th Florida, had a minie ball in his right thigh, was transferred to West's Buildings, paroled and exchanged at City Point 8/63, and admitted into a Richmond hospital. He returned to his regiment and surrendered at Appomattox.

W. W. Hunt
Co B 2nd Ga Batt
Macon, Ga

Wilkins W. Hunt, Co. B, 2nd Georgia Battalion, was gunshot through the right hip and thigh, was transferred to West's Buildings, paroled and exchanged at City Point 9/63, and admitted into a Richmond hospital.

R C Wimberly
Co B 3rd Ga

Richard Columbus Wimberly, Co. B, 3rd Georgia, had his right arm amputated, was transferred to West's Buildings, paroled and exchanged at City Point 9/63, and admitted into a Richmond hospital.

Lient J J. Schlandt
)Co([sic] B 21st Geo
Regt

Was unable to locate Schlandt, or variations of the name, in the Compiled or Unlisted Service Records, or prisoner rosters.

D C Montgomery
Co H Reg 3rd Geo

D. C. Montgomery, Co. H, 3rd Georgia, had his left arm amputated, transferred to West's Buildings, paroled and exchanged at City Point 9/63, and remained on wounded furlough.

Capt. G A Graves Co I
22 North Carolina Reg
Locust Hill N C

Captain G. A. Graves, Co. I, 22nd North Carolina, was wounded in the right arm and sent to Johnson's Island in 9/63. In 5/64 he was transferred to Point Lookout, paroled and exchanged.

R T Harper
1st Lient Co E
5th Texas Regt
Washington
Texas

1st Lieutenant R. Thomas Harper, Co. E, 5th Texas, was wounded in the thigh and shoulder, sent to Camp Chase, and transferred to Point Lookout in 3/65.

W H Belton
1st Lt Co "E"
11th Miss Reg
Crawfordsville
Miss

1st Lieutenant William Henry Belton, Co. E, 11th Mississippi, was wounded, transferred to West's Buildings, then to Johnson's Island. In 3/64 he was paroled at Point Lookout and exchanged at City Point. Retired from service 10/64.

Z A Blanton
Capt Co F 18th Va Regt
"Address" Farmville Va

Captain Zachariah Angel Blanton, Co. F, 18th Virginia, was wounded, exchanged from Point Lookout 5/64 and retired from service because of permanent damage to the right side of his face and tongue.

Wm T Johnson
Capt Co H 18th Va Regt
Evergreen Va

Captain William T. Johnson, Co. H, 18th Virginia, was shot in the left groin, transferred to West's Buildings, then to Ft. McHenry, then to Ft. Delaware by 6/64. One of the Immortal Six Hundred, he was taken from Morris Island to Hilton Head to Beaufort, South Carolina where he was exchanged 12/64.

J S Dowell
Co (A) 7 Tenn Reg
Alexandria Tenn

Jonathan S. Dowell, Co. A, 7th Tennessee, was gunshot in the right thorax, transferred to West's Buildings, then Ft. Delaware, where he was released 2/65.

T J Sneed, Jr (Private)
Co A 7th Regt Tennessee
Alexandria

Thomas J. Sneed, Co. A, 7th Tennessee, was wounded, "sent under guard from West's buildings hospital, Baltimore for safe keeping to Ft. McHenry", then transferred to Point Lookout in 1/64. He was Sam Watson's cousin. [See letter, page 78, and Provost Marshal file].

C H Woolley (3rd Sgt)
Co A 4th Regt Ala Vols
Benson

Sergeant Columbus H. Woolley, Co. A, 4th Alabama, was wounded, transferred to West's Buildings, paroled and exchanged at City Point 11/63. He would be killed at the Wilderness. [See letter Provost Marshal file].

Genl Hospital
Near Gettysburg, Penn.
Aug. 13th, 1863

Away with care
And dull Despair!
Let no one dare disturb us!
To night we'll drink,
And never think
Of those that may observe us!
The boys fillup,
The rebels cup,
Tho' captive chains do bind us!
Drink deep—drink deep!
And 'wake from sleep
Mem'ry of those behind us!

Toast

Here's to Miss G!
The girl of my song!
Her heart's all right,
May her life be long!

May her bright eye
Have no cause for tears!
May her proud soul
Be bowed by no fears!

God bless her now-
God bless her always!
We'll think of her, boys
In all coming days!

Then fill your glass
With glorious wine,
and drink with me-
"This creature divine!"

Your friend
Thos. D. Houston
1st Lieut. Co. "K"
11th Virg. Infty.

Toast.

Here's to Miss G!—
The girl of my Song!
—Her heart's all right,
May her life be long!

May her bright eyes
Have cause for no tears;—
May her proud soul
Be bowed by no fears!

—God bless her now—
God bless her always!
We'll think of her, boys,
In all coming days!

Then fill your glass
With glorious wine

1st Lieutenant Thomas Dix Houston, Co. K, 11th Virginia, was gunshot in the right hip, transferred to West's Buildings, then to Johnson's Island where he was released in 3/65. He had three brothers in the same regiment at Gettysburg, one killed [David], one wounded [Andrew], the third [Edward] survived to Appomattox. The entire Houston family played a large part in Pheme's activities during her exile and after the war. [See Diary]

In behalf of my Cousin. My thanks are due to Miss Goldsborough for her kindness to (S.H.W. [Sam Watson]), my Cousin. An exile from home, and debarred from pleasures in which he was wont to indulge, arising from social delights, we can only appreciate this manifestation of kindness from a daughter of Maryland. In his behalf, I, therefore, tender my heartfelt thanks.

With all the hardships and dangers of a soldier's life, there are no pleasures like those which are associated with the memories of home, and with the daughters of the South, whom in former days we were wont to love. The mere thought, the suggestion, of a woman's kindness or a woman's love awakens memories of the past.

The joys of a mother's tenderness and affection seems as of yesterday—as when I look up through the blue silence of the sky, fresh stars shine out where at first none could be seen. Wherever I have wandered since this war begun, I have found the women of the South were ever the same, developing new excellences of character which I had thought peculiar to the sex of my own home in the West.

Fresh memories and the half-forgotten tones of those I have loved are awakened by the kind words and kind attention of the Lady of Baltimore to my little Cousin. An affectionate Mother, a kind and loving Sister will bless thee, Miss Goldsborough, for the kind attention given to an absent Son and Brother.

Will you now accept my thanks?

T J Sneed, Jr.

Thomas J. Sneed, Co. A, 7th Tennessee, see previous entry on page 75.

M. W. Taggart, 1st Sergt
Co H 11th Ala Regt
Reform Ala

1st Sergeant Moses W. Taggert, Co. H, 11th Alabama, was wounded in the left arm, transferred to Ft. McHenry 10/63, then to Point Lookout for exchange 11/63, and entered the Invalid Corps.

H G Nobers
Co H 11th Regt Ala Vols
Reform
Ala

Horatio G. Nobers, Co. H, 11th Alabama, had his right leg amputated, was transferred to West's Buildings, paroled and exchanged at City Point 11/63.

Lieut John D. Perkins
Co M 2nd Fla Regt
Perry's Brigade

Lieutenant John Day Perkins, Co. M, 2nd Florida, was wounded in the left leg, hand, and side and lay on the field for two days. He was sent to Ft. McHenry where his leg and thumb were amputated. In 3/64 he was paroled, exchanged and furloughed.

Major A. D. Crudup
47th Regt N C
Lewisburg
Franklin Cty
N. Ca

Major Archibald D. Crudup, Field & Staff, 47th North Carolina, was wounded in the breast, neck, left arm, and left hip. He was sent to Ft. McHenry 10/63, transferred to Point Lookout 1/64, paroled and exchanged at City Point 3/64. He resigned from the service with a "completely shattered constitution."

Will S. Rankin
Lieut Col 21st N. C. Vol
Hokes Brigade
Early's Division
Ewell's Corps
Home address
Greensboro
N Carolina

Lieutenant Colonel Will S. Rankin, 21st North Carolina, was wounded in the right thigh, transferred to Johnson's Island in 9/63 and exchanged 3/65.

R. W. Martin Lt Col
53rd Va Vols
Armistead's Brigade
Pickett's Division
Longstreet's Corps
Home address:
Pittsylvania C.H.
Virginia

Lieutenant Colonel Rawley W. Martin, 53rd Virginia, went over the wall with Armistead, was wounded in both legs, transferred to West's Buildings, then Ft. McHenry, then Point Lookout where he was exchanged 6/64, and admitted into a Richmond hospital. Pheme visited his home both during and after the war. [See Diary, Provost Marshal file, and Appendix 6].

James R. Herbert
Lt Col 1st Md Infantry
CSA
Sept 10 1863
left hand

Lieutenant Colonel James R. Herbert, 1st Maryland, was wounded in the leg, arm, and abdomen, transferred to West's Buildings, then Johnson's Island, from where he was released 10/64. [See letters in Personal Collection section and Provost Marshal file].

Lamar Hollyday
Co A 1 Md Battalion

Lamar Hollyday, Co. A, 1st Maryland Battalion, was "dangerously wounded", transferred to West's Buildings, and admitted into a Richmond hospital 11/63 "permanently disabled for field service." He then served as a clerk in the medical department. [See Diary]

J W Laird
Sergt Maj
1st Md. Infty
C.S.A.

Sergeant Major James W. Laird, Co. H, 1st Maryland, was wounded, transferred to West's Buildings, paroled and exchanged 11/63.

Dr. R. L. L. Walsh
Jerusalem Mills,
Hartford Co Md

Dr. R. L. L. Walsh was not listed as a contract surgeon and most likely volunteered his service to the Confederate wounded.

A. D. Shekill M.D.
Georgetown D C
No 151 High Street
(office)

Dr. A. D. Shekill is listed at this address in the 1863 Washington City Directory. He was not listed as a contract surgeon and most likely volunteered his service to the Confederate wounded.

E. M. Bean
2nd Lt. Co G 5th Texas
Address Cameron

2nd Lieutenant Ellwood M. Bean, Co. G, 5th Texas, was gunshot in the right shoulder, transferred to West's Buildings, then to Point Lookout in 2/64 where he was exchanged 5/64.

W Burton Owen
Chaplain 17th Miss Regt
McLaws Division
Richmond Va
address:-
Cockrun P.O.
DeSoto Cty Miss

Chaplain William Burton Owen, Field & Staff, 17th Mississippi, "left with the wounded at Gettysburg Penn", transferred to West's Buildings 10/63 and was exchanged at City Point 11/63.

C. H. Toy
Chaplain 53 Ga Regt
Semmes Brig,
McLaw's Div
Norfolk, Va

Chaplain C. H. Toy, 53rd Georgia, was appointed 12/17/62, and according to his records retired from service 8/8/63 to become a teacher.

A. M. Houston
Co K 11th Va Vols
Rockbridge Co
Va

Captain Andrew Matthew Houston, Co. K, 11th Virginia, was wounded in the arm, transferred to West's Buildings, then Ft. McHenry, then Point Lookout, exchanged 4/64, furloughed and joined the Invalid Corps 1/65. Brother to Thomas Dix Houston and one of the four Houston brothers to fight at Gettysburg, he died 7/21/69 from the effects of his wound. [See Diary]

Wm. W. Goldsborough
Major 1st Md Battalion
Baltimore Md

Major William Worthington Goldsborough, Field & Staff, 1st Maryland Battalion, shot in the left lung, transferred to West's Buildings, then Ft. McHenry, and Ft. Delaware. In 6/63 he was transferred to Ft. Pulaski, Georgia, received back at Ft. Delaware from Hilton Head, South Carolina in 3/65. He was one of the Immortal Six Hundred. [See Thomas Sneed's letter, Provost Marshal file]

Wm. M. McGalliard
Lieut Co E
8th Louisiana Reg
Winnsboro
La

Lieutenant William M. McGalliard, Co. E, 8th Louisiana, was wounded, transferred to West's Buildings, then to Ft. McHenry and Ft. Delaware. He was paroled and exchanged in 9/64.

P. L. W. Thornton
1st Lt Co "H" 21st Va

1st Lieutenant Presley L.W. Thornton, Co. H, 21st Virginia, was gunshot in the right arm and left thigh, transferred to West's Buildings, then to Ft. McHenry, then to Point Lookout in 1/64, then to Ft. Delaware 6/6/64. No date of release but he shows up in a Richmond hospital in 12/64; retired from service.

Azra P. Gomer
1st Lt Co "F"
3rd Va Infty

1st Lieutenant (promoted to Captain 7/4/63) Azra P. Gomer, Co. F, 3rd Virginia, had his legs shattered below the knee, left leg amputated, was transferred to West's Buildings, then to Ft. McHenry, then to Point Lookout in 1/64, paroled and exchanged 3/64, admitted into a Richmond hospital, and retired from service 8/64.

J. A. Allen
Co "K" 3rd Va Infty

John A. Allen, Co. K, 3rd Virginia, was wounded in the left shoulder and right knee. He escaped from Camp Letterman, was recaptured, transferred to Point Lookout, where he was exchanged 2/65.

J. C. Warren
1st Lt co C
52nd N C Regt
Lynchburg, Va

1st Lieutenant John Crittenden Warren, Co. C, 52nd North Carolina, was wounded in the leg, right wrist, & left thigh, transferred to West's Buildings 10/63, then to Ft. McHenry, then Point Lookout 1/64 where he was paroled and exchanged at City Point 3/64.

Daniel Parker
Asst Surg 8th Ala Regt
Wilcox Brigade
Anderson's Division
Hill's Corps

Assistant Surgeon Daniel Parker, Cos. A & D, 8th Alabama, was transferred to West's Buildings 10/63 and exchanged at City Point 11/63.

R. G. Southall
Asst Surg 6th Ala

Assistant Surgeon Robert G. Southall, Co. I, 6th Alabama, was received at Ft. McHenry 10/63 and sent to City Point for exchange.

J. M. Hayes
Surg Rodes Brigade
Rodes Division

Surgeon J. M. Hayes, Field & Staff, 26th Alabama, O'Neal's Brigade, has no information in the Compiled Service Records before 5/64.

H A Minor Surgeon
9th Regt Ala Vols
Macon C S A
Noxubee Co
Miss

Surgeon Henry Augustine Minor, 9th Alabama, was "left with wounded of his brigade at Gettysburg", transferred to West's Buildings 10/63 and exchanged at City Point 11/63.

Robt McCulloch
Capt Co "B"
18th Va Inf
Garnett's Brigade
Room No. 70   *Pickett's Division*
Gettysburg College Hosp   *A.N.V.*
July 24th 1863
"Aide toi et Dieu t'aidera"

Captain Robert McCulloch, Co. B, 18th Virginia, was wounded, transferred to West's Buildings, then to Johnson's Island where he was exchanged in 3/65. Capt. McCulloch is one of the most prominent figures in Pheme's diary.

For your kindness

Thanks for yourself remembrance "Here to-day—gone tomorrow, such the destiny of a soldier. Such the fate of created things. Words may express ideas but were never intended to express feelings. Looks, action and memory are the agents of the emotional soul-

[unsigned]

General Hospital
Gettysburg, Penn
August 6th, 1863

Miss Goldsborough,

In bidding you adieu it affords me pleasure to write a few lines over my autograph as a slight testimony of the high appreciation I have of your kindness not only to myself but to the wounded of our Army, at this place and the College Hospital. Words, however, fail me in expressing the feelings of my heart. I am too sad at the thought of leaving this place made pleasant by the smiles and cheering words and kind friends to go to some dungeon where tyranny and oppression reigns supreme.

Time may roll on, the varying fortunes of war may come and go with us, years may pass by, but your cheering smile and kind attentions will never be forgotten.

In years to come after we have achieved our National Independence and returned to our quiet and delightful homes your name will ever be remembered.

Should you ever visit the land of Flowers, the land of free speech, brave men, and lively women, my appreciation of your kindness will be shown not in empty words but with kind offices of friendship not only by myself but by one of the loveliest and best of women, my dear wife.

Respectfully your friend,
Wm. Bailey
Capt. Co. (G), 5th Fla Regmt.
Tallahassee, Florida

Captain William J. Bailey, Co. G, 5th Florida, was gunshot in the right hip, and sent to Ft. Delaware. He was transferred to Morris Island, South Carolina as one of the Immortal Six Hundred, sent to Hilton Head prison. Included in his war records is a letter he wrote in 12/64 requesting a parole to go home behind Confederate lines to die and send back a Union captain in exchange. The request was denied and he died March 5, 1865 of "inflammation of lungs."

The Diaries of Euphemia Goldsborough 1863-1868

"Arrested by the yankee government..."

Euphemia Goldsborough's diaries spanning the years 1863 to 1868, were written throughout the "Hospital Books" between the entries made by the wounded Confederate prisoners under her care at the Pennsylvania College Confederate Hospital and Camp Letterman. They were written most often in pencil, sometimes pen. Most entries are run-on with little punctuation. They were not entered in date sequence. They are transcribed here verbatim. The only changes made were indentations for clarity and organization of date sequence. Parenthesis are Pheme's; brackets are mine. Only identified people and places are referenced in the endnotes. All military units referenced are infantry unless otherwise noted.

These personal memories give us a picture of Pheme through her arrest, exile, and subsequent visits to Virginia after the war. Her humiliation, loneliness, patriotism, love, and despair flow through the record of the war years. In the latter part of the diary there is a conspicuous lack of comment on anything outside her private sphere. She must have witnessed the heavy hand of Reconstruction. The attempted rescue of Dr. Watson [See Appendix 7] occurred in the same time frame as her visit to Rockbridge County, yet she makes no reference to it. Only social activities were listed in the post war years, albeit full of Confederate men and women.

What was recorded in diary form in the third book that was stolen can only be guessed. Surely Pheme would have recorded her meeting with General Lee when he signed his photograph to her. The lack of information concerning the resolution of her relationship with Mr. Douglass is indeed frustrating. Yet what we do have is a fresh, subjective piece of history and it is a privilege to be taken with Pheme on her journey.

Arrested by the Yankee government Nov 23rd at 12 o'clock PM Locked up in my room alone until the next day Nov 24th 11 AM Through a hard rain taken before the Military Authorities under guard. Sentenced to banishment during the war. Allowed to remain at home until Nov. 28th under strong guard day & night.

Saturday Afternoon, Nov 28th at 4 PM put on board the Steamer Adelaid (in a fainting condition) for Fortress Monroe[1] with military escort.

Reached the Fortress at daylight Sunday morning Nov 29th, raining fearfully. Taken to Beast Butlers HdQtrs[2] about sunrise the same morning. Found The Beast not up. Wet & cold sat shivering in his office until a fire was made. Finally he came (this 2 headed monster) I was turned over into his hand by the guard and evidence handed in. Strong enough: the beast said to cost me my head "under any other Government than the mild & glorious stars and stripes" Again banished for the war with orders that if I attempted to return, to be shot. But what was sentence of death & banishment at the hands of these cruel tyrants that I hated then & now with all the intensity & fervor of my passionate nature? Freedom to breath for a brief time the pure breath of our glorious Confederate Nation.

Euphemia Mary Goldsborough circa 1863.

Held a prisoner until Wednesday night 8 PM. Dec 2nd Put on board the U.S. Truce Steamer, New York.[3] before starting was striped [sic] of all my clothing. rudely examined by two Yankee women open doors with all around, Yankee soldiers laughing & jesting at my expense. If I live for half a century I can never forget the humiliation of that hour. My blood seems turning to fire even now while I write of it. Although it belongs to the Shadowy past.[4] Alone, save a guard reached the steamer by way of a tug-about 10 o'clock PM. Lay at anchor all night in the [Hamp-

The U.S. truce boat **New York.**

ton] Roads. Introduced to Maj (now Gen) [John Elmer] Mulford [the Exchange Officer] More of a gentleman than any I ever knew in Yankee blue treated me most kindly. My heart swells with grateful emotions at the remembrance of the same. I was <u>so desolate then</u>, that a kind word fell like oil upon troubled waters.[5]

The next morning Dec 3<u>rd</u> we were to have started up the James by daylight but the boat got aground and it was sunrise before we got off.[6] Passing the wrecks of the Congress & Cumberland[7] off Newport News and many other points of interest. indeed every foot of ground along that noble river has been rendered historical by the great struggles for independence on its banks. The evening of the 3rd we reached City Point about an hour before sunset.[8] There was a French Frigate anchored in the stream. Our own [the Confederate] Truce Boat had not arrived. I had never been up the James River before. The country is picturesque & beautiful & the night clear & faultlessly lovely And I past an hour alone on the gard's of the boat looking for the Schultz, watching the signals from a station on top of a hill hard by. And the Stars as they came out one by one like sentinels guarding their posts. Had a visit from one of the officers of the French Crown. invited me to breakfast next morning, which, I was obliged to decline being still a prisoner.[9]

When I awoke in the morning Dec 4<u>th</u> our Boat had arrived and with a light & bounding heart I bid Goodbye to Yankee rule & tyranny. And for the first time found myself seated on our little Boat with the Starry Cross, the flag of the free waving over me. I forgot to say that horrid woman Bell Boyd, was sent up on the same truce boat with me, but enough of her.[10]

I reached Richmond about Nightfall the same evening Dec 4th was escorted up to the Spottsswood Hotel by Gen. [illegible] Smith.[11]

The hotel was dark & cheerless. The Parlor shadowy, with gay groups sitting around laughing & chatting. Officers and ladies all strangers to me. I alone, the Gen having gone to order my room. My very heart died within me & I felt truly that I was alone "a stranger in a strange land." After supper the first familiar face was Willie Gill's.[12] I retired early, tired & dispirited.

Dec 5th went down to breakfast, found Willie G. and Lev Lake[13] waiting for me, took breakfast with me. Had no sooner reached the parlor than our dear Jack came, then the Rev Mr. Wilmer, Lamar Hollyday, Craig Lake, Tom Pratt, Mr. Elder, Charles Steele[14] all old friends. before 12 o'clock I had some 15 friends & the feeling of loneliness was wearing away. In the afternoon Mr. Garnett, Cousin Em, Maj. Griswold, Col. Calvert, Dr. McGill, Dr. Boyd and Mr. Charles Hodges came.[15] After tea Willie Gill, Charlie Steele, Maj. John Mason, Gerves Spencer, Jack & my dear friend Willie Hollyday.[16] Introduced to Maj Owen[17] of the Washington Artilery.

Sunday Dec 6th went to St Pauls Church in company with Jack and Willie H. they knew everyone & pointed them out to me our great people. For the first time I saw our great and glorious President Mr. Davis. knew him from his strong resemblance to his photographs

Remained at the Spottswood until Wednesday Dec 9th seeing many old friends and making many new ones. Went to Mrs. M. T. Southalls, Cor of Grace and [illegible] Streets—on the 9th to board. A pleasant household. Introduced to Dr. R that night. Heard from home for the first time since banishment. Jack brought me the letter, via underground, per hand of a K, a brave and faithful man. The letter was from my dear Mother, did not read it until after retiring to my room. Cried all night.

Received an appointment in the Commisary Gen'l office, through the agency of Dr A Y P Garnett[18] & Jack. the same day went before the examining board Dec 15th Passed.

Christmas day was lonely and miserable. went to church in the morning Saw Jack, Willie and others in the afternoon & evening.

1864

Entered on my duties at the Department 1st of Jan 1864. How different from other I had past with the friends of youth gathered around.

Jan 9th Left Mrs. Southall's to board in a private family on Main Street near 3rd from no fault but that of reducing expenses Found a pleasant home with Mrs. Judge Nicholas. Staid with her until her son was married. Roomed with a sweet lovely girl from Clarksville, Tenn.

Jack left for Texas April 30th

Went back to Mrs. S-s May 9th Roomed with Mrs. Seldon from Norfold found a dear kind friend in her. Battles raging all around. Sounds of cannon ringing in my ears day & night. Days of sorrow with our bravest & best being brought back to us dying & dead.

Left Richmond July 18th 1864 to visit Rockbridge [County] Va. Capt. Houston[19] met [me] in in [sic] Lexington. brought me to his home. A sweet lovely spot with the beautiful blue mountains piling up one above the other on every side His family, God bless them. I can never forget for their kindness to the homeless exile.

Returned to my Post Sep 14th reach[ed] Lynchburg that night in company with Capt A Houston who escorted me to Barkville [Burkeville] Junction.

Reached Richmond Sep 15th with Col [paper worn away] with a head cold. Sick several days. Many Marylanders and friends wound[ed] in the Hospital. My time divided. Department in the morning, Hospital in the afternoon until entirely broken down. Mrs. Southall's board raised to $50 per day, five extra Obliged to move on that account.

Nov 15th went to board with Maj Young. Corner 6th & Leigh. A Q M [Quartermaster] & most extravagant home. very sick with jaundic. Nearly all the while throat much congested & but for kindness of outside friends should have suffered for everything. Got up for the first time Christmas Day. A large dinner party was present at the table but ate nothing. Sick in bed nearly all the week after Dr. G. attending me twice a day.

1865

Jan 1st left on the Danville train to visit Dr. Martins family, had known Col M[20] at Gettysburg. Went in a box car, the only lady on the train escorted by Maj Wood, Q M of transportation.[21] Reached D. 1 o'clock A M Found Col M waiting for me at the Depot. knocked them up at the Tunstal House[22] got in about 2 A M

Provost Marshall pass dated January 2, 1865 for 10 days to Danville. Pheme was traveling to Pittsylvania County, Virginia to visit the home of Colonel Martin.

Next morning Jan 2nd started for the [illegible] House. A most uncomfortable day. Beside being sick rode 20 miles in a snow storm. Found his mother & sisters sweet and lovely & kind and God will reward them, for their kindness to the weary wanderer.

Staid with them, making many new and pleasant acquaintances until Feb 16th (A day long to be remembered & regaled)[23] That night reached Danville about 8 P M. Started at 10 P M on the train for Richmond Meeting all the refugees from Columbia S C—old & young pushing & rushing "fleeing from the wrath to same" Lay on the road broken down. a greater part of the next day. Violently sick several hours. the same day. reached Richmond at 12 o'clock that night.

Feb 17th went to board with Cousin Em Garnett, cor Grace & Jefferson. A week passed pleasantly enough. (Early I was on) walks in the balmy sunshine dreaming the happy hours away. A month of weariness, hard work at the office, doubts for the success of our beloved Cause the safety of our Capital, headaches and heartaches. Again comes sunshine For when did not sympathy & kindness make glad & bright the heart.

March 22nd Our prisoners from Johnson's Island returned. Brave Soldiers & gentlemen how my heart warmed toward all of their kind. Thursday Mch 23rd had a perfect reception at my office, of officers & friends I had known on the bloody field of Gettysburg, when it had been my happy privlege to nurse & attend them.

March 26th Sunday morning. I left Richmond in company with Capt T D Houston[24] to visit his dear home again, little dreaming the terrible fate of our glorious Capital in a week's time. Met Capt. Mc'Cullough[25] at Dehnville [Danville], Col Kane[26] a Marylander Sam Sulivan & others made up our party. reached Lynchburg that night, found the canal boat not running.[27]

Left L [Lynchburg] Tuesday morning Mch 28, in an Ambulance & pair of condemned mules to journey over the mountain a distance of 40 miles, (with Capts [Tom] Houston & [Robert] Mc'Cullough) which we were two days accomplishing. The first night stoped in the mountain at the house of a Stranger & asked for lodgings. With true Virginia (All honor to the brave old state) hospitality we were received by the owner whose ancient name & blood had it's heading in the veins of Cavaliers. Mr. Minor & his daughters were indeed a charming family in whom beauty of both soul and mind shown fourth [sic]. Early next morning we started, reaching the home of Capt. McC about 4 P M where we were most cordially greeted, he having returned from an imprisonment of two years.

In deep sorrow & humiliation I must record the evacuation of our much loved City Richmond Apr 2nd 1865. Apr 5th I came to Dr Houstons[28] and here the news of Gen Lee's Surrender Sunday Apr 9th reached us on Monday afternoon Apr 10th. I could not believe it at first, but in a few hours our weary, worn, crush[ed], and bleeding soldiers began to come, returning through the mountains Our army disbanded, their muskets stacked our people scattered to the four winds. Oh! days, & weeks of agony & fears. With no word of comfort of hope or of home.

June 19th My Dear Father came for me. Left Rockbridge June 27th. Reached home July 2nd, Sunday morning before breakfast 1865....

1866

Jan 11th 1866. Came to Virginia. Stoped in Richmond two weeks with my cousin Mrs. [Emily] Garnett. Attended a large ball at the Exchange Jan 16th. Snow on the ground all the while. A pleasant visit notwithstanding.

Jan 21st went to Danville. Reached Dr Martins Jan 22nd. A most cordial reception. Spent two months delightfully. Mch 26th returned home escorted by Lieut Whitehead.[29] At Richmond Mrs. Garnett joined me & returned home with me, also Maj Q[30] of Gen Jenkins Staff Got home to breakfast the morning of the 28th of March. Much improved in health. Jack arrived Apr 5th staid two weeks with us most happily.

To "Miss Effie Goldsborough" from "R.E. Lee 18 Jan '66." Pheme was in Richmond at this time, but the presentation was not noted in the remaining diaries.

(Courtesy Randy Herrell)

Journal for 1866 [Book II]

Aug 7<u>th</u> Left home at 3 1/2 A M on the Washington train. After many <u>trials</u> left that city on the O & A R R [Orange & Alexandria Railroad]. Thankful that I had gotten my escort so far safely on the way. a strange old man he was, going to the Rockbridge Alum Springs.[31] The journey was a most <u>thrilling</u> <u>one</u> every foot of the ground from Alexandria to Gordonsville is teeming with interest, rendered so by the many & fearful battles which have taken place along the route. Reached Lynchburg the evening of the same day, with a sick headache Capt Mc [McCulloch] (the kindest & best fellow in the world) met me at the Depot. Staid all night at the Norval House.[32] Had a visit from Col. Withers[33] a pleasant gentleman & great friend of Mc's. Also a visit from a good hearted accomodating [sic] Jew who is ready to wait on anyone. Had a good supper & got up much refreshed. Left on the Canal boat for Balcony Falls.[34]

Aug 8th Fell in with a very pleasant party from Ala. Mrs. Horner & family on their way to visit the Natural Bridge. Received a cordial greeting from the household.[35] Mary[36] is looking thin and badly.

Aug 9th spent pleasantly talking over the days that are gone. Mag and Fannie Mohler, Maj and Mrs Mohler[37], spent the evening with us. I'm sure Capt Mc is sick but he will not admit it.

Friday Aug 10th Tom Houston returned after a tour through the South since the Surrender.[38] All glad to see him. A visit from Miss Bettie Paxton & Capt. Obenchain.[39] Such eyes. I call him the handsome Capt.

Aug 11th Spent the evening at Col Mohlers.[40]

Sunday 12. Went to falling Spring Church. had a good sermon from Mr. Junkin[41]

Thursday Aug 16th Went up to High Bridge Church on horseback to a revival going on there. Went home with Mrs Houston[42] to dinner & staid all night.

Friday morning 17th introduced to Dr. Fairfax. returned home on this evening Mr Rutherford came with us. Found fat Tom Gordon here. Staid all night and all next day. Prayer Meeting here this afternoon Aug 18th.

Friday, Aug. 24th. Went up to High Bridge. Horses ran up on a bank nearly turned over the carriage within a few feet of the river. Capt. McCullough hurt himself. Tuesday night came home by moonlight.

Thursday Sep 9th Went up to Mrs. Houston's to stay. Returned with Mc & Mary [McCulloch] on the next Wednesday. Back again to Natural Bridge Friday, Sep 14th to witness a Tournament. Much pleased with the riding.

John Echols Knt [Knight] of "Seven Stars"
John Campbell " "Flying Cloud"
Robt McCulloch " "Lost Cause"
Mc Paxton " "Hard Times"
Wm. Rex " "Silver Cross"
Horace Houston " "Milton"
E. M. Houston " "Yankee Hat"
Jake Arnold " "Silver Heel"
J.A. Armistead " "Bay Pony"
Tom Burks " "Silver Arrow"
Frank Jordan " [blank][43]
Miss E. M. Goldsborough
Miss Fannie Mohler
Miss Emma Paxton
" Betty McCullough

" Annie Weaver
" Cassie Burks[44]

Went to the Ball. Felt like a fool being crowned. Not at all satisfied to receive the honor from the Victor. Introduced to Senator Preston Cable.[45] Got back to Mrs. Houston's 2 0'clock A M, escorted by Mac [Robert McCulloch], Ed H [Edward Houston], T D H [Tom Houston], & Mr. Garth.[46]

Sunday 16th went to Falling Springs Church with Martin Trevilian,[47] Mr. and Mrs. Garth & Ed Houston in double carriage. Capt T D Houston Mr Rutherford Houston[48] & Dr. Fairfax outriders. Returned with Mrs. John's.[49] Road over to the schoolhouse horseback to hear Gen Pendelton[50] preach. Introduced to him after Sermon.

Monday 17 Sep. Spent the day at Mrs. John's. Company to spend the evening Maj Mohler & wife & sisters. Annie Weaver & others. had a dance.

Tuesday Sep. 18 After breakfast returned to Mrs. Houstons. Escorted there by Capt. T D Houston. Dr Fairfax to dinner.

Thursday, Sep. 20th Dr Fax [Fairfax] to dinner. Caught in the Equinox. Staid all night Also Jennie Houston[51] Tom & I had a quarrel but soon made up.

Broadside announcing the tournament on September 14, 1866.

Photo taken at the jousting tournament. Pheme is on the right, Bettie McCulloch on the left.

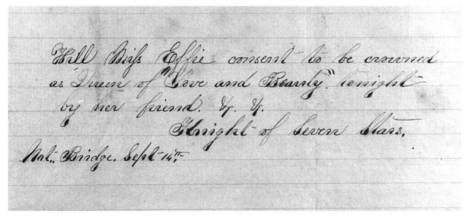

"Will Miss Effie consent to be crowned as Queen of 'Love and Beauty' tonight by her friend. A. Y. [Affectionately Yours] Knight of the Seven Stars, Nat. Bridge, Sept. 14th."

Friday 21 Sep. Dr. Fax still with us

Saturday 22nd bright & clear. Dr. Fax to dinner again. Bettie Houston[52] also.

Sunday 23rd went to church on horseback with Capt. Houston.

Tuesday 25th Went to a Big Picnic under the Natural Bridge given in honor [illegible]. Had a pleasant time. Wandered far up the stream & on an old rock had a delightful flirtation with Dr. Fax.

Thursday 27th Mac [McCulloch] came for me, returned with him to dinner.

Tuesday Oct 2nd Spent the day by invitation at Mr. Preston Paxtons,[53] very pleasantly.

Wednesday 3rd Spent several hours at Mr Mohlers in the afternoon & came home with Mac. A nice walk. The handsome Capt. Obenchain came in after tea. Those glorious eyes. Came to say Goodbye to us. going to Texas.

Introduced to Mr. Douglass[54] Oct 8th 1866. Monday afternoon in the lane leading from Hawthorn to the river He escorting Annie Weaver, on horseback. Mary, Bet, Mac & myself walking, on our way to Mr William Paxtons.[55] Monday 8th Spent the evening at Mr William Paxtons quite a large party and good supper. Crossed the James in a flat boat, & then walked two miles. Got home broken down. All next day 9th staid in bed.

Sunday 14th Rode to church on horseback with Mac. A week past pleasantly, riding horseback &c &c.

Dined at Mrs Houstons Friday 17th with Dr Fax & others.

Thursday 18th At Mr Mohlers to supper & a dance, walk home by midnight with Mac.

Sunday 21st Rode to church horseback again with Mac. in the afternoon walked down to the River & rested on still winding banks for some time.

Monday Oct 22nd up long before day. eat breakfast just as day was breaking. tooke the Boat on my way home. Mary Mohler Annie Weaver Bettie McCullough Mac Paxton Davis Mohler[56] came as far with me as [the] Boat Ferry. Had a song from Mary & Annie on the Guitar. The scenery more surpassingly beautiful than anything I ever saw with all the varid tints of Autumn. Who would not die if Death's approach was heralded as beautifully. Reached Lynchburg at 4 P M in a very heavy rain Storm. [illegible] at the Norval House in company with Mrs. Johns & Mrs Glasgow[57] visit from Mr. Ecols [John Echols] Knight of the Seven Stars before ten. Company after tea. Senator Bowcock [Bocock] daughter and sister in law Mrs. Bowcock from Alabama. Miss Annie Weaver sing on the Canal Boat Oct 22nd '66

Tuesday 23rd Escorted to the B & A railroad by Mr. Echols & Mrs John's Met Lieut Warren[58] at the Depot. glad to see him Pleasant chat about dear old Confederate times with Mr B[59] who was Speaker of the House in our Congress. Mrs & Miss B came on with me enroute to the latters Grand Pa's Mr. Falkner's of Martinsburg.[60] On the train a lady approached me, with some question in regard to the trains reaching Baltimore. She proved to be the sister of Gen Mulford U.S. who commanded U.S. Truce Boat Steamer New York. The only yankee gentleman I ever met. Received great kindness at his hands, while a prisoner in his charge, for which I shall ever be _profoundly grateful_. Found Miss M _much of a lady_. She had often heard her Brother speak of me. I told her of his polite attention & kindness when I was in so much sorrow & for my life I could not help crying as I thought & spoke of my forlorn and lonely desolate condition & of his kindness to me under such circumstances. Reached home at 8 P M Found Pa at the depot to meet me. All well at home.

1867

My dear Uncle Maj Richard Hayward died at his home in Talla-hassee Fla Jan 1867. May he rest in Peace.

Tuesday Feb 12th 67. Dear Fenton[61] came this morning, bless her heart. I am so glad to see her. Thinner than when I last saw her Saturday, March 25th 65 in Richmond just one week before the sur-render. We've had a talk & cry over the days that are gone, Confed-erate times that can never return.

Went to the most magnificent party I ever attended at Mrs. Seldon's. Feb 18th 67. Got home at 4 A M 700 invitations.

Diary for 1867 of My Summer Trip

Left home Tuesday July 30th in the 4 P M train for Lynchburg in company of Miss Carry Campbell. She left me in Washington. Trav-eled all night. And arrived in L. at day light. The weather very cold for the season. Found Mr Echols at the train to meet me. Went to the Norval House, took breakfast, which was a _grand one_, beef stake ham eggs, French roles, cakes, good coffee & delightful cream. Met an old acquaintance most unexpectedly at the breakfast table Came over, took breakfast with me & then escorted me up on the canal boat. July 31st Had a grand flirtation "_An old song well sung_", gave me his photograph. Capt Mac [McCulloch] met me at the landing received a most cordial welcome from all the family. Mary is as sweet as ever, & Bettie more improved than any one I ever saw.

Thursday Aug 1st. Company all day. in the Morning Miss Nannie Braidy, two Yankee ladies from Philadelphia, & Mr Frank Jensin and Col Mohler. In the evening Mr Davis Mohler The time past pleasantly Mary & I singing duets & music. My foot paining me all the while very much

Friday Morning Aug 2nd spent laughing & talking with Capt Mac & the girls In the afternoon a nap

Saturday Aug 3rd Past pleasantly at home until afternoon. Bettie & Mrs Mohler went to prayer meeting also Mrs Johns. Capt Mac & I took a sharing ride on horseback. the country is looking beautiful & I enjoyed it much. Mr M staid to tea.

Sunday Aug 4th went to Church in the morning, heard a good sermon from Mr. Junkin. Slept all the afternoon.

Monday Aug 5th Company, Miss Moffit Mr Moffit, Miss Fannie Echols, & her brother.[62] Mr M asked us to take a sail on the river.

Tuesday Aug 6th busy making a pair of slippers.

Wednesday Morning Aug 7th a visit from Mr. Mohler and Dr Arnold.[63] The latter is looking very handsome. Afternoon A thunder storm.

Thursday Aug 8th Mr Bryan[64] & Col Mohler in the Morning. Afternoon a fearful thunder storm. The lightning struck very near here. Mr. Mohler that night.

Friday Aug 9th Still busy with my slippers. Afternoon, Mr Moffit thinks he's in love with Mary.

Saturday Aug 10th Morning Mr Mohler, Bettie's most devoted, made a short visit. At noon a good rain. Afternoon went to prayer meeting at Dr. Watsons[65] with Col Pogue[66], on horseback. A very nice little man and a brave Soldier Bettie & Mrs Mohler Mary & her brother got back in time for tea. The Col & Mr M came in & staid until 9 o'clock P M.

Sunday Aug 11th Went to Church this morning at Falling Spring, got there very late. had a good sermon from Mr J [Junkin] & a cordial shake hands with him Afterwards. Then a renewal of former acquaintance with Col. FitzHugh[67] & ex Confederate Congressman. The gallant little Col escorted me to the carriage. So much for a campaign I have planned against him but more of this hereafter. Afternoon a walk with Capt Mac, Mr Mohler Bettie & Mary. Rested on the road side & watched the moon rise cloudlessly & beautifully from behind the Stately Mountains. enjoyed the moonlight for a while & came home.

Monday Aug 12th Johnnie Echols came in the morning, brought us some peaches. Staid to dinner. about 4 P M Col FitzHugh called. teased Mary and Mr. Echols nearly senseless. left about sunset.

Exacting a promise of us to join them on the river after tea & see them drag a fish net. The description I will leave to a readier pen than mine. Rode down to the river on Belle. Moonlight splendid. Sat on the bank & sang until the boat came with our party. Quite a party but caught no fish. had music & got home at 11 o'clock. Been in bed about a half hour when we were surprised by a serenade.

Tuesday Aug 13th Just as hot as it well can be. No company until evening. Alex Paxton[68] and Dave Mohler.

Wednesday Aug 14th. Still hotter. done nothing all day but try to keep cool. An engagement to spend the evening with Mrs McChesney[69] but was disappointed by a heavy rain.

Thursday Aug 15th Raining hard all day. Had the blues so badly have not know what to do with myself

Friday Aug 16th Very pleasant nice breeze & clearing. Visit from Mac Paxton. Mary & Capt Mac [McCulloch] went to the [Natural] Bridge to a Circus, & animal show. Dave Mohler spent the day with Bettie and I.

Saturday Aug 17th went to ride in the morning with Capt McCulloch. In the afternoon went to ride again. Was knocked out of the saddle by running against a dead limb of a tree, draged and very much bruised, brought home & put to bed.

18th 19th 20th 21st 22nd 23rd Stiff & I am scarcely able to turn over in bed. Afternoon of Friday 23rd better.

24th went to ride again, enjoyed the ride much. Afternoon went to prayer Meeting at Mr Mohlers. Capt McCorkle[70] Mac Paxton & Dave Mohler came home with us Spent the evening & night here, very pleasantly.

Sunday 25th All the gentlemen & Bettie went to Church to hear old Mr Junkin. Mary & I staid home. Mr Junkin & his brother came home with them, took dinner here & preached at the School House. A very good Sermon. We all went Had several escorts.

Monday Aug 26th Feeling very badly again, stiff & sore. About 11 o'clock Capt Houston came. So glad to see him. Mr. Endes[71] came with him. Dave Mohler also came & invited us all to a dunking party at Dr. Chandlers[72]. Rained very hard and could not go. In the evening Dr. Arnold & Mr McClintick[73] came, all spent the night & we had a pleasant visit or rather evening.

Tuesday Aug 27th After breakfast Dr A & Mr McClintick left. Capt H & Mr E staid all day. Still raining. to all day myself. Could scarcely limp about noon. Mac Paxton & Dave came. All left in the afternoon In the evening feeling better. Took supper by invitation at Mr Preston Paxtons. came home after dark—first crossing the river & then rode home by horseback.

Wednesday Aug 28th Spent pleasantly Invited to spend the evening at Mrs Mohlers. Nice supper & dance afterward. Very pleasant evening until Maj Garber & Jos Baldwin[74] arrived Afterward the "Etc.'s" were almost too heavy.

Thursday Aug 29th In the Morning Several gentlemen called Also Miss Mollie[75] and Bettie Paxton. Afternoon went up by invitation to spend the evening at Dr. McChesneys.[76] had a nice time Dave went with us.

Friday Aug 30th Miss Fannie Watson & her brother[77] feeling sick all day.

Saturday Aug 31th Sick still Afternoon went to prayer meeting at a neighbors with Mac [McCulloch] Dave & Bettie Mary & Mac P [Paxton]. had a jolly good time coming home and romped away the last hours of summer. how cloudless & beautiful the sun went down upon us. Will we all meet again when the summer days return, with the same buoyant feeling? But why reach forth to the future, the curtain is down, & our vision ends with the happy present. After tea we had some music & a game of cards and so ends the summer of '67. Alas Alas. Why will not past joys return?

Sunday Sep 1st Went to Falling Spring. Communion Sunday. Came home with Molly Trevilian & Capt Houston to spend a week or ten days. found Mrs Houston very well. Dr Fairfax here to dinner.

Monday Sep 2nd Lounged [illegible] & talked all day.

Tuesday 3rd Helped Mollie about her dress; in the afternoon went over to Bannbrooks. Got some nice Peaches grapes, Cider &c. &c. Mr Endes left in the morning for Pittsylvania [County].

Wednesday 4th Dr Fairfax & his cousin Mr. Fairfax.

Thursday 5th Went to a big Pic Nic at the Bridge gotten up by Capt Mac in Compliment to the Miss Withers from Lynchburg, daughters of his old friend & Col. Had a most charming time, went with Capt Houston but saw very little of him during the day. Capt Mac upset me in the water, got as wet as possible but did not come home for it. After dinner went to the Hotel.[78] had music, a game of ten pins, and then a nice dance in the ball room. Started home about sundown. My Saddle turned on the Bridge. Dr Fairfax pulled me over & I received only a bruised arm. The Miss Withers are pleasantly pretty and wild. Dr and Mr Fairfax took tea here.

Friday Sep 6th A Quiet day While at Supper Wm. Houston[79] came.

Saturday 7th Sacramental meeting begun. Mr Heart & daughters Miss Lizzie Heart from Richmond & Mr Fairfax came back with Mrs Houston to dinner. Miss L H. & I have many mutual acquaintances They left after dinner.

Sunday 8th Went to Church. Dr F, Mr McClintick escorted us to the church, the latter gave me three letters, one from [illegible], Pa, & Dora,[80] glad to receive them of course. Ed Houston was down from Lexington Came home to dinner, also Dr & Mr Fairfax. a rainy afternoon or rather a cloudy one.

Monday Sep 9th in the morning raining. Cleared at Noon. Miss Mattie Houston[81] came in about dinner time. After dinner Ed & Mr Will Houston left for Lexington. Capt Houston & I had a long talk in the afternoon. He's more changed than any one I ever saw in every respect. No longer the genial, happy, companion of olden times, but reserved & indifferent to his Confederate friend & sister. Well Such is life, the "world wags & I shall wag with it." but not without a sigh of regret for the friendly Brotherly chats of other times. About Sunset, Bettie McCullouch & Mr. Mohler came, on their way to the Peaks of Otters,[82] inviting me to be one of their party. They staid all night.

Tuesday Sep 10th Made an early start. Dave & Bettie, Capt Houston & myself on horseback, for this noted point of interest. Met the River crowd at Gilmore Mills. Went on to Skidmore Ferry, there expecting to meet the rest of our party but in this we were disappointed. crossed the river on flat boat's Horses & riders resting under the shade trees on the other side. After waiting an hour we took up our line of March. Capt Houston & I in advance followed by Guss Watson Joe Paxton Ella Paxton Joe Watson Mr Canany Bettie Mr F Mr Mohler, Mollie Paxton & Col Fitzhugh.[83] At two o'clock halted at spring on hill side about 5 miles from the Peaks. Unpacked our "Happy Sacks" had a nice lunch, which we enjoyed. After resting about an hour, we remounted & moved on toward the Peaks. Now the country grows picturesque romantic & beautiful, and if my companion had been just a Little more amiable, I should have enjoyed the ride so much, however, being an invitation, we must overlook his Manners Arrived at the Hotel[84] at the foot of the Peaks, between 4 & 5 o'clock. After resting a while getting water &c. &c. we remounted again & began the assent. for about a mile our horses toiled wearily up the steep rugged path, winding like a huge serpent down the mountain sides. Then the road becomes impassable except to the pedestrian. The order to halt is again given, dismounting our horses are made fast to the trees. And from this point we hear, "Fall in-forward." Provided with heavy shawls, we join hands with our escorts and begin to climb from rock to rock. in some places they are almost perpendicular. again they slip from under us, & go rolling down the mountain side, but bracing our nerves, we go onward overcoming every obstacle in the hope of reaching the top before Sunset. The rocks grew larger & larger & to climb over them seemed almost impossible, but breathless & exhausted we struggle onward through the thick undergrowth. When suddenly, we come to an opening in the trees. And fatigue is forgotten in the grandeur that has bursted upon us, but the top is not yet <u>reached</u> & the road is steeper & rougher than before but we dash onward & the <u>summit is gained</u>. I thought then and am <u>still</u> thinking of words to express what I felt. <u>admiration</u> is tame, extacy but little better. All other feeling was lost in this one: <u>What a God is our God</u>, how boundless in all his abilities. <u>Hugh hugh</u> rocks are dashed together in wild confusion on the summit of this notable place, as though some great convulsion of nature there occurred. Standing on these lofty rocks, shaking with cold, even in our heavy shawls, we gazed out upon a panorama baffling all description. Rivers hills fields & villages are like toy landscapes far <u>far</u> below us, and all around us, peaking one above the other, as far as the eye can reach, stretch the gloriously magnificent mountains. On this scene of grandeur, which words fail me to patray, the Sun goes down. And its rays still linger on the mountain sides, making them beautiful beyond description.[85] The approach of twilight or rather the moon coming up in solemn beauty over the Eastern Mountains warns us of the hour, & that we are nearly two miles from the Hotel, & we begin to retrace our steps which to <u>me</u> was <u>more exhausting</u> than the journey up. reached my horse thoroughly broken down. Upon reaching the Hotel, we found the balance of our party awaiting us, Dr. Chandler Mr Harmon Miss Burks Cap Kable Mr. [illegible], Miss Becham, and Miss Gwinn.[86] The Landlord[87] a long faced old fellow gave us a very good supper after which came into the parlour & plaid for us to dance until nearly 1 A M. Slept about two hours. At 3 1/2 A M, Again in our saddles groping our way through bushes over huge rocks and <u>almost</u> impassable pathes in <u>perfect darkness</u>. Capt Houston threw a white blanket over his shoulders which enabled me to follow or rather to keep the horse in the path. In the darkness we again dismounted, and commence our pilgrimage to the top hoping to see the Sun rise. Weary & worn we reached the rocks which cap the summit just as day began to break. A fire was soon lighted, which with shawls & a swallow of coniac kept us moderately comfortable. The mist & fog was dense, & nothing was to be seen for a time. Grouped together, we chatted & listened to the rushing of the winds over & around us. Then the vapors begin to rise & float in great rolling clouds past us, gradually they grew thinner & again we see the beautiful gloriously magnificent view at our feet, but alas we were disappointed in the object of our early trip, for the sun was up before

Sunny Knoll was the name of the Houston home. This photo was taken circa 1940. The woman in the middle is Maude Houston, Thomas' daughter.

(Courtesy Leyburn Library, Washington & Lee University)

the vapors rolled away. Two hours past merrily when hunger prompted us to return to the Hotel. Leaving our names on the walls of a ruin, which had once been a rough house[88] just below the rocks With many a lingering look at this mighty work of God's creation, we hurry forward, down the mountain. In due time we find our horses, & gallop back to the Hotel. Breakfast is ready before we are, but is none the less palatable when we reach the table. Capt Houston was just as good and kind as a <u>Brother could</u> have been, like he was in the early days of our acquaintance, after we arrived at the Peaks. I cannot account for his ill humor on the journey, except that the trip was too much for him. At 11 A M we remount & turn our faces <u>homeward</u>. Had seen the Peaks, been lost in admiration of their grandeur and bid Goodbye to them <u>forever</u>. As soon as Capt H tired of riding he was as sharp as a needle and rough as a chestnut burgh, just <u>quarreled</u> with me all the time. I'm sure I did nothing to offend him & certainly never had my feeling so wounded in my life nor did any other gentleman venture to say so much to me before. I could not have controlled my feeling if I had said anything, so rode much of the way in silence. Ah! well he has forgotten to [illegible] of his old friend and sister with kindness.

Reached home Wednesday afternoon, Sept 11<u>th</u> 4 o'clock perfectly broken down. Went to bed & slept all that afternoon & night. All the next day Thursday 12<u>th</u> In the evening Dr. Fax came over, but I retired soon after supper just tired to death.

Friday 13<u>th</u> A house full of company Mr & Mrs Garths & two Miss Garths, & Tom Houston. Dr F in the evening, pleasant day. Moon in eclipse.

Saturday 14<u>th</u> Went with the Miss G's to see the Bridge. Capt T D H. [Tom Houston] & Capt A M H. [Andrew Houston] & Mr. Garth. Capt Mac joined us there. he Capt Andrew H & I sat on the rocks & had a nice chat. Went back to Sunny Knoll[89] to dinner and in the afternoon came back to Mrs. John's. found Col Fitzhen [Fitzhugh], Mr Echols Mr Mohler Col Mohler Mac Paxton, Mr Thompson[90], Mrs Mohler & Fannie Mohler hear. After tea had "Whist."

Sunday 15<u>th</u> Capt Mac's birthday. he, Mr Thompson, Mary & I went in the carriage Bettie & Mr Echols on horseback, to church. Came back & dined with us.

Monday 16<u>th</u> Mr. Thompson went back to Lexington. <u>joy</u> go with him

Tuesday 17<u>th</u> Spent quietly with Mary & Bettie.

Wednesday 18<u>th</u> Got up at day light & rode down to the boat to say goodbye to Mollie Travalian Mary Bettie & Capt Mac. Met Ed

Houston at the Point[91] Expected Capt A M Houston to come home with us, but he was sick in bed when Mollie & the Garth's left, so we were disappointed. Had a long chat with Col Fitzhugh on the boat & invitation from the Capt, to go down & meet the returning boat but could not accept it having an engagement to spend the evening at Mr Wm Paxtons. Afternoon, Mr Echols came for us in his boat. Mr Mohler & Miss Fannie went with us, had a splendid boat ride. Col Fitzhugh was also along Mr E had peaches & grapes which we enjoyed mightily, had a jolly good time, a real good supper, & came home by moonlight a beautiful night.

Thursday 19th Mr Echols came & spent the day. at 4 P M we were to start on a chinkapin [chestnut] hunt, but the Miss Paxtons kept Mr Echols waiting & the boat did not come for us until Sundown. So we only had a boat ride up the river. Stop in at Mr E & got any quantity grapes & peaches & got home to supper.

Friday 20th. Mary went to Singing School & brought Mr Echols & Capt McIntosh the singing master home with her.

Saturday 21st Mary Bettie Capt McIntosh, Capt M Mr Mohler & I all went on horseback to Singing School. Bettie Lizzie Gilmore[92] and myself not members, so we sat in the choir with Capt McCorkle Mac Paxton & Mac. Had a funny time, eat dinner under the trees. Every body around the county out. The country singing schools are great places. Afternoon had a heavy rain, came home after it was over, accompanied by Mis Fannie [Mohler] Davis [David Mohler] Capt McCorkle Mac P[axton] Mr Grigsby.[93] The [illegible] first came in & spent the evening also Mr. Echols Fannie & Baxter[94] staid all night, owing to the rain.

Sunday 22nd All went to church on horseback. Mary & Mr Echols, Bettie & Davis, Mac Paxton & myself had a merry ride. Mr. E took dinner with us. About sunset took a walk, painted ourselves with pokeberries & [illegible] to our heart's content.

Monday 23rd Mary sick in bed, a quiet busy day. Mending up bodies torn to pieces romping with Capt Houstons pet dog Lee.

Tuesday 24th Cool & bracing, but feeling badly.

Wednesday 25th Mrs. Mohler & babies were here & Davis spent the evening with us also. Mrs. M. staid all night. Some how I don't fancy her, although she tries to be very agreeable.

Thursday 26 & Friday 27th quiet days. not at all well. Friday afternoon had a most charming ride on horseback.

Saturday 28th went to singing school. had the best kind of a time. A good time with Mr Douglas[s], he's the boy for me, the one I've been looking for all this time. Saturday night Mr Hamilton[95] came home with us and spent the night.

Sunday 29th A sermon from old Mr Ewin[96] Afternoon Davis Miss Fannie & Mrs Mohler.

Monday 30th Cool & delightful. Mr Anderson[97] spent the night here, no other company. Miss Emma [Paxton] Capt Mc's sweetheart came home, after an absence of 4 months.

Tuesday Oct 1st A quiet day but a charming one.

Wednesday Oct 2nd Pleasant morning & beautiful afternoon walked down to Mrs Mohler's & staid until Sundown. Davis & Capt Mac walked home with us. Spent the evening playing cards. <u>Blues</u> most awfully. An unkind word wounds me deeply A <u>small matter</u> my feelings have grown to be, & with the coming sunshine of tomorrow will forget or at least try to.

Thursday 3rd Not at all well. All went to see Miss Emma Paxton but Mrs J [Johns] and myself. Amused ourselves by writing letters & playing on the Guitar, a fearful thunder storm after dark. Felt mighty lonely about [illegible]. The girls got home about 11 P M

Friday 4th A rainy day. Capt Mc made <u>fireworks</u> for our amusement.

Saturday 5th In the morning too rainy for singing school. Cleared about noon. Went to prayer meeting at Mr Wm Paxtons in the afternoon, had a delightful ride & a nice long letter from Dora. John C's gone back to [illegible]. God speed him say <u>I</u>, I [illegible] him there forever. Oh! Breathe not a word of our love.

1868

Waited of Capt McCulloch & Emma Paxton June 18th/68.[98] Served with Mr. Douglass and had a lovely time. Went to the Peaks of Otter with Mr. Douglass Aug 4th/68 Had a time to be remembered. Dinner at Mr Douglass' by invitation first time Aug 8th, 68. Spend the night & returned home. Sunday afternoon [illegible] 9th at Sunset. I wish I could go home in the boat tonight for though I am very happy, I am sure trouble is in store for me. I <u>wish I could hate him</u>.

Went to Mrs Houston's Aug 11th with Dave Mohler.

Aug 22th Saturday Mr Douglas came for me & brought me back to St. Johns.[99]

August 23th Sunday Dave took Bet & I to Church today in the yellow waggon. dined at Mrs Douglas,[100] Mr D came home with us & he lost my gloves.

Aug 24th An engagement to go to a Pic Nic at the Bridge with Mr. Douglas. Could not get a horse. So all went in a farm horse waggon. Dave, Bettie Fannie Mohler Mollie [Paxton] Ella [Paxton] [illegible] & self. Mr D. on horseback. Left Fannie & [illegible] at

Fancy Hill, Mr D. got in the wagon then. got home at 9 P M It was raining, but I was <u>oblivious</u> to <u>that</u>. And so were other people. A happy ride for us <u>all</u>.

Monday Sep 7<u>th</u> dined at Mrs Morgan Poagues.[101] Mr Douglass took me, Dave Bet. Another happy day all around.

Mr Douglas came for us Sep 8<u>th</u> in the double carriage & took us to his Mother's. Spent the day & night real pleasantly.

Sept 9<u>th</u> Went back to St Johns with Mr D & Dave. found the house locked up. Unable to get in so dined at Col Mohlers, and in the afternoon went to Oakland. A <u>good time</u>.

Oct 11<u>th</u> 68 Sunday. an event in my life not likely to be forgotten. How fair and beautiful earth seems to be.

Oct 12<u>th</u> Mrs. Douglas Mrs Whitney Miss Annie & Mr D dined here, a pleasant day for us all.

Oct 17<u>th</u> 68 Under the rose bush [illegible] on the front porch pillow after coming from prayer meeting at Mr Preston Paxtons I <u>listened</u> to the <u>romance of my Life</u> in few words, but they came from an <u>honest heart</u>. Oh! for a look into futurity.

Oct 24<u>th</u>/'68 Saturday Prayer meeting at Mac Paxtons Somebody came for me. I walked home with Mr Thom. We walked the back porch for two hours. He is in trouble but will not tell me the cause but has promised to do so before I leave. Made an engagement to take me to church tomorrow, Oct 25<u>th</u> my last Sunday in the country.

Sunday 25<u>th</u> A happy day that will never be forgotten. Dined at Mrs D's by invitation, & stopped at P O [Peaks of Otter] on our way home. These happy days are <u>almost</u> over.

Oct 26<u>th</u> a long walk with the girls. saw him on the road in his farm clothes & he looked embarassed.

Oct 27<u>th</u> 68. He came & took me to the boat in the buggy. The <u>beginning</u> of <u>trouble</u>. If I could only know how it will end. All the young men & girls in the neighborhood spent the evening with us at Capt Echols to see me off. Edward went with me to the third lock & then said goodbye.

My <u>treasure</u> came Nov 12<u>th</u> 1868, and my first letter.

The Provost Marshal File of Miss Euphemia Goldsborough

"Treasonable Plans and letters & Traitorous Poetry"

G 327 1863
Cit

Papers of <u>Miss E. Goldsborough</u> containing much that is disloyal
Ten [sic] enclosures

Head Quarters, Middle Department
8th Army Corps.
Baltimore, Nov. 23, 1863

Lt. Col. Fish
　Prov. Mar.
　　I am directed by the General Commanding to enclose to you for
your perusal a letter addressed by a Rebel prisoner to Miss E. M.
Goldsborough 49 North East corner Courtland & Mulberry Streets
with instructions that you at once send a discreet officer with a suffi-
cient guard to the house indicated arrest Miss Goldsborough search
the house in every part take possession of all papers and any contra-
band or suspicious articles search the persons of the inmates and
retain in close custody Miss Goldsborough until further orders.
　　The General desires that you will conduct the matter with much
secrecy and dispatch as to take by surprise all the inmates of the
house to possess yourself of all evidence that there is in the house of
the intercourse of its inmates with the Rebels

by command of Major Gen
[Robert C.] Schenck
Alexander Bliss[1]

[illegible]

　　Please preserve & return the letter & envelope & report the result tonight to the General.

Provost Marshal's Office,
HEAD-QUARTERS MIDDLE DEPARTMENT.
Baltimore Md., *December* 22 186 3

PRISONER.

M ^{rs} Goldsborough

RESIDENCE.

City

CHARGE.

SEE CASE OF

Treasonable Plans

and letters & Traitorous

Poetry.

The name and location of the recipient of this letter is not noted. It was doubtless confiscated for the anti-Union sentiments.

Baltimore
Rich Richmond B
March
Rich Richmond
Baltimore, March 1st 63

My Dear Cousin,
Your kind letter was duly received and attended to. I have been feeling quite uneasy in regard to the shoes as you wrote—since you had sent them, but they had never been received, however, I find from your letter the fault was the Cap's & some of yours or mine he did not bring them up until the night before he was to have left & was to call for them the next morning at ten but it was such an awful day I could not get out of the house but as Mr. Mc[illegible] was going over on Saturday I [illegible] you would get them even sooner than by the other opportunity. I hope you have received them and that they may fit you. I got the music for you yesterday which I shall send through the P. office. I suppose you have had a most delightful time during the wedding. I should like above all things to have looked in upon you, & enjoyed the nice things that were in such plenty. Miss Nutt had a most charming visit—she was scarcely content herself at home now, I do not know what she would do if it did not chance to be Lent which of course will not permit us to join in gayeties [sic] for a season at least. I quite lost my heart with Mr. Barsay but Miss Nutt brought bad news about him, that he is a <u>union man</u> he did not talk that way to me, or rather I thought him not strong either way but more Southern than otherwise. we go [sic] along nicely although I did put it down on the Yankees <u>most unmercifully</u> but if he is for this <u>hated hated Union,</u> away with all fancies. I rather see <u>the Devil himself and</u> rest in his fiery arms than have a Yankee Emancipated man come near me. I just hate the very air they breathe and would like to kill every one I see. I suppose Miss Nutt told you all about our Masquerade & how gay we have been this winter. I've often thought of you & wished you could walk in upon us. We have a piano now, & enjoy it much. Brother had a birth night party on the 16th of Feb. there were between 40 & 50 people here the next night we all went to a party at Jami Johnsons which was the last night before lent.

Mis E Goldsborugh [sic]

The signature is not in Pheme's hand and her last name is misspelled. The hand is very much like Col. Fish's with the same "G".

Baltimore

Twas on the nineteenth of April last,
    Baltimore, Dear Baltimore
When Lincoln's soldiers thought [to] pass
    through Baltimore, Dear Baltimore
But when they came along Pratt Street
    A shower of bricks they chanced to meet
Which made the Yankees use their feet
    Through Baltimore, Dear Baltimore

Now when they got to the depot
    Baltimore, Dear Baltimore
They thought they then were sure to go,
    From Baltimore, Dear Baltimore
But Marshal Kane[2] with his Police
Made them all scatter like geese,
And took away one gun apiece
    Baltimore, Dear Baltimore

🐚 🐚 🐚

This undated newspaper article included in Pheme's file concerning the death of Brigadier General Robert Seldon Garnett was the inspiration for the poem "I Am So Cold." Boatner gives this explanation of "Carrick's Ford: (Cheat River), WV, 13 July '61 (West Virginia Operation in 1861): When Garnett at Laurel Hill learned the night of the 11th that Pegram had been defeated at Rich Mountain, he retreated the next morning to Kaler's Ford on the Cheat River. Garnett's movement was slowed by rain and by his desire to save his trains. After a delaying action at Carrick's Ford, Garnett was killed at another ford, a short distance away, while commanding a small rear guard of 10 men. His troops continued their retreat to Monterey. The Federals reported a loss of 53, and estimated the enemy's loss at 20 killed, 10 wounded, and 50 prisoners. About 40 wagons and a 'fine piece of rifled artillery' were reported captured."

The Cheat River Battle

The Death of General Garnett—The Brave Georgian—The Dead and Dying—A Shocking Scene

The correspondent of the Cincinnati Gazette accompanying General McClellan's army, gives the following graphic account of the death of General Garnett, and the scenes accompanying the retreat of his army:

As soon as the proper arrangements could be made, Gen. Garnett's body was conveyed on one of his own litters, thrown from their baggage wagons by his flying soldiers to hasten their retreat to Gen. Morris' headquarters. There, fresh clothing was procured from a Georgia trunk in one of the captured wagons, and the body was decently laid out.

The brave boy who fell by him was taken to the hills above the headquarters and buried by Virginia troops. At his head they placed a board with the inscription: 'Name unknown. A brave fellow who shared his general's fate, and fell fighting by his side while his companions fled.'

When Gen. Garnett fell it was only known that he was an officer attempting to rally the flying rebels. He wore a colonel's uniform with his epaulette changed, and the brigadier general's silver star glittered on the shoulder strap. Over this he wore a fine black overcoat. The ball struck him in the back (as he was turning on his heel to rally his men), passed traversely through his body and came out on the left side of his breast. He wore a dress sword, with plated silver hilt, which had been presented to him by his old friend, Gen. G. M. Brook of war of 1812 distinction. This, his gold chronometer, the opera glass slung across his shoulder, a fine topographical map of Virginia, and his pocketbook containing sixty one dollars in Virginia currency, were taken from his person by Major Gordon, to be kept at headquarters till an opportunity should offer for returning them to his family.

General Garnett was a slightly built man, with a small head, finely cut and intelligent features, delicate hands and feet, black hair, and with full beard and moustache, kept closely trimmed and just beginning to be grizzled with white hairs. His features are said, by those who know him, to have retained their natural expression wonderfully. He was instantly recognized by Major Love, Gen. Morris and Capt. Bentrain, all of whom were intimately acquainted with him. Major Love had been for four years his room-mate at West Point, and had always cherished a warm friendship for him.

Returning from the bank where Garnett lay, I went up to the bluff on which the enemy had been posted. The first object that caught my eye was a large rifled cannon (a six pounder) which they had left in the precipitate flight. The Star Spangled Banner of our regiment floating over it. Around was a sickening sight. Along the brink of the bluff lay ten bodies, stiffening in their own gore, in every contortion which their death anguish had produced. Others were gasping in the last agonies, *and still others were writhing with horrible but not mortal wounds, surrounded by the soldiers whom they really believed to be about to plunge the bayonet to their hearts. Never before had I so ghastly a realization of the horrid nature of this fraternal struggle. These men were all Americans—men whom we had once been proud to claim as countrymen—some of them natives of our Northern States. One poor fellow was shot through the bowels. The ground was soaked with his blood. I stopped and asked him if anything could be done to make him more comfortable, he only whispered, 'I'm so cold!' He lingered for nearly an hour in terrible agony.*

Another—young, and just developing into vigorous manhood— had been shot through the head by a large Minie ball. The skull was shockingly fractured; his brains were protruding from the bullet hole, and lay spread on the grass by his head. And he was still living! I knelt by his side and moistened his lips with water from my canteen, and an officer who came up a moment afterward poured a few drops of brandy from his pocket flask into his mouth. God help us! what more could we do! A surgeon rapidly examined the wound, sadly shook his head, saying it was better for him if he were dead already, and passed on to the next. And there that poor Georgian lay, gasping in the untold and unimaginable agonies of that fearful death, for more than an hour.

Near him lay a Virginian, shot through the mouth, and already stiffening. He appeared to be stooping when he was shot: the ball struck the tip of his nose, cutting that off, cut his upper lip, knocked out his teeth, passed through the head, and came out at the back of the neck. The expression of his ghastly face was awful beyond description. And near him lay another, with a ball through the right eye, which has passed out through the back of his head. The glassy eyes were all open; some seemed still gasping with open mouths; all were smeared in their own blood, and cold and clammy with the dews of death upon them.

But why dwell on the sickening details?—May I never see another field like that. There were on it ten corpses—two more died before they could be removed to the hospital, three died during the night; another was dying when I left.

Every attention was shown to the enemy's wounded by our surgeons. Limbs were amputated, wounds were dressed with the same care with which our own volunteers were treated. The wounds on the battle field removed all differences—in the hospital all were alike, the object of a common humanity that left none beyond its limits.

The following poem is exact as are all transcriptions in this file.
Here [sic] notations are omitted as they would affect the meter.

"I Am So Cold"

The North man treads the Southern shore
He stains the Southern stream with gore
The land he has so long decried
Its claim for right, or peace denied,
With pleas familiar to the strong,
He tramples now, with his last wrong-
The last—than triumph of such foe
The land can reach no further woe
The Assyrian, Persian, Roman chain,
The symeter of Tamerlane.[3]
The Norman Austrian, Russian yoke,
So proud a People never broke.
The torture never touched a flame,
So sensitive to pain or shame,
The conquered to his foe may lend,
Never to him he once called friend.
The last—should this dark effort fail,
No fond delusion shall prevail;
With Liberty, again to trust,
That Power is kind, or good, or just.
So hope the Common Strength of all,
May not the weaker still enthrall
Whenever she wins one foot of sod
She'll put her trust, henceforth in God
And hold her smallest spot of land
Through him by her own armied hand.

Brave Garnett dies without a stain
He bounds beyond the soiling chain
The iron enters not his soul
It rises on the battle roll
Virginias mountains on it fills
And soon to the eternal hills
He joins on high the Martyr throng,
Who still their glittering line prolong,
As day by day their numbers swell
From scaffold, field, or prison cell
Of those, while Begots[4] still refine
On things, or numbers right devine
Of order, government, and law.
With prompt instinctive duty draw
Against the invader of their land;
The unaggressive battle brand:

Virginia writes another name
Upon her scroll of spotless fame,
Of Sons, who answering to her call
Have staunch, to guard her menaced throne,
And never yet, for hers alone
But ever for the rights of all.

Here lies a stripling by his side.
A boy unknown, he nobly died
And evermore shall his young fame
With Garnett shine, in blended flame,
He was a battler from the hills
Whence Chattahooche draws its rills,
Or fair Savanah rolling wide
Upon whose banks Pulaski⁵ died.
The Georgian lad—the veteran Pole,
Both have the high heroic soul
An <u>unknown</u>, and a <u>wide known</u> name,
A dawning became a noon day flame,
Both lit at Freedom's sacred shrine,
By the eternal fire divine.
Both quenched in a disastrous day,
When for a time, the wrong had sway,
Both met the death to freemen meet,
To pass to glory, from defeat.
Not that vain glory of the crowd,
Which fills the earth with clamorous loud,
And even that—good men regard
But that which is its own reward
The glory of a race well run,
Of earnest duty, nobly done.
The glory which befits the soul,
As wide the heavenly gates unroll
To enter on that untried sphere
Humbly, but without death or fear,
And with its powers schooled below,
In that expanding field to glow,
From glory into glory turn
In infinite progression burn;
Still mounting nearer to the Throne,
Without a bound, save God alone.

And here another victim lies-
The death film gathers oer his eyes.
The light of battle on his face,
Melts off into a softer grace:
Virginia see thy faithful son
Faithful to death, his task is done

The trumpet call, the cannon roar,
Shall rouse his parting soul no more,
The hopes, the visions of his youth
His manhood's struggle for the truth
Roll back—once more a feeble child
As when the night dank chill and wild
Close cowering in his little nest,
He yearns for the maternal breast.
Oh! Mother clasp him to thy heart,
And let the gushing tear drops start
As close his stiffening limbs you fold,
Hear his child words "I am so cold."

"I am so cold," that touching word,
Has all the founts of feeling stirred:
The warrior on Manassas hill,
The Maiden by [illegible] rill,
The mighty leader of the war,
The weakest victim, flying far,
<u>All</u>, touched, by that pole suffered woe,
All let the melting torrent flow.
To him who braved the adverse tide
And with his struggling General died,
And in disastrous battle wild
Passed from the earth like some young child.

"I am so cold," that sad, low word,
A million Southern homes has stirred:
That plaintive note has sent its thrill
Through every vale and swelling hill
And melts a million hearts in one
Each makes the sacrifice its own;
And taught how great that sacrifice,
A hero's life, beyond all prise,
Each gives, as dearer he becomes,
Its victims—all those willing homes,
One soft wide wind, uprising heaves
The boundless forest, countless leaves,
One tide floods on the under-sweep
Of ocean, and deep calls to deep;
To its profound abysses stirred,
It waves to that low whispered word.

"I am so cold," that saddening word,
Shall yet in Northern homes be heard.
For sorrows voice in battle din,
Still whispers, all mankind are kin,
The aged chief whose practised hand,

Sheds blood upon his native land.
Bringing upon his soldier's pride,
A foiled attempt at Matricide,
Dimming a life of dassling[6] fame,
With that unutterable shame.
The loving wife, the tender maid,
The mother, for a while betrayed,
To give their sisters homes, to flame,
To slaughter, and to woman's shame.
Shall listen yet to sorrow's tone,
Happy, if it be not their own.
That voice shall reach the inner cells,
Where nature's healing virtue dwells.
The Angel, from Indras[7] sky,
Though Rome's fierce eagles flutter nigh,
And priestly pride, disdains to bend,
On wings of mercy shall descend
And this Bethesda's[8] troubled pool,
Oh may they wash, and make them whole.

Oh children of the Northern clime,
Hold back your hand from this great crime.
The wise may wrangle o'er a word,
But when the strong drives home the sword
Against a weaker Brother's breast,
Doubts and distrust are put to rest,
And all men see the murky stain
The mark upon the murderer Cain.
And earth & Heaven hear that sound,
The cry of blood, from ones own ground.
Blood consecrates the victims land,
But ever stains the slayer's hand.
Tis yours to strike and to forbear.
Ours to struggle and to dare.
Strike—we will answer blow for blow,
Till treads our soil no armed foe.
Strike and the battles refluent tide,
May waste your land with ruin wide.
Strike—and the still unswerving feud,
May drain your childrens veins of blood;
For fear no Southerner will be found,
With fire and sword on Northern ground,
Unless again, with mutual hand,
To drive the foeman from our land.
Unless, once more, for you to free,
The pathways of the boundless sea.

On the order of Major General Butler[9] commanding the United
States army at New Orleans, relating to the ladies
of that city
May 1862

Is there a single manly heart, on all the Earth's expanse
Whose tender feelings instant start, at Woman's slightest glance?
That heart will dash upon the brute, Alas! of woman born,
The Hayman[10] Butler, and his race, its bitterness of scorn.
What? shall our Sisters of the South, the pure, refined, and good,
Hear their sweet names, in his foul mouth, & shall his soldiers rude,
With Governmental license clutch, with insult drag along,
Whom, even to save, no man can touch, but with vice scuse[11] of a wrong.
Oh! shall the female victim shriek, be heard forever more,
Beneath the coarse New England power? and on a Southern shore?
Is there no corner of the world to which the weak may fly,
And rest in peace, no neth[12] on Earth? no pity in the sky?
Oh, scorching brand of servitude! this Anatic[13] shame,
This Sepoy[14] vengeance of our foes, in torture more than flame,
Our women helpless in their power! Oh God! must this be borne?
Oh! think of Mary, blessed Christ, & of thy natal morn;
Of all thou hast in woman shrined, mercy, redemption, love,
The beauteous source of human life, blessed fount of that above;
Oh take her gentle form to Heaven, and leave to men alone,
To struggle on this blasted Earth, for Power's blackened throne.
When Ussa[15] heedless, touched the ark, Thy vengeance Thou let fall,
When Benjamin[16], the Woman wronged, the sword consumed them all.
Is there no bolt of vengeance left, with wrath extremest red
To strike from off the shrinking Earth, this bestial despot dead?
Oh! in our agony to Thee, where can we else we turn?
And in this depth of misery, Thine awful will would learn,
From shame and suffering, virtue springs, nations are born in woe,
This pang with Earth, our Mother wings, is Nature's final throe.
Eight lustres[17] of increasing wrong, could scarcely send away,
Some natural ties, which linger long, this snaps them in a day.
Another Nation lives in flames, the true heart knows no more,
The power which seeks our Sisters shame, our kinsmen's death and
    gore.

❦   ❦   ❦

Baltimore, Apr. 9th [1863]
To Mrs. William H. Hollyday,

Dear Madam,

A few days back, I was the honored recipient of a short letter from your son Willie,[18] he was _very well,_ & returned to camp, the _day after_ writing, having been on furlough for six weeks, he wrote in very excellent spirits, and desired me to try & find out _all_ I could in regard to you, if you were _still_ in Philadelphia &c &c in which case asking me to write, and tell you of his well-being, & with much love to you _all,_ begs that you would write to him _very soon,_ a _long letter,_ as he has never heard, _but once,_ from _home,_ since his advent in the army. Every day it becomes more & _more_ difficult to communicate with those _far away_ from the _comforts_ & _endearments_ of _home._ Nevertheless if you _wish_ to write & will do so _immediately,_ a gentleman _who has influence_ has promised to get it through, _probably by way of_ "Fortress Monroe." I have heard Willie _so often_ speak of you all, that I scarcely feel as though I was writing to a stranger, but at the same time, _politeness required_ that I should ask your indulgence for thus addressing you.

With kind regards to yourself and family (stranger though I am) and the earnest desire for the _safety, honor, welfare,_ and _return,_ of your son, believe me dear Madam

Very respectfully yours
Euphemia M. Goldsborough

Direct & enclose
to Miss E M Goldsborough
Corner of Courtland & Mulberry Sts
Baltimore Md.

Private Wm. H. Hollyday.

KILLED, June 3d, 1864, at Gaines' Farm, in an engagement with the enemy, Private WM. H. HOLLYDAY, 2d Maryland Infantry.
☞ Baltimore papers please copy.

Newspaper clipping about Private Hollyday's death.

~ ~ ~

For Miss Goldsborough

-Florida Boys-

Died in College Hospital, Gettysburg Pa-

1. Corpl. R. J. Wolf	Co. D	2nd	Fla	July 8,	1863	
2. " W. D. Kenedy	Co. A	2nd	Fla	" 12	"	
3. Private E. French	Co. I	5th	Fla	" 7	"	
4. " R. Wilson	Co. G	2nd	Fla	"		
5. " A. A. Brown	Co. D	5th	Fla	" 14	"	
6. " Wm. Bryant	Co. A	2nd	Fla	"		
7. " B. Inmand	Co. A	2nd	Fla	" 21st		
8. " [Barton] N. Hillhouse	Co. F	5	Fla	" 4		

Officers from Florida

> Capt R. N. Gardner
> Lieut A. J. Peeler
> Capt Wm Bailey
> Lieut B. F. Wood
> Lieut H Bruce
> Capt Livingstone [sic]
> Lieut J W Malone
> Lieut E. P. Dismukes
> Lieut F. M. Bryant
> Lieut J. W. Hall
> ――――――
> Lieut Wm Ross

[Captain Richmond N. Gardner, Co. K, 5th Florida, Lieutenant Anderson J. Peeler, Co. I, 5th Florida, Captain William J. Bailey, Co. G, 5th Florida, [See Hospital Books].

[1st Lieutenant B. F. Wood, Co. H, 5th Florida, was wounded in the left thigh, captured on 7/3, admitted into West's Buildings 7/25, sent to Johnson's Island 8/63, transferred and exchanged at Point Lookout 3/65.]

[1st Lieutenant Hector Bruce, Co. B, 8th Florida, was wounded in the right arm and leg. He was sent to Johnson's Island and exchanged 2/64. One of T. D. Houston's messmates, he was described as "an intelligent and educated young scotchman with dark hair and whiskers, beautiful teeth and a very expressive 'grin', but like all of his countrymen obstinate in his opinions for he would suffer death rather than give up a principle." —Houston Letters]

[Captain Tailiferro B. Livingston, Co. E, 8th Florida, was wounded on the left side, spent some time at Chester Hospital in Philadelphia, was sent to Johnson's Island, then to Ft. Delaware in 4/65.]

[Lieutenant John W. Malone, Co. B, 8th Florida, was wounded in the right shoulder, sent to Johnson's Island, and exchanged from Point Lookout in 3/65. Another Houston messmate, he was described as "(commonly called the 'Fat Baby') weighing about 200 pounds, red hair, one of the best natured faces in the world, possessing a manly and generous heart." —Houston Letters]

[Lieutenant Elisha Paul Dismukes, Co. F, 8th Florida, was wounded, sent to Johnson's Island and paroled and exchanged at City Point 2/64. Another Houston messmate, he was described as "small and good looking, talkative and sensible. He is a young member of the bar and loves arguments and potatoes. He enjoys the good things of the world and laughs at misfortune." —Houston Letters]

[2nd Lieutenant Francis M. Bryant, Co. K, 8th Florida, was wounded in the right thigh, sent to Ft. Delaware and paroled in 10/64.]

[Lieutenant John W. Hall, Co. I, 2nd Florida, was wounded, sent to Ft. McHenry, then Ft. Delaware and Johnson's Island and exchanged from Point Lookout in 3/65.]

[Lieutenant William J. F. Ross, Co. C, 2nd Georgia Battalion See Hospital Books]

ϡ   ϡ   ϡ

General Hospital Sep 3rd [1863]

Lient Peeler,[19]
The long looked for letter arrived safely on Sunday night last. Need I tell you I was happy to hear pleasant tidings of those <u>chance</u> *had thrown us with in the hour of suffering during "Our College days"; but enough. Probably you will be some what surprised to hear we are all still in Camp—& so far have all kept well, except for an occasional Headache or* <u>Heartache</u> *I scarcely know which. I am glad to know you have the same pleasant party together at Sandusky [Johnson's Island] that you had here & trust most sincerely the days of your captivity may be short. When you write tell me if you are allowed to receive boxes &c &c how long letters I may write, as I know little in regard to such correspondence. Remember me most kindly to—Caps B & G, Col L Lieuts G[20] [illegible]—indeed to* <u>all</u> *I have the pleasure of knowing with my best wishes for comfort and speedy exchange. Say to Capt G. I should be glad to hear from him whenever he has a spare moment from thoughts of Miss L[21]. Write* <u>very</u> *soon and direct as before to your Friend sincere   EMG*

ϡ   ϡ   ϡ

Sergt-Maj Ross[22]

Your letter was received about ten days back, with much pleasure I assure you & should have been answered sooner, but for the fact of my waiting to see if the letter you were expecting was coming. So far there has been nothing for you, but I do not feel that I can allow another day to pass (though a letter has not yet arrived) without the pleasure of answering your letter being mine. Please do not think I have been neglectful, or forgetful of absent friends. I have thought of your <u>party</u> very often & missed you from your tent across the way each day more and more. Mr. Betton[23] with his quiet good morning. Sergt. Haines in his merry way particular to himself, & last but not least, the [illegible] cordial greeting of your respected self. You said you should have prefaced your letter with an apology for waiting. You should have done nothing of the kind, <u>friends</u> should <u>forget such formalities</u>. Your friends remaining here doing well. Cap G S & G H Jones[24] have both been sent off to your hosp. no doubt seen them both by this time. I am glad to hear you have been treated with kindness since you left Gettysburg & trust you may continue in the same, and above all the days of your captivity may be short.

[no signature but in Pheme's hand]

❧   ❧   ❧

West's Hospital
October 28th, 1863

Miss E. M. Goldsborough,

I am happy to acknowledge the reception of your present for which accept my most sincere thanks. I was delighted to find that I had a friend in the City who thought of me while a prisoner.

My kindest regards to all of my Gettysburg acquaintances & also to your Sisters.

I am as ever your
friend C. H. Woolley[25]

❧   ❧   ❧

West Building Hosp Baltimore Nov the 20th 1863
Miss Gettysburg

My very Dear Friend,

In a very unexpected way I received your very welcome letter a few days ago but owning to inconvenience of dispatching I have failed to answer. As you will see from the date of my last letter I had written it *several days before I could get it off so I hope you will not charge me with negligence. I feel very unpleasant when you tell me you have been disappointed in not hearing from me. If I could write an interesting letter and could get them off I am sure it would be a source of great pleasure to me to write to you every day—particularly if I could get answers to them but being wholly incompetent to perform the first part of my proposition I cannot see but you are profited instead the loser of my not writing more frequently whilst I am very perceptibly loser by it. I believe they will not allow any one to come to the Hospital now. I thought I saw a couple of your sisters last Sunday afternoon coming towards the hospital—they turned to the left at the head of the dock and crossed the Bridge, was it them? I can scarcely see how I can come and see you unless I take the <u>oath, must I do it</u>? or would you allow me to come then. Miss G I shall hope for a better day when I can. I might drop in there one of these nights wholy [sic] unexpected to you and myself but I cannot tell how long it must though I hope in a few days. Did you go to Gettysburg to the grand to do?[26] I guess they had a very nice time up there (<u>in their way</u>). I am truly sorry Miss G that you had to submit to such outrages.[27] I wish I had it in my power to relieve you. I am will [sic] to start back to another Maryland Pennsylvania or any other kind of Campaign that had for its object the deliverance of Baltimore as soon as I get to Dixie. Such tyranny cannot always exist. It will be done away with one of these days and then if not before I hope to be able to come to see you untrameled [sic]. You wish to know who went off in that lot the other day, W. W. Smith, J. H. Brown, C. H. Woolley[28] and I believe every body else that you know except my <u>little</u> self. I am here as it were all alone. We have but five wards in the hospital now. I have been transferred from ward "G" to ward "A". I am night watch in there. I never sit down five minutes every night after every thing gets still but I think of my friend whom I am now writing. Miss G if you could see me every night whilst sitting all alone I know you would say <u>poor unfortunate Rebel Tom</u> but I think I will survive my imprisonment. Then I'll have a good time will I not? I did receive the package of tobacco for which allow me to return my sincere thanks. I am very much obliged to you for writing to Callie.[29] I know she will be pleased to answer it. It is a pleasure to me [to] even write her name on paper. You remind me of Callie on one respect. Callie will write me a <u>little short</u> letter and exact a long one from me. That's the way with you. I have received nearly a page from you in your last. If I did not write any more than that to you, you would be like you was once before. You would say you did not write me a long letter, what is the reason? I dislike to ask you why you did not write me a long letter when you* tell me at the outset that you have not time. Must I accept that as an excuse at this <u>critical</u> time? Well I guess I'll have to for this letter Miss G. Tell Miss Addie[30] (not wishing to be extravagant in the way of capital letters) I am very much pleased with my envelope and papers and will comply with her request as soon as she answers my letter also I am truly thankful for the same. Bouknight[31] did not leave any Fans with me. I asked him before he left if he had anything of the kind and he told me he did not. I have a couple on hand that one of the boys gave me before he left, one I intended for Miss Addie. You can tell her I have the fan she wished and will send it to her the first opportunity. You can have the other if you wish to. I have had them on hand ever since the Boys left. I have just heard of the capture of Col. Gibson[32] I do not believe [it]. It is reported that they captured him and five others. Have you heard anything of it Miss G. This is a very interesting letter so I will cease to write. I know you are tired of it. I have nothing to write about. Smith, Brown, and Woolley requested me to remember them to you as often as I wrote. Maj G[33] thinks he is getting better, feels very well this morning. I have seen his brother from Liby [sic] Prison.[34] Have you seen him? Did you receive a ring on that package of letters I spoke to you about? I sent it to Miss Gertie.[35] Was one of the three that you did receive from me. I have never heard you say a word about it. You merely informed me you received three of them. I was anxious for you to get that letter. Were you acquainted with Miss Duvall up at Gettysburg who had a wounded brother there?[36] It is reported he took the <u>oath</u> yesterday. I hope it is not true. I do not give it as true only as rumor. Well Miss G I will close by asking you to write to me very soon and believe me to be one of your best Friends,

T. J. Sneed, Jr.[37]

❧   ❧   ❧

Addressed to: Prisoner of War
Lt. Col. James R. Herbert
1st Maryland Bat, Johnson's Island
Sandusky City
Ohio

Baltimore Nov 24th[38] [1863]

Col. James R. Herbert,
    My dear friend (for so I am sure you will permit me to call you). Your letter was received with great satisfaction a week ago today. I had quite given up the hope of being honored with the remembrance

of your respected self and was <u>beginning</u> to think the remark which irritated you so much "out of sight, out of mind" made while at Gettysburg was <u>about to be verified</u> but your pleasant and <u>highly appreciated</u> letter put all such conjectures at rest. I am happy to know you have recovered the use of your hand. I had quite forgotten until your letter reached me that your wound was in the <u>right arm</u> and therefore a <u>letter, quite an undertaking</u>. I do hope you will manage to keep comfortable during the cold weather that is fast approaching. I often think of those it was my fate to meet under such <u>trying circumstances</u> and sigh that I cannot give them the comforts of their <u>homes</u>. You ask after Maj G[39] he is here at West Building Hospital, <u>still suffering</u> an <u>awful cough</u>. I have sent him many little things but have never yet had but <u>one</u> note from him. Some days he is better <u>than worse</u>. Do you know Col I have quite given up the hope of his recovery? I <u>hate</u> the <u>thought</u>—and yet I do not see how we can <u>longer contend</u> against it. His brother Dr. Charles has been exchanged arrived two weeks ago but I do not think that will have the <u>least bearing</u> upon the <u>Maj exchange</u>. Alice was here the afternoon of the same day your letter reached me and I gave your messages to her. I'm sure Mrs. G would send you her love, did she know I was writing. Your letter was handed me just as I was starting downtown with two lady friends. I told them what you said and but for the publicity of <u>Charles Street</u> would have given them such a kiss to which they were <u>most willing</u> to <u>submit</u>. Others said they <u>objected</u> to the <u>agent employed,</u> but would be happy to receive it from the Col <u>himself.</u> I am quite shocked that you should have concluded to be a flirt "when this cruel war is over". Ladies are <u>perfectly harmless</u>. I do assure you and there is no reason why you should be afraid of the "dear creatures". I am sure Col Herbert did not live so long in Baltimore without owing allegiance to some fair one. <u>Every heart</u> must have <u>a shrine, however</u> [illegible]. Otherwise <u>life</u> would not be worth enduring. Of course you remember John Hanson and Emily Pickney. They were married last Wednesday and had a great wedding. And Miss Anne Poltney & Garrith Folhner took each other for <u>better</u> or <u>worse</u> two weeks ago. I really do believe people are quite beside themselves on the subject of getting married. And unless the <u>war</u> is over soon Col H will not find <u>many to make love to</u>. If <u>I am in Baltimore</u> when that wished for time arrives I think I shall warn all <u>not</u> to be deceived by promises <u>only</u>. You asked me to write you a long letter, have I not done so? Remember me to all friends and let me hear from you soon. Believe me there is no one I should be better pleased to hear from than yourself. Hoping you are well I remain your True friend EM Goldsborough

On the envelope of the following letter is the address: "Lient. Col. R. W. Martin, Ft. McHenry"

Written above the address: "Dr. General This is one of many but will answer to satisfy some of her loyal (?) friends who will doubless [sic] call on you.   W S F [Col. William S. Fish]"

Baltimore, Nov. 23rd[40] *[1863]*

Col. Martin[41]*—Dear Friend,*

    I received a letter from you with very great pleasure on Saturday last which I shall <u>answer soon</u> letters <u>sub-vosa</u> are only <u>notes</u> from the <u>way side of the heart</u> which I am happy to find by your letter of Wednesday you can <u>honorably receive</u>.[42] *I cannot tell but this <u>may be the last</u> letter Col. M will [illegible] be troubled to decipher from me as I fear I am <u>implicated most seriously</u> in the <u>attempted</u> escape of a prisoner. A letter <u>directed</u> was found on his person and probably I shall go to "Sweet Dixie" sooner than <u>you</u> however I am not one <u>bit afraid</u> & <u>defy</u> the whole <u>Yankee Nation send me where they will</u>. I am <u>able</u> & <u>willing</u> to <u>suffer hardships</u> & <u>loss</u> for <u>myself</u> for the sake of a <u>country</u> & <u>people that I love</u>. But probably it will all <u>blow over</u> & my friends may be <u>unnecessarily alarmed</u> at any rate I have never in my life been <u>more</u> at ease on that subject than <u>now</u>. I have been so busy <u>lately</u>. I wish I could see you that we might have one of our <u>old timed</u> talks but that cannot be until the war is over I fear. A friend has promised to secure me a pass into the "<u>Prisons</u>" around us. I hope & trust most earnestly, he may be as <u>good as his word</u>. If I am allowed to remain in my home. A pass to see my friends would be my greatest pleasure & <u>privlege</u> [sic]. I send you the chess men and board. I never cared for the game therefore did not have a set but got you a <u>small set</u> that you could easily carry about with you. I also send you a box of colobles*[43] *which I hope <u>yourself</u> Lient. Perkins, Warren, & Maj Cudrup*[44] *may enjoy. I have understood your lives <u>so well</u> at "Fort McHenry" that not many things are <u>dainties</u> but suppose nevertheless you will manage to consume the box. My kind regards to <u>all</u>. I hope <u>Col. M,</u> will remember to think of his friend often or rather <u>sometimes</u> & believe me always the same. <u>Truly</u> & <u>Sincerely</u>,*

                              Miss E Goldsborough

ʃʘ   ʃʘ   ʃʘ

Rebels

Rebels tis a holy name,
The name our fathers bore,
When battling in the cause of <u>Right</u>,
Against the tyrant in his might,
In the dark days of yore.

Rebels tis our family name
Our <u>father, Washington</u>,
Was the arch-rebel in the fight,
And gave the name to us—a right
Of father unto son.

Rebels tis our given name,
Our Mother, <u>Liberty</u>,
Received the title with her fame,
In days of grief, of fear and shame,
When at her breast were we.

Rebels is our sealed name,
A baptism of blood;
The war ago, and the din of strife;
The fearful contest life for life,
The mingled crimson flood

Rebels tis a patriots name;
In struggles it was given:
We bore it then when tyrants raved;
And through their curses twas engraved
On the doomsday book of Heaven—

Rebels tis our fighting name;
For peace rules on the land,
Until they speak of craven woe—
<u>Until our rights received a blow</u>,
From foe's or brother's hand.

Rebels tis our dying name
For although life is dear;
Yet freemen born and freemen bred;
We'd rather lie as freemen dead;
Than live in <u>slavish fear</u>.

Then call us rebels, if you will,
We <u>glory</u> in the <u>name</u>;
For bending under <u>unjust laws</u>,
And swearing faith to an <u>unjust cause</u>,
We count a greater shame.

The last two letters contained in the Provost Marshal file appear to have been of little use to substantiate charges of treason. One page of an undated letter, author unknown.

Dear Pheme,
I am so sorry I could not get Mr. Ross to send the [illegible] to day. There would be no surety of your getting them but that is not the reason. after he told me he would send them, I think he might do so, but some people are too mean to him. I was surprised to hear [illegible] and [illegible] had arrived, they brought the good news that Pa had some thing to do, one of my objects in writing is to ask some of your plans with [illegible] a good long letter by Saturdays boat as I have not heard from home in two weeks. Cousin Anne wants one of the girls to get her one of these envelopes of paper at [illegible] with a pair of [illegible] buttons inclosed & send them down on Saturday to Knights wharf where our [illegible] always goes on steamboat days for papers. give them to the Captain. I cannot [illegible] as I am in a very great hurry indeed I am so sorry about the [illegible] but you know I cant help it. I shall write you a long letter on Monday next and there are one or two little things I want you to send me. I guess I shall go to Talbot [County] in about ten days with much love to all I remain yours with love Pheme I shall go to Springfield on Friday if [illegible] looks
[end of page]

Bell Air Aug 7 1861
Dear Aunt,
    Pheme intended writing to you this morning but some gentlemen just called to see her, so I write a few lines to ask you and Uncle to come down on Saturday next to see us our Mellons [sic] are ripe and Lewis wants you both to come if you only stay a day or two we would [sic] to see you all if you all could come. We are going over the Weighs this car tomorrow to [illegible] I am so sorry we cannot induce Pheme to stay longer with us I've been sick every [sic] since she's been here on Saturday we had company and I was taken very sick with Bellows colic had to leave the company and all with Pheme and get to bed. I've had such a sick time this year if you will come home on Saturday Lewis will be over at [illegible] wharf for you Pheme says this in her [illegible] [illegible] for life and death our love to you all do come it [would] do you good and I want to see you here Lewis Clinton & Pheme join me in love to you all
            [illegible]
                affect Niece Ann

The remainder of the Provost Marshal file consists of notecards which appear to have been plans for a series of tableaux. There is no date and it is in Pheme's hand but mostly in abbreviated notes. Some of the scenes are Queen Elizabeth knighting Sir Walter Raleigh, Cinderella trying on the slipper, *Taming of the Shrew*, etc. There is one titled the Conscript's Departure which indicates war time. Of more interest to the Provost Marshal would have been the list of people who were to participate. Coupled with the fact that Pheme put tableaux on to help finance her activities for the Confederacy, one could assume that the people involved as actors may have also been involved in her other activities. The list is as follows:

```
Pheme Goldsboro—
Kate        do      [ditto]
Gertrude    do      [her sister]
Mona        do      [her sister]
Mrs. Carr
Miss J Johnson      [possibly Jami Johnson previ-
                     ously mentioned in a letter]
  "  J  Ohrendorf
  "  M  Love
  "  A  Love
  "  L  Caldwell
  "  L  Bowie
Mrs  Levering
Miss  Thomas
  "      Todhunter
  "  A  Owings
  "  L  do
  "  E  do
Mrs D Johnson
Miss Sanborn
  "  J    do
  "      Keys
Annie Price
Joe       do
Mrs. Buckner
Miss Berryman
  "     Gettings
  "        do
  "     Lutton
```

Personal Collection

Letter to Sam Watson's mother now missing from collection.

Balto Sept. 22, 1863

Mrs. Harriet Watson,
Dear Madam,
   I suppose you have already received intelligence of your son, Sam H. Watson being wounded at the battle of Gettysburg. His right arm was amputated and for a time he seemed to be getting on nicely, but unfortunately for himself, and those who loved him, an abcess [sic] formed under his arm, which, with sorrow be it said, terminated his young life. It was my privilege to nurse him six weeks, during which time I looked to his comfort as I would my only brother and learned to love him <u>just the same</u>. He died in my arms, Sunday evening, Sept. 13, <u>just at sunset</u> his precious brown eyes fixed in mine, without a struggle, and his last fleeting breath I caught upon my lips. He spoke of both you and his sister during the day and asked his cousin, Thomas Sneed from Texas, to return to you two plain gold rings that each had given him. Also a likeness of himself taken about four months back and to say "he had come for a soldier, <u>done his duty</u> and died for his country." I know every word I am writing will carry <u>grief to your heart</u>, and yet, judging you by myself, I feel that you would like to know all. I had him buried with my own, the Episcopal Church service, and marked his grave. Mrs. Watson, you <u>must not</u> feel that your son died in an enemy's country with <u>none</u> to <u>love</u> or care for him. His whole Brigade loved him as did all who came in contact with him, <u>even those</u> who were opposed to the glorious cause for which so many brave and noble have already been sacrificed, and many were the bitter tears shed over his untimely grave. If this should ever reach you, may I ask that you will answer it. I hope that we may meet after this

unhappy war is ended and that I may be able to give you back your <u>darling son's</u> dying kiss. Hoping I may hear from you and with a heart full of sympathy and sorrow for your loss, with profound respect I remain

Your friend,

E.M. Goldsborough

Direct to Miss Euphemia M. Goldsborough
   No. 49 Courtland St. Balto, Md.

Enclose it to Jackson Douglas, 1st Auditor's Office, Richmond, Va. and he will send it through <u>underground</u> to me. Excuse a faulty letter. I have no control over my feelings while writing or thinking of this subject.

❧   ❧   ❧

Letter now missing from collection.

Johnson's Island
November 11, 1863

My dear Miss Goldsborough,

   I cannot refrain from dropping you a few lines from my present abode expressing my admiration for your many kind acts and devotion to the poor wounded soldiers at Gettysburg. you and your collaborators, Miss McKee [Henrietta McCrea], Miss [Maggie] Branson, Miss [Annie] Long and others will not be forgotten. May God bless you all and I am sure he will. Well, I suppose you would like to hear of your patients. As far as I know they are all doing well and if they could see you, or get some of the milk punch made by your own fair hands they would be as happy as possible under the circumstances. We are all very comfortable here but expect very cold weather ere long, but we will grin and bear it. What on earth has become of Major G?[1] How is his wound. I have written but have got no answer. I have not heard from him since I came here. He knows that until lately I have been unable to use my hand or I would have written to him often. Give my love to his mother who was just as kind to me as my own mother. Write me if you can find him, and just as long a letter as you please. I can receive it. Has Dr. Goldsborough got home from Libby prison yet. I hope so, especially on his brother's account. We amuse ourselves here in various ways, chess, backgammon, checkers, cards, etc. It will be entirely too cold for the Major at this place. This winter it would certainly kill him. And Lt. Ferguson[2] got well, I hope and trust he did. I never saw anyone bear such suffering with more Christian fortitude. He is a noble man. How are all the girls. You can kiss them for me if you choose and if they submit. I believe when this "Cruel War is over" I will make love to all and no one in particular. I am rather afraid of the "Dear creatures", would you believe it? But 'tis a fact. But I would be glad if you would make as many as possible write. I am sure if they know with how much pleasure they are read they would write. You, now, have so many correspondents, more agreeable ones, I can only claim a very small share of your thoughts. With many wishes for your happiness   I remain your friend

James H. Herbert

       ᔡ   ᔡ   ᔡ

Transcripts from undated, unnamed newspapers in Pheme's scrapbook announcing her exile:

Ladies Sent South—Misses Virginia Lomax, Nannie Lomax, Julia Lomax and E.M. Goldsborough were arrested by Government officers a few days ago and taken before Col. Fish upon the charge of corresponding with parties in the South. Previous to their arrest the officers had unmistakable evidence of their guilt. The three first named, we believe, are from Westmoreland County, Virginia. They were all ordered to be sent South with the understanding that if they return before the war is ended they will be treated as spies. On Saturday afternoon they left in the Fortress Monroe steamer under guard, and will be sent to City Point by the first flag-of-truce steamer.

More Banishment—Miss E.M. Goldsborough of Baltimore, of wealthy parents, beautiful and refined has been detected in correspondence with "rebels" and sentenced to banishment.

As to the Lincoln government with it's heel of despotism crushing the liberties of Maryland has given that state the fitting soubriquet of 'The Poland of America'. They have chosen the Southern Confederacy for it's 'Siberia'. The Ape apes the 'Czar of all Russia' in more respects than one.

Sent South—Misses Virginia Lomax, Nannie Lomax, Julia Lomax and E.M. Goldsborough were arrested in Baltimore a few days ago on a charge of corresponding with parties in the South. They were ordered to the South, with the understanding that, if they returned before the war is ended they will be treated as spies. The first three are from Westmoreland County, Virginia. Valiant soldiers.

ﻉ   ﻉ   ﻉ

Lewisburg, Va
Jan. 5, 1864

Miss Goldsborough

I have just received a letter from my brother in Richmond announcing your arrival as he failed to mention the first name, I don't know that I have the pleasure of your acquaintance. But as we are both from old Maryland and I having been absent so long, my great anxiety for the welfare of my dear friends induces me to write this letter and if it be congenial to your feelings I would be most happy to receive an answer that I may know something of my friends. Brother mentioned that you brought Uncle Howe's picture over. I hope you left him well and that the picture was intended for me. Congratulations on your safe arrival in the land of living, I remain with highest regard,

R. Chew Jones,[3] enrolling officer
Greenbrier County, Va.

ৈ৵   ৈ৵   ৈ৵

Letter now missing from collection

Louisiana Hospital,
March 16, 1864

My Dear Friend,
*   Please accept my gratitude for your past kindness at Gettysburg*
and Johnson's Island. I messed with Capt. Gardner, Lt. Peeler, Lt.
Minor[4] and a number of your other friends at Johnson's Island, all of
whom I left behind. Poor fellows, I am sorry for them. I wish I had
time to call and see you. I could tell you all about your friends. I
leave tomorrow but will return in a few weeks.

*   Your friend,*
*   Jack Barnes*
*   Col. 59 Ga Regt[5]*

ৈ৵   ৈ৵   ৈ৵

Poem written by Col. W. S. Hawkins, C.S.A.[6] (prisoner of war at
Camp Chase, Ohio), a friend of a fellow prisoner who was engaged to
a Southern lady. She proved faithless to him. Her letter arrived
soon after his death and was answered in the following lines:

Your letter came, but came too late
For Heaven had claimed its own;
Ah! sudden change from prison bars
Unto the Great White Throne.
And yet I think he would have stayed
For one more day of pain
Could he have read those tardy words
Which you have sent in vain.

Why did you wait, fair lady
Through so many a weary hour?
Had you other lovers with you
In that silken, dainty bower?
Did others bow before your charms
And twine bright garlands there?
And yet, I ween, in all the throng
His spirit had no peer.

134

I wish that you were by me now
As I draw the sheet aside
To see how pure the look he wore
Awhile before he died.
Yet the sorrow that you gave him
Still has left its weary trace
And a meek and saintly sadness
Dwells upon that pallid face.

"Her love" he said, "could change for me
The winter's cold to Spring."
Ah! trust of thoughtless maiden's love
Thou art a bitter thing:
For when these valleys fair, in May
Once more the blossoms shall wave
The Northern violets shall blow
Above his humble grave.

Your dole of scanty words had been
But one more pang to bear;
Though to the last he kissed with love
This tress of your soft hair.
I did not put it where he said
For when the angels come
I would not have them find the sign
Of falsehood in his tomb.

I've read your letter, and I know
The wiles that you have wrought
To win that noble heart of his
And gained it; fearful thought.
What lavish wealth men sometimes give
For a trifle light and small;
What manly forms are often held
In Folly's flimsey [sic] thrall.

You shall not pity him, for now
He's past your hopes and fears;
Although I wish that you could stand
With me beside his bier.
Still, I forgive you; Heaven knows
For mercy you'll have need;
Since God his [sic] awful judgment sends
On each unworthy deed.

Though the cold wind whistles by
As I my vigil keep.
Within the prison dead-house where
Few mourners come to weep.
A rude plank coffin holds him now
Yet Death gives always grace,
And I had rather see him thus
Then clasped in your embrace.

Tonight your rooms are very gay
With wit, and wine, and song;
And you are smiling just as if
You never did a wrong.
Your hand so fair that none would think
It penned these words of pain;
Your skin so white - would God your soul
Were half as free of stain.

I'd rather be this dear, dead friend
Than you in all your glee
For you are held in grievous bonds
While he's forever free.
Whom we serve in this life, we serve
In that which is to come.
He chose his way; you yours, let God
Pronounce the fitting doom!

Balcony Falls, Virginia
March 2nd, 1867

[Pheme must have obtained a copy of the poem during her visit.]

&a   &a   &a

The marriage contract between Euphemia Goldsborough and
Charles Willson was written by the latter with a great deal of humor
shortly before the marriage took place.

Marriage Contract

Entered into this 11th day of April 1874 between _____
party of the first part and Miss _____ party of the second
part. Witnesseth that the said party of the 1st part doth agree to

become the lawful husband of said party of the 2nd part for the following considerations, hereinafter stipulated, to be performed by the respective parties.

Viz. that the party of the 2nd part shall make over all real and personal property to the said party of the first part and to his present heirs, forever, and without reserve or recourse to law. If said property shall not be valued at one hundred thousand dollars, or shall fall below this amount, then shall the party of the first part not be required to fulfill his part of the contract.

It is further stipulated that the party of the 2nd part shall be required before marriage to procure from one of the best Dentists a full new set of teeth of the most improved pattern.

It is further stipulated that the party of the 2nd part shall furnish herself with a complete bridal outfit, to be selected by Miss Effie Goldsborough, not to exceed twenty five hundred dollars to consist of five hundred dollars worth of rouge and perfumeries to beautify and purify the person of the party of the second part.

It is further stipulated that one thousand dollars shall be expended in purchasing underwear to consist of chemise, petticoats, corsets, wadded and inflated bodies, false calves, hosiery and other unmentionables, all of the most improved style and of best materials.

Five hundred dollars shall be expended in purchasing a mask to be worn in the day and five hundred dollars to be expended in purchasing elaborate veiling to be worn at night, or at retiring, to prevent the necessity of having to put the head under the bed clothes.

One thousand dollars shall be expended also for wrappings, silken drapes, furs, etc. etc.

One thousand dollars shall also be expended for decorating the bridal chamber; wreaths of beautiful flowers shall be suspended from the bed posts, and other decorations that shall lend to the same.

It is further stipulated that the sum of two thousand dollars shall be expended in the purchase of carriage and horses to be at the disposal of the party of the 1st part, and also of Miss Effie Goldsborough, in consideration of valuable services rendered the bride-elect in beautifying and renovating her person for negotiating the contract for said parties to this contract.

It is further stipulated that an annuity of five hundred dollars shall be paid promptly to said Miss Effie Goldsborough for bringing matters to a happy issue, said annuity to be paid as long as either of the parties to this contract shall live. It is further stipulated that should the party of the first part outlive the party of the second part, and thus be left a widower, it shall be his duty to make an offer of marriage to Miss Euphemia Goldsborough in consideration of successfully financiering for the party of the first part (and thus elevating him to a position that the "Gods may well envy") that it is fair and just that she should share a fortune she has virtually secured to the party of the 1st part.

The party of the 1st part shall present to the party of the 2nd part five children for her motherly consideration to be trained in the way they should go. Also a body free of disease or hereditary afflictions, corpulent and weighing 185 lbs. has no earthly goods worth speaking of, has a big heart and a willing mind all of which he proposes to offer as a sacrifice to the Goddess of Love in exchange for the considerations mentioned in this contract.

The party of the 1st part furthermore agrees to visit home nightly, not to be out later than 11 o'clock, if no questions are asked, not to take a drink oftener than he thinks for the good of his health and to keep his spirits up should they flag, or before embracing his bride-elect, to lend zest to the occasion.

It is further stipulated that the party of the 2nd part shall in no instance have bad breath, which shall be sufficient grounds for divorce.

It is further stipulated that is, after living together for a reasonable time the party of the 2nd part may change her home, or travel for a change of climate or scenery, she shall be permitted to do so with the express understanding that she must not return to claim bed and board, but receive an annuity of five hundred dollars which should satisfy any reasonable woman.

The happy part of this contract can only be fully appreciated after marriage; may this crowning act of our lives call forth loud applause for posterity, who will rise up and call us blessed. To our many friends we would say the die is cast, wish us joy; may you all reach the same acme of expectations and happiness, and may you all have your beauty preserved as well as the party of the 2nd part to this contract. A world of future is before us. I hope none of the friends of the 1st party to this contract will dare to presume that she has been actuated by sinister motives when the world is before him and "any man can marry any woman if he will but persevere." Witness our hands and seals this 11th day of April, 1874.

Money   (seal)

Pure Love (seal)

Transcript from fragment of a letter written to Ann, Euphemia Goldsborough Willson's daughter concerning a dress handed down to her by her mother. The author, obviously an aunt, is unknown.

Now let me tell you about the war dress. My sister bought the dress of Mrs. General Gracie in Richmond. Mrs. Gracie was a niece of Mrs. Lt. Gen. Winfield Scott[7] of the U.S.A. Commander-in-chief of the Federal Army. Mrs. Scott was in Europe during the Civil War and it was such a terrible effort to get anything in those days. Mrs. Gracie wrote to her aunt, Mrs. Scott, to get her some clothing and send it to her from Paris by the Blockade runners. Mrs. Scott did so and paid one hundred dollars in gold for that black and white silk. It was 1200 in Confederate money. It took the blockade runners very long to escape the strict watch of the U.S. steamers kept on the coast and all the seaports so of course it was some time getting to Richmond and a few days after Mrs. Gracie got the box there was a battle and General Gracie[8] was killed. Then Mrs. Gracie sold all the fine clothing and went in deep mourning. Your mother bought that dress and I always thought it ought to be kept very sacred for it's connection with the "Lost Cause" and with the dead. Your mother prized it most highly.

This dress was presented to the museum at the Visitor's Center in Gettysburg by Euphemia's granddaughter, Mrs. Elizabeth Crim, on October 10, 1993.

Appendix 1

Name Index by State to Hospital Books

ALABAMA

Cloud, Thomas J., 3rd Alabama, Co. C
Hayes, Surg. J. M., 26th Alabama, Field & Staff
Minor, Surg. Henry Augustine, 9th Alabama
Nobers, Horatio G., 11th Alabama, Co. H
Parker, Asst. Surg. Daniel, 8th Alabama, Cos. A & D
Southall, Asst. Surg. Robert G., 6th Alabama, Co. I
Taggart, Sgt. Moses W., 11th Alabama, Co. H
Woolley, Sgt. Columbus H., 4th Alabama, Co. A

ARKANSAS

Brushear, Sgt. Richard H., 3rd Arkansas, Co. H
Tshear, Sgt. Napoleon N., 3rd Arkansas, Co. I

DISTRICT OF COLUMBIA

Shekill, Dr. A. D., civilian doctor

FLORIDA

Bailey, Capt. William J., 5th Florida, Co. G
Beck, William H., 5th Florida, Co. H
Betton, Sgt. Julian, 2nd Florida, Co. M
Gardner, Capt. Richmond N., 5th Florida, Co. K
Givens, Lt. Thomas Wilkes, 8th Florida, Co. K
Peeler, Lt. Anderson J., 5th Florida, Co. I
Perkins, Lt. John Day, 2nd Florida, Co. M
Shine, Thomas W., 5th Florida, Co. K
Woods, Sgt. Francis Marion, 5th Florida, Co. G

GEORGIA

Davis, E. J., 3rd Georgia, Co. F
Ganey, Jacob, 3rd Georgia, Co. F
Griffith, John J., 50th Georgia, Co. I

Hunt, Wilkins W., 2nd Georgia Battalion, Co. B
Hutchins, Robert Maxwell, 53rd Georgia, Co. E
Jones, George H., 22nd Georgia, Co. B
Montgomery, D. C., 3rd Georgia, Co. H
Ross, Sgt. Maj. Wiliam J. F., 2nd Georgia Battalion, Co. C
*Schlandt, Lt. J. J., 21st Georgia, Co. B
Smith, John J., 22nd Georgia, Co. E
Toy, Chap. C. H., 53rd Georgia
Wimberly, Richard Columbus, 3rd Georgia, Co. B

LOUISIANA
Day, Edward M., Moody Battery
McGalliard, Lt. William M., 8th Louisiana, Co. E

MARYLAND
Goldsborough, Maj. William W., 1st Maryland, Field & Staff
Herbert, Lt. Col. James R., 1st Maryland
Hollyday, Lamar, 1st Maryland Battalion, Co. A
Laird, Sgt. Maj. James W., 1st Maryland, Co. H
Walsh, Dr. R. L. L., civilian doctor

MISSISSIPPI
Belton, Lt. William Henry, 11th Mississippi, Co. E
Dodds, William P., 17th Mississippi, Co. D
Dunlap, John R., Jeff Davis Legion, Co. C
Moore, Robert W., 17th Mississippi, Co. K
Owen, Chap. William Burton, 17th Mississippi, Field & Staff
Reddick, Robert H., 21st Mississippi, Co. F
Sharpe, W. G., 13th Mississippi, Co. C
Thompson, John M., 21st Mississippi, Co. F
Wells, John W., 17th Mississippi, Co. F

NEW YORK
Teale, George Massingburd, 83rd New York

NORTH CAROLINA
Crudup, Maj. Archibald D., 47th North Carolina, Field & Staff
Gales, T. L., 43rd North Carolina, Co. I
Graves, Capt. G. A., 22nd North Carolina, Co. I
Griffith, Josiah H., 43rd North Carolina, Co. B
Hancock, John, 2nd North Carolina Battalion, Co. B
Lewis, William A. G., 26th North Carolina, Co. F
Liles, Wesley, 7th North Carolina, Co. E

Loyd, Andrew J., 32nd North Carolina, Co. C
Mason, Israel H., 30th North Carolina, Co. F
Peeler, William D. C., 4th North Carolina, Co. K
Pittman, B. F., 2nd North Carolina, Co. B
Rankin, Lt. Col. Will S., 21st North Carolina
Rouse, T. B., 2nd North Carolina, Co. F
Seavers, Henry J., 4th North Carolina, Co. K
Sparrow, Thomas A., 55th North Carolina, Co. A
Walkins, David, 14th North Carolina, Co. E
Warren, Lt. John Crittenden, 52nd North Carolina, Co. C
Watson, J. W., 3rd North Carolina, Co. I

PENNSYLVANIA
Sturdevant, Asst. Surg. S. B., 139th Pennsylvania

SOUTH CAROLINA
Adkins, William, 1st South Carolina Cavalry, Co. H
Bouknight, S. J., 7th South Carolina, Co. M
Gaillard, Cpl. T. E., 2nd South Carolina, Co. I
Grant, Alexander D., 8th South Carolina, Co. C
Haltiwanger, J. L., 3rd South Carolina, Co. H
Haltiwanger, Sgt. J. S., 3rd South Carolina, Co. H
Hanson, Joseph, 7th South Carolina, Co. M
Hollingsworth, Robert L. T., 3rd South Carolina, Co. B
Marsh, James A., 2nd South Carolina, Co. A
Parker, Britton, 2nd South Carolina, Co. G
Ross, A. A., 1st South Carolina Cavalry, Co. H
Wilson, Sgt. Joseph D., 8th South Carolina, Co. F

TENNESSEE
Dowell, Jonathan S., 7th Tennessee, Co. A
Dunbar, Thomas G., 14th Tennessee, Co. B
Hamilton, John H., 7th Tennessee, Co. H
Lockert, Col. James W., 14th Tennessee
Sneed, Thomas, J., 7th Tennessee, Co. A

TEXAS
Bean, Lt. Ellwood M., 5th Texas, Co. G
Brown, J. H., 5th Texas, Co. F
Ford, J. F., 5th Texas, Co. K
Harper, Lt. R. Thomas, 5th Texas, Co. E
Watson, Samuel H., 5th Texas, Co. E

Allen, John A., 3rd Virginia, Co. K

Bartley, Lt. Nathan T., 7th Virginia, Co. C

Blanton, Capt. Zachariah Angel, 18th Virginia, Co. F

Brown, William Clay, 18th Virginia, Co. A

Bruchett, James M., 8th Virginia, Co. K

Burroughs, Christopher Frank, 2nd Virginia Cavalry, Co. D

Burroughs, James B., 2nd Virginia Cavalry, Co. K

Daniel, John H., 1st Virginia, Co. A

Elam, Sgt. William Robert, 18th Virginia, Co. H

Gaskins, Sgt. William H., 8th Virginia, Co. K

Gaulding, John R., 57th Virginia, Co. F

Gomer, Capt. Azra P., 3rd Virginia, Co. F

Houston, Capt. Andrew Matthew, 11th Virginia, Co. K

Houston, Lt. Thomas Dix, 11th Virginia, Co. K

Johnson, Capt. William T., 18th Virginia Co. H

Maloney, Clem H., 18th Virginia, Co. K

Martin, Lt. Col. Rawley White, 53rd Virginia

McCulloch, Capt. Robert, 18th Virginia, Co. B

Middleton, Jonathan W., 27th Virginia, Co. H

Parker, Cpl. Calvin Lee, 1st Virginia, Co. I

Reynolds, Samuel T., 14th Virginia, Co. E

Robinson, Lt. James H., 9th Virginia, Co. K

Thornton, Lt. Presley L. W., 21st Virginia, Co. H

Weymouth, Lt. J. E., 18th Virginia, Co. E

Whitesill, Sgt. John Wesley, 19th Virginia, Co. B

Worsham, Sgt. John B., 24th Virginia, Co. D

*Schlandt may be incorrect; no war records were found under this name.

Appendix 2

The McCrea, Branson Letters

It had been said that "the men, the soldiers, were the strong right arm, the mighty body of the Southern Confederacy, as with spirit undaunted they trod, with bleeding feet, the way of the Southern Cross. But as the men were the body, so were the women the soul....What was the depth of their dolor, none but the All-seeing Eye could discern. But those who were with them, who were bound to them by ties of blood or affection, know this, at least, that the Southern women never hesitated or faltered; that every rich sacrifice on the altar of country, but confirmed their resolution to surrender whatever else remained; that, in fine, they were joined to the Southern cause to love, to honor, to obey—for richer or for poorer, for better or for worse, and until death them should part!"[1]

The following letters were received by Captain Thomas Houston while imprisoned at Johnsons Island. They illustrate both the close bond that evolved between nurse and patient and the commitment of the women of Baltimore to the Confederate soldier. Houston had been one of the wounded in the College Hospital where Hettie McCrea and Maggie Branson nursed. The women were part of the group from Baltimore. He affectionately refers to them as honorary "cousins". The letters relate a service done for him and his family; the removal of the body of brother, David, from a grave on the field of Gettysburg to interment in the McCrea family plot in Greenmount Cemetery in Baltimore. The letters are part of the Houston papers housed at Leyburn Library at Washington and Lee University and appear here by their permission. The text is edited.

Baltimore, May 30, 1864

My Dear Cousin,
I now hasten to reply to your letter on the 11th instant. I did not wish to answer it until I could tell you something definite regarding your brother's grave. On Friday last I

*took your letter and started for Gettysburg determined to find
it if possible from your graphic description of position. We
very soon found the barn but it was not brick, a part of it
was stone, the rest board. Pickett's Headquarters was at a
farm house on the banks of Marsh Creek, at the foot of this
hill is Breans' [Bream's] Mill. Your brother died in Curren's
barn [almost across the way from Black Horse Tavern on
what is known today as the Fairfield Road] and is buried
upon the roadside. It is marvelous that the tiny board still
remains to mark the sacred spot. Upon it is cut quite deeply
"Captain D. G. Houston, aged 25 Co. D. 11th Va. Infantry."
This mound is upon a sandy hill and is no longer safe. I felt
I had no right to remove his remains until I had consulted
you. My desire is to remove him at once to our beautiful
cemetery "Greenmount." Would you prefer his remains being
put in a vault with the view of taking him in the future or
would you be willing to have him interred in our family lot.
I must urge this matter to be decided at once as it is getting
so warm. Oh! I could not bear to have him so far away.
Cousin Sallie [Houston, a real cousin] and I have just returned from our tour. I have much I should like to tell you
but am too sad. In treading on these grounds, visiting the
dear old college camp [College Hospital where Pheme also
nursed] I forgot I was a woman and wept as a child. I stood
with my hands on door latch of room "No 76" [room where
Thomas Houston and Robert McCulloch were kept-See Hospital Books] but dare not enter, so conscious was I that the
cold eye of the world was upon me. I send you a little sprig
which I plucked from the grave of a noble brother; when you
write me be sure to tell me his size and the color of his hair.
My sister unites with me in love to you. Let us hear from you
very soon....*

"Rettie" [Henrietta] McCrea

Miss McCrea is noted in connection with assisting Southern families to locate their dead after Gettysburg up into the 1870s. The
second letter, in which it is evident Thomas gave his permission for
exhumation is from Maggie Branson.

Miss Branson nursed at Gettysburg where she met the
wounded Lewis [Powell] Paine, one of those convicted in the Lincoln assassination plot. It was believed that she helped his escape from West's Buildings in Baltimore. At the time of the
assassination, Lewis Paine was staying at the Branson boarding

house, whose residents were arrested en masse. But that ordeal was almost a year away when she wrote to Thomas:

Baltimore, July 18, 1864

My Dear Cousin,

...Cousin Rettie called early this morning and after break- fasting with me, went to Greenmount "That lovely city of the dead." Mrs. Gibson, your cousin, Miss "S", and a little daugh- ter with Cousin Rettie and I were the small flock that sur- rounded the grave which was to rest your great beloved brother. Think not though his spirit had fled to its eternal home twelve months no tears were shed. Yes, many fell, both for the living and the dead and though it was the first sod broken in the lot, he will not sleep alone, tomorrow three of his comrades will lie by his side. It will ever be Rettie's and my sad, but pleasant task, to twine flowers and evergreens over and around the grave, of our cousin brother. It will not be a grave of a stranger, but ever fondly watched over and loved. I culled there little flowers from a vine overhanging the head of your brother; while stand- ing there, I could think of nothing save our glorious resurrec- tion, when all would be again reunited. I have not forgotten the conversation I had with a friend at the back of his tent, one lovely summer morning, in which he told me he was inclined to be skeptical. I hope he will not always think as he did then. You cannot imagine how much I would love to see you all....

Maggie Branson

Appendix 3

"Looking Back to the Days of 1863"

— THE BANISHMENT OF MISS EUPHEMIA GOLDSBOROUGH —

Those who lived in the stirring times of the Civil War find the circumstances of that direful period often crowding back without any effort of memory. They are written in letters of fire upon the pages of almost every family history and are feeling now, in tones that cannot be hushed, by change of time or state.

A poet sings "There are feelings that words cannot measure, there are tones that we cannot forget." Those tones are of voices silenced long ago by the enemy's shot and shell, but they call aloud at this time to the sons and daughters of the "lost Cause" to provide for their widows and war-worn comrades in arms. The cry will be heard and the faithful will take up the woven web and wind in and out golden threads of active patriotic effort and secure the success of the Confederate Relief Bazaar. The following story will be just one little thread in the warp of the great movement.

When the guns at Gettysburg had ceased to volley and thunder many of the ladies of Baltimore offered their services to nurse in the hospitals there. Among these ladies, Miss Euphemia Goldsborough, who was one of the most active spirits of the Southern Cause in Baltimore, hurried with Miss McCrea and Mrs. Dubois Eagerton and many others to the scene where they were assigned to duty as hospital nurses and to other departments of usefulness.

Miss Goldsborough was first put to work in the College Hospital. The North was a new field for active operations and the fight at Gettysburg found the people of the town unprepared for the emergency thrust upon them by the "Rebels." The College was the only suitable place they could make use of and was bare of all necessary comforts.

While the confusion was greatest and heros [sic] were lying without pillows on the bare floor of the ward legless and armless, waiting for their time to come for attention, Miss Goldsborough found it her privilege to support, in his last moments, the gallant Col. Patton, a Virginian, whose bravery has since been the theme of many tongues.

The surgeons in charge decided that it was imperative to place Col. Patton in practically a sitting posture to prevent suffocation. Being shot through the lungs, and unconscious, it was impossible to save his life unless he could be propped up, and there was absolutely nothing to be had to prop him with. Seeing the difficulty, Miss Goldsborough decided to offer herself as the necessary agent. Accordingly she seated herself on the bare floor, feet extended, the surgeons tenderly placed the dying officer against her back and secured him there. She sat there, still as a wooden image never daring to move lest the slightest motion should bring on a hemmorrage [sic] and death insue [sic].

I have heard her describe the numbness that stole over her as she sat the night through, holding up the fast dying officer. It was said by a veteran afterwards, that of all touching sights in his memory, the recollection of that picture would stand before him. "Midnight, a brave soldier, for whom the last taps were sounding, a young frail woman sitting by the light of a flickering candle supporting the dying hero of many hard fought battles, surrounded by the dead and dying and some grown old in wars."

All efforts to save Col. Patton were futile, he died soon afterwards and was brought to Baltimore I have heard and buried in Greenmount.

A few months from the time of the Gettysburg incident, Miss Goldsborough found herself in exile in the city of Richmond, where Col. Patton's family sought her out, having heard of her efforts to save his life, and insisted that she should make her home with them during the war. Though appreciated, this kind invitation was not accepted.

An amusing incident occured [sic] while in Camp [Letterman] Hospital. There were one hundred men assigned to Miss Goldsborough's ward, fifty federal and fifty confederate soldiers, some officers and some private soldiers. Among them was a great need of suitable clothing and, for some reason known only to men in authority, it was against the rules to provide them with new boots and clothes, but Miss Goldsborough was determined that one at least whose needs were especially great should not be sent to a northern or western prison destitute as he was. She feigned an excuse to go into town, secured a permit and started off in an army ambulance that was going there that morning. After securing the longed for treasures and what articles she could find, she happened upon a friendly spirit who I have forgotten now however. They tied the boots securely under the immense hoop-skirt Miss Goldsborough rejoiced in and all the other traps that could be fastened on and then started off bravely to camp. But on reaching the official place to meet the ambulance, to [her] dismay, there stood the dreaded Yankee officer instead of just a teamster. The officer officiously insisted upon assisting her to get in the ambulance her fears of detection were something appalling. She was sure the boots would bump against the side of the ambulance as soon as she attempted to get in it. However, she made a desperate effort and got in safely. Neither of the boots dropped down or bumped against each other. The camp was reached safely. The officious Yankee assisted her out and she reached her tent in safety. Then, when the opportunity presented itself, she smuggled the effects to the rejoiced "Reb" and went on her way tending the wounded and dying. Her entire time was passed, nursing day and night except such time as sleep was absolutely desired, for fully nine weeks.

She returned to us the most delapidated [sic] young girl that tongue or pen could describe. During the nine weeks of camp life and hard work at nursing she had worn out all supplies taken there and sent to her by her family and the traveling garments she wore up to Gettysburg, were things of the past. The hornets had built a nest in her bonnet and so it was necessary for her to return to Baltimore in her nurse's attire.

We did not know her at first. It was the 13th of September, 1863, a warm afternoon. Our mother was lying down taking an afternoon nap as usual, the writer sitting near her. Suddenly a vague consciousness of another presence was felt and looking up a figure standing in the doorway explained the sensation. At first we scarcely knew her, so worn and changed, so utterly exhausted with the sights of the battlefield and death bed scenes in the hospitals. The awful sights of those days, the anguish and suffering, witnessing the operations in the hospitals where legs and arms were sawed off like those of cats and dogs and where blood poured in streams from the operating tables, where she stood beside the poor boys in grey and heard their last messages and prayers. Little wonder to us of mature years that the life and youth in this frail woman's body was almost exhausted, for in truth she was never the same joyous girl again. Such things leave red letter marks that time never effaces.

We mingled our tears with hers as we listened to descriptions of the closing scenes of young lives sacrificed to duty and honor and country. Some were mere boys in years but brave and "counting it gain" to die in such a cause while far away from home and friends with only a stranger's hand to close eyes that would never again behold the dear home faces or respond to other eyes that would watch in vain for the soldier's return.

CHAPTER SECOND

On the 23rd of November following at midnight Col. Fish, who was then in charge of this department sent three officers and a number of guards to arrest Miss Goldsborough for treason. The soldiers surrounded the house, 49 Courtland Street, Corner of Mulberry, now a Priest's house but at that time a neighborhood well known and popular as a residence locality.

The Yankees filed into the house and took up formidable attitudes, while some stood guard outside. They had enuf [sic] powder and shot along to kill a company, but the idea in those days was to over-power whereever [sic] they could. This was not such an easy matter as they sometimes found out to their loss. Southern women are not cowards and some of the besieged families were [not] frightened, though of course excited, for the arrest was made at a serious time. There were hampers packed and waiting to be smuggled into Fort McHenry that very night, and it was almost impossible to get them unpacked and hustled out of sight without attracting the attention of the guards. The family was large however, seven daughters, all with their wits about them and a father and mother especially on the alert. The unpacking was accomplished while the searching party was upstairs looking all over the house, in bureau drawers, in old closets, wardrobes, and every empty and occupied room being looked over for evidence of treason; this little pleasantness, had been vouchsafed before, when the Yankees reported finding a wagon load of guns secreted. In reality, not a gun had been in our house for the past twenty years, at least.

A detective made the arrest first, and then after asking Miss Goldsborough if she had nursed at Gettysburg and she had told him "yes", he put his hand on her shoulder and said, "You are my prisoner, consider yourself under arrest." Then my Lord Cardinal called in his gallant officers and guards with their little swords and guns and all rushed upstairs and spread over the house like the darkness that spread over Egypt.

Before leaving the hall where all this took place one very knightly officer told the guard that if Miss Goldsborough attempted to move to shoot her down. She quietly remarked "I'm not coward enough to run." After an hour spent in ramsacking [sic] desks for papers, they departed, actually telling us they were tired and sleepy; but only the officers left, and the guards locked up the prisoner in a cold room, and took position on the outside of the door. They had strict orders not to allow any members of her family to speak to her, but they did. Each one as he went on duty said if we would not tell the next guard he would let us see and speak to our sister and one kind hearted soldier, when he found she was in a room with no fire, and the weather bitterly cold, even went so far as to assist us in getting a stove into the room, and each guard kept up the fire as he came on duty during the time she was locked in that particular room. We can say now, after the lapse of so many years, as we said then, that the private soldiers were very kind and full of sympathy; it was the higher class of officers who acted in the South like beasts. At least in our experience it was always so.

The news of the arrest spread on the wings of the wind. Friends and strangers in sympathy with the South full of interest and genuine feeling. There were no idle curiosity seekers abroad in these war times. About eleven o'clock the following morning a detective came to escort Miss Goldsborough before the great Col. Fish of pestilential memory. She said unless he brought a carriage he would have to see Col. Fish alone as she had no intention of walking through the public streets with him to Col. Fish's office. He insisted and she steadfastly refused so he had to go and bring a carriage though as a matter of course he could have forced her to go on foot.

Our father was greatly grieved but he accompanied his daughter to the Provost Office and there heard them pronounce the sentence of banishment for the war. She was given permission to carry two trunks and just exactly $225 in federal money, not another cent and was told if she tried to come back before the close of the war she would be tried for her life and shot as a spy. But in the face of this, when the war suddenly closed, she was arranging to run the blockade to visit us, and she would have come too and we would have hidden her away as we did Maryland boys who came and stayed with us in the face of all danger. Rebel boys home to see family and sweethearts found plenty of their rebel friends here ready to hide them away for weeks at a time and take chances of discovery and all the punishment the government saw fit to deal out to us. There are some living today who can recall just such cases as I describe. If the old Courtland house could speak it could tell some curious tales of refugees from Fort Delaware and Camp Chase; of the Baltimore boys who wore the grey and slipped home sometimes the underground route, as blockade running was called; of piles and piles of clothes stacked up to be sent down South as soon as the opportunity presented itself; of hundreds and hundreds of letters destined to be sent to the Army by the Confederate blockade runners, but in one instance a few were destroyed and that was after the war was over. Our little "Reb" did not come for them in time and so, we had to destroy them. Among the articles sent our house to be forwarded

South were some boxes marked quinine. They were received under the assurance that it was to go South to be used for the soldiers in Richmond hospitals. After the surrender, the Confederate mail, which was buried in our cellar together with these boxes, was dug up; the letters burned, but the boxes were opened to find a clue, perhaps, to the owner so as to notify him to get them. Imagine the astonishment of everyone when instead of quinine there lay snugly packed in rows hundreds of false teeth. Afterwards it was discovered that the man who brought them to us, to risk our liberty in sending, was sending his partner in Richmond these false teeth to make money and not as he said to relieve the sick in the hospitals. He must have been born North of the Mason and Dixon line!

But to return to Miss Goldsborough's banishment. It would take volumes to retell her experience and a gifted pen. She was sent South after about five days, under escort. She left the house about three o'clock in the afternoon. The streets, doorsteps, windows and every available spot was packed with an eager sympathetic crowd to see her leave under such painful circumstances. Not a sound disturbed the peace! All seemed to feel it a funeral instead of a military banishment. She faced the crowd bravely but fell forward like a dead woman as soon as she was seated in the carriage. She was determined to show no signs of fear or distress before any possible enemy in that dense crowd, so she threw off our father's assisting arm and with erect head passed down the steps to the carriage alone, followed by the gentlemen and friends of our family, and the high official who was there to see his orders carried out.

She arrived in Richmond after various experiences, some sad, some annoying, some amusing and others that made her southern blood jump. One of the amusing instances was at Fortress Monroe. The Truce boat was expected to meet the Exchange boat that carried the prisoners and exiles. While waiting off at some point on the route a French Frigate of War was recognized lying near them. Soon a boat was launched and manned. An officer descended and took his seat then and the seaman rowed rapidly to the Exchange boat, pulled up and the officer came on deck. Bowing and smiling he said he called to pay his respects to the Miss Confederate whom he was told was on board. He was dressed in full uniform, low cut shoes and silk stockings, evidently arrayed to make a call of ceremony. Miss Goldsborough was presented, the officer paid her all the compliments his limited command of language allowed, placed his hand over his heart, bowed and returned to his ship. Other interesting events transpired but as it is not my intention to fill all the journal, I must pass on to the end. Upon arriving in Richmond, Miss Goldsborough was welcomed right royally, feasted - not as they could have done before the war - but generously and proudly. Many doors were opened to her and many hearts.

Mr. [President Jefferson] Davis instructed [Commissary] General [Lucius Bellinger] Northrope [sic] to offer Miss Goldsborough a position in the Treasury Department, which was filled to overflowing. When informed there was no vacant position for Miss Goldsborough he said, "Well, then make one!" The Maryland Line sent a formal invitation to Richmond for her to dine with them in camp and from far and near came letters from the wives and mothers of officers and men who had been nursed at Gettysburg. On one occasion when the Maryland troops were in Richmond and were passing through the streets, Miss Goldsborough was recognized in the crowds of Department Ladies, who were eagerly watching the troops. Word passed along the line; every man lifted his cap and cheered.

When the war closed she came back to Baltimore, married a Marylander of Frederick County, Mr. Charles Perry Willson, an ex-confederate soldier. They removed to Summit Point, Jefferson County, West Virginia, where their hospitality was soon acknowledged and will be long remembered. Twenty years ago it was a real privilege to meet there in winter and all gather round the blazing fire, when host and hostess and many guests would recall their war experiences. Sometimes the guests would be snowed in and we would have a house party for days of the bachelor veterans of the war and there we would sit for hour after hour in the old southern home, the soldiers with their favorite dogs that followed them everywhere, stretched at full length before the huge fire of logs that burned away only to be replaced while first one battle scene and then another was repeated by some who were in the fight. This would go on for days and never get tiresome. Finally Mrs. Willson devoted the same energy to church work that she had given to the Confederate cause and the beautiful stone church standing now at Summit Point is largely due to her efforts.

In 1896 this earnest, active, self-sacrificing Southern lady with the spirit of Joan of Arc quietly joined the great army of martyrs and laid down the cross in the shadow of the Rock and was laid to rest in Virginia, the State she dearly loved, near the little town of Berryville in Clark[e] County, beside her husband and children.

Mrs. R. P. McCormick
[Mona Goldsborough]

Appendix 4

Highlights from Lt. Colonel Fish's Court-martial

Lieutenant Colonel William S. Fish, 1st Connecticut Cavalry, took position in July 1862 as Provost Marshal in Baltimore. He was cashiered from service 4/21/64. These edited court-martial proceedings are from RG MM1356.

Charge I: "Conduct prejudicial to good order and military discipline." All specifications occurred in Baltimore except 12th, 13th, 14th, 15th

specification 1st: (December 13, 1862) put in a claim which was paid for a horse he said was his that was actually a captured animal and property of the U.S. and was paid $175.13

specification 2nd: (February 1863) converted to his own use a diamond breastpin of the value of $250 seized from blockade-runners that was then property of U.S.

specification 3rd: (February 12, 1863) converted to his own use a quantity of dry goods and hosiery valued at $411 seized by military authorities at Harpers Ferry.

specification 4th: (April 1863) seized and converted to his own use trunks containing ladies wearing apparel belonging to Mrs. Otley and Miss Seldon valued at $500.

specification 5th: (May 6, 1863) obtained possession of Confederate Cotton Bonds valued at $12,500, delivered them to his clerk and detective, Andrew Thompson, and ordered Thompson to proceed to Europe to sell the bonds, furnishing $300 from U.S. funds to finance the trip.

specification 6th: (April 10, 1863) "embezzled and wrongfully misapplied" Southern bank notes valued at $998, delivered them to Henry Wilson with orders to sell them in New Orleans and paid Wilson $213.05 from the proceeds.

specification 7th: (February 25, 1863) released two prisoners, Gogenheimer and Hentzler, and restored their money to them, upon the solicitation of B. F. Ulman after receiving from Ulman a diamond breastpin valued at $125.

specification 8th: (April 1863) possessed and then restored a large sum of money, including $3,700 in gold belonging to one L. Mann, at the solicitation of B. F. Ulman, receiving a consideration of $200.

specification 9th: (May 1863) possessed and then restored a large sum of money belonging to two prisoners, named Irene and Lipzen, upon the solicitation of B. F. Ulman, receiving a consideration of $200.

specification 10th: (continual practice February, March, April, May, June, July, August, September, and October, 1863) possessed a large number of prisoners and large sums of money, permitted B. F. Ulman, a pawn broker and liquor dealer, access to prisoners, refusing audience to responsible counsel, refusing to release prisoners or return their money until they paid Ulman large fees for his services in their behalf, and received consideration from Ulman in presents of money, jewelry, wines, liquors, and cigars.

specification 11th: (May 1863) accepted and retained a bribe of $480 through Samuel White, to allow one Hutzler and others to go South through military lines, arrested the people who paid the bribe, discharged them, and sent them North.

specification 12th: (June 15, 1863) procured arrest of one Louis Cohen in New York city by a lieutenant and three detectives under his command, discharged Cohen after he paid a bribe of $600 which was divided between Fish and the three detectives, and when threatened with exposure by one Emanual Pike delivered to Pike a gold watch and chain and notes valued at $600, and continued to keep the three detectives in his employ.

specification 13th: (April 14, 1863) in violation of his duty, sent South beyond the military lines of the United States at Baltimore, Harpers Ferry and Winchester the following prisoners: Henry Guntz, H. Frank, Sarah Davis, Louis Morse, and Tobias Diddenhofer.

specification 14th: (April 15, 1863) sent South beyond the military lines of the United States through Harpers Ferry and Winchester, a prisoner one Lewis Moss, at the request of Ulman for the fee of $25.

specification 15th: (April 17, 1863) sent South beyond the military lines of the United States through Harpers Ferry, Winchester, and Newton, Virginia, four men, Bernard Rees, Simon Rosenfels, Herman Husch, and Hicks, at the request of Ulman, for the fee of $100.

specification 16th: (April 1863) possessed a sorrel horse, property of the United States, caused the government brand to be removed, convert the horse to his own use, and sell and deliver the horse to Lt. S. W. Hawley of the 1st Connecticut Cavalry for $100.

specification 17th: (March 1, 1863) "embezzled and wrongfully misappropriated" a silver watch valued at $12, the property of the United States, and gave it to Pvt. Richard Hills of the 1st Connecticut Cavalry.

Charge II: "Using false accounts and vouchers, knowing the same to contain false statements, for the purpose of obtaining the approval of false and fraudulent claims against the United States, contrary to the statute in such case made and provided."

specification 1st: (May 6, 1863) presented to his commanding officer, Major General Schneck, an account against funds intrusted to him for the use of secret service, in the amount of $300 to be used by his detective, Andrew Thompson, to travel to Europe to dispose of the Confederate Cotton Bonds [noted in Charge I, specification 5th], with knowledge that Thompson only went as far as New York and had not expended a sum exceeding $20.

specification 2nd: (October 1, 1863) presented to his commanding officer, Major General Schneck, an account for $96.94 as an additional expense for Thompson to go to Europe, but was used for Thompson to travel from New York to Canada to escape arrest and punishment for an attempt to travel from New York by steamer to Europe to sell "treasonable papers".

specification 3rd: (October 1, 1863) presented an account to his commanding officer, Major General Schenck, which contained the entry of $998 [noted in Charge I, specification 6th] charged as "counterfeit and broken bank bills", but sold and retained by Fish.

Charge III: "Violation of the thirty-ninth Article of War

specification 1st: (February 23, 1863) "did embezzle and wrongfully convert to his own use" $452.60 taken from deserters

Charge IV: "Conduct unbecoming an officer and a gentleman."

specification 1st: (January, February, March, and April 1863) "visited a public house of prostitution kept by one Emma Morton habitually as often as three times a week, wearing his uniform as an officer of the army, and there conspicuously dancing in his uniform and associating with prostitutes.

specification 2nd: (March 22, 1863) "attended a ball at a public house of prostitution kept by one Annette Travers, wearing his uniform as an officer of the army."

specification 3rd: (January, February, March, April, May, June, July, August, September, October, November, and December 1863) "habitually frequented a public house of prostitution kept by one Annette

Travers, wearing his uniform as an officer of the army, and conspicuously associating with prostitutes."

specification 4th: (February 22, 1863) "attended a ball at a public house of prostitution kept by one Nancy Thomas, wearing his uniform as an officer of the army."

specification 5th: (February 1863) ordered his assistant under his command whose duty was to "enter with his patrol all houses of prostitution for the purpose of arresting officers and all soldiers found there without passes, not to enter the house of Annette Travers, a public house of prostitution which said Fish was in the habit of frequenting."

꙳   ꙳   ꙳

Lt. Col. William Fish, age 30, was arrested and sent to Washington, D.C. on January 25, 1864. He pleaded not guilty to the above charges. He spent time in Carroll Prison and Old Capitol prison, places that many Southern political prisoners were kept. On April 19, 1864 the military court sentenced him "To be cashiered, to forfeit to the United States all pay and allowances due and to become due to him from the United States and to pay the United States a fine of five thousand dollars, and to be imprisoned in the Penitentiary at Albany, New York, or in such other place as the Secretary of War shall direct, until such fine shall be paid, provided that such imprisonment shall not be less than one year."

The sentence was approved by President Lincoln on April 21, 1864.

This welcome event was noted in the Baltimore *Sun* on April 25, 1864: "Col. Fish Sentenced to Penitentiary—Col. Fish of the First Connecticut Cavalry, (formerly provost marshal of this city, under General Schenck), who has been undergoing a court martial trial in Washington for misdemeanor in office has been sentenced by the court to one year's imprisonment in the Albany penitentiary. The finding of the court has been submitted to the President for approval."

Appendix 5

Obituary of Mrs. Euphemia Goldsborough Willson

Written by her sister Mrs. Mona Goldsborough McCormick
Date written on manuscript: March 10, 1896

The recent death in Baltimore, Md. of Mrs. Euphemia Goldsborough Willson, daughter of the late Martin Goldsborough, formerly of Talbot County, closed another historical page in the annals of Maryland's brave, patriotic women.

Mrs. Willson was one of the central and most active figures in the late war, so far as Maryland was interested. She devoted her youth to the Southern Cause, was almost unequaled in her successful efforts in sending supplies, and sometimes arms, to the officers and men of the Maryland line.

Into every Federal prison in the United States where Confederate soldiers were confined went articles of comfort, both of food and raiment, to the suffering prisoners, while she worked day and night to procure funds to further that purpose.

After the Battle of Antietam, Miss Goldsborough went at once to Frederick City where the wounded had been conveyed and gave the Confederate soldiers assigned to her ward unremitting care.

Immediately after the Battle of Gettysburg she offered her services as a hospital, or field, nurse and with other Baltimore ladies was assigned to duty in the College Hospital at first and the Camp [Letterman] Hospital later on, having fifty Federal soldiers and fifty Confederates in her ward. The U.S. soldiers were placed there to insure her discharge of duty without treason to the government.

Miss Goldsborough recognized the importance of showing no partiality, and many of both armies owed their lives to her good nursing, common sense and justice, while she gladly forgot party spirit for the time and saw the necessity of sacrificing self to the good of the Southern wounded, and discharged her obligations to the many in order to secure the care of wounded, dying soldiers of the Confederate Army. She remained there nine weeks, working incessantly, forgetting the world and self, living only to comfort and support the suffering and dying. Finally exhausted nature demanded rest and she returned to Baltimore.

But only to be arrested on the night of Nov. 23rd, 1863 and banished from the United States on charge of treason. There are many still living who will remember the occasion of her banishment. The excitement, the popular indignation, the crowded streets, the packed sidewalks before her home, the burst of indignation from the crowd when Miss Goldsborough, accompanied by her father and under military guard, left her home to be driven to the Norfolk Boat enroute to Fortress Monroe.

An examination was held in military quarters by General Ben Butler and Miss Goldsborough banished for the war with the severe penalty of being shot should she venture inside the Federal lines before the close of hostilities.

No sympathy was shown this heroic Southern girl by Gen. Butler. No regard for her tender age or youth, but he sternly demanded to know what she had been sent to him for. Her reply was "For feeding the hungry and clothing the naked." She refused to reply to another question or a shaft of bitterness, but calmly awaited his decision. Though subjected to the most rigorous search personally, and her trunks upset in [sic] the floor and examined, she nevertheless carried through to Richmond certain dispatches and delivered them safely at headquarters. This, in the face of a Northern prison - even death itself - she ventured and accomplished.

Belonging to an old colonial family, she was widely known and friends and some relatives used every effort to secure official influence, and succeeded in getting her removed for a time from the damp cold cellar where General Butler had her confined while awaiting the flag of truce boat to convey her to City Point.

On arrival in Richmond President Davis appointed her to a position which she successfully filled until the surrender. The Southern people welcomed her royally to the Confederacy and to their homes, whose doors were wide open to her, and many life-long friendships were formed.

On one occasion, when the Maryland troops were passing the War Department, she was recognized by someone. The word passed rapidly along the line and Maryland's bravest sons paid tribute to her, exiled daughter, and while cheering, the entire regiment passed her with hats off—a compliment to her personally.

Acknowledged as a genius with pronounced intellect, she was urged to write reminiscences of the war for Southern History—but falling into ill health she never complied with the wishes of her many friends.

And so a varied life has closed and shut up the treasure house of a brilliant memory. Like many for whom she risked her life and liberty, she has passed - fully prepared tho' untrumpeted [sic] to a glorious reward. Thus with tears for her loss, regret for her sorrows, we lay with reverence the laurel wreath upon her grave.

Appendix 6

The following are transcripts of letters found in the Rawley White Martin file in the Manuscripts Division of the library at Duke University, published with their permission.

Baltimore, Sep 24th

Lient. Col. Martin
Dear Friend,
 Yesterday morning I was the fortunate & happy recipient of your nice long letter, need I tell you I was glad to hear from you? But <u>that</u> you mustnt [sic] doubt, for had I not desired the correspondence, I should not have written the first letter. I am glad to hear you are improving & trust you may soon be well enough for exchange, which happiness I feel soon [sic] will <u>now soon</u> be yours since the great & glorious victory in the Southwest - God <u>Bless</u> our poor people. <u>I love them all</u> & <u>their</u> sufferings are <u>mine</u>. I am <u>so sick</u> this morning can <u>scarcely work at all</u>, therefore my friend Col. M must excuse a short incoherent & <u>faulty</u> note, but I will promise to answer his "Sweet Letter" better the next opportunity. My love to Liet. Perkins,[1] and all friends in your tent. Write me a mile long letter by Miss Saunders[2] and believe me the same faithful friend.

Pheme

PS If you care to have a card of my plain face & self, I am perfectly willing, when they come from under the hands of the artist. Goodbye.

❦ ❦ ❦

Baltimore Oct. 21st

Col. Martin - My Dear Friend,
 Your letter which had been most anxiously looked for, coming the post three days, has reached me safely. An assurance of how welcome it was & how <u>happy</u> I was to be the fortunate recipient of same, would I trust be <u>useless</u>. And then it was such <u>a nice, long, kind</u> & may I add <u>dear letter</u> that it could not

fail to bring happiness folded within its seams. It becomes either a singular coincident [sic] that Col. M & his friend should have [been] <u>alike employed</u>. Sunday afternoon as <u>my</u> last letter was written at that time, therefore, I have no ground <u>whatever</u> to reproach his "Lordship" with breaking <u>one</u> of the <u>ten</u>. Those I like <u>most</u> I most frequently write on Sundays. <u>There is no sin</u> that I can see and if there is I hope there is also <u>forgiveness</u> for the same. Before going further, there is one thing I'm going to tell you of. One part of your letter I feel to be a <u>rebuke</u> for my <u>enthusiasm</u>. <u>Why ridicule</u> my unfortunate ignorance by asking me to suggest a spring campaign for <u>one</u> with intellect <u>little short of a God's!</u>; I would not <u>dare</u> venture soon one opinion, in the presence of one so profoundly learned as Gen Lee. Col that was not kind of you. Ah! well <u>probably</u> it was a just & (illegible) rebuke. I know I'm <u>sinfully</u> bitter & vindictive on the <u>Yankee question</u>, but I cannot help it, <u>indeed I do not try to</u>, for I glory in the strength God has given me to hate them with. We are of <u>Indian descent</u> seven generations removed but <u>their "iron will"</u> has been faithfully handed down to <u>me</u> to which <u>every</u> pulsing of <u>my heart</u> bends in <u>submition</u> [sic]. Do you know I never understood <u>anything</u> in <u>my life</u> without going through with it however that is probably because I never grasp at <u>impossibilities</u>. To have faith & <u>believe one can</u> is I think equivalent to the success of her desire. Matters not how softly they are. You say "Never say Gettysburg to me." Why should I not? There is no <u>eulogism too great</u> in my opinion, to be given the brave & chivalrous and may I not justly add, <u>invincible</u> people who fought that great battle. I have never been fortunate enough to read Gen Lee's report but that was <u>not</u> necessary to prove the <u>will</u> & <u>determination</u> with which the gallant "children of the Sun" pressed the enemies [sic] line, had there been a <u>doubt</u> on the subject, the hundreds & thousands of suffering & dying, it was <u>my error</u> & <u>misinformation</u> to see, would have set the matter <u>far beyond conjecture</u>. I have seen you twice since it was my privilege [sic] to hold communication with you through the medium of the pens and each time it has seemed to me <u>more forcibly</u>, how <u>inhuman</u> to forget those who would give <u>anything</u> with the <u>love of reason</u>, to exchange the cordial greeting dictated by friendship & for aught. <u>I knew</u> our (illegible) sister may have an offering of leave to add to the beautiful <u>gem</u> which your humble is ever ready to give to all who fear themselves <u>worthy</u>. While I think of it let me tell you when next I pay you a visit, (either reasoning the order of things, don't you think so, *for ladies to visit gentlemen) don't you look at me, as you did this afternoon. upon my word I was as near as should be, laughing on tight, and just expected one of those hateful Yankees to take hold of me every moment. now do you not honestly think it the most foolish thing you have ever known them guilty of, not to allow prisoners the privilege [sic] of speaking to their friends. I am sure there are no such restriction in R. if there chances to be one friendly heart to Yankeedom in our "Rebel Capitol" [sic]. Our people are above such petty meanness [sic] Well my dear friend this is the fourth letter I have written since I came to my room tonight. and tonight it could not under any circumstances fail to be a pleasure to write to Col. M. Still I feel sure he will pardon me for being tired & sleepy too and moreover everything is so deadly quiet & still. the very scratching of my pen makes me nervous. So with the promise to fill this out to a good length tomorrow morning and with wishing him pleasant dreams of Mrs M to be will most reluctantly say "Good Night." Was not the heart of my friend never glad by once more seeing the sweet face of his sister of yesterday afternoon (dangerous things to control sometimes) I met her on Baltimore Street, & told her you were out & I felt (illegible) expected her down & so with frequent requests to go back with her which I could not do. She stated you must not think of her as gloomy, and disappointed at not getting home. She is much of a philosopher & takes things as she (illegible) without mourning of what which cannot be helped. indeed I do not think I should be far from right if I was to tell you that not being able to gain admittance into West's Buildings is at this particular time giving her more sorrow than not getting home. can you account for this? It would be no vanity on Col. M's part if he was to say & think it was because he was there. I hope your names have been taken down to be sent off. is it true? I took you down a basket of fruit & a package of needle cases yesterday for Lts. M & P, Maj C[3] & yourself. Miss Moffit said she had sent Lieutenant Warren[4] one. Mary Told her you had received one also if so I guess you will be able to find some one [sic] who needs it. When you write again tell me which of my sisters you thought like me? Was it the one with me as we passed up the street yesterday? or the smaller (short girl) one? When they came home the evening you spoke of both said they knew Col M from what I had told them & was sure he & others should have had a boquet [sic] long ago. by the way I must tell of what a coward I was yesterday. My fall bonnet had just*

gotten home with "red, white & red" flowers on the inside. Af-
ter I was nearly down to your Hotel, it occurred to me, with
such treasonable colors[5] I might not be safe so I went in a store
& took out [th]is ill fated "white [illegible]" Now would still
wish to have my spirit—in many.....[rest of letter missing]

❦ ❦ ❦

The following is a transcript included in Martin's files. The original is missing. As Pheme's penmanship was very difficult to read,
there are, I believe, a number of errors in transcription. I bracketed
what I felt was the correct word.

Baltimore November 1
Col. Martin Dear Friend:

An opportunity occurs, by which I can send you a letter, free
from inspection and I gladly avail myself of the same. Trust-
ing I may receive a reply though the same channel—she is faith-
ful—regardless of the shade. On Thursday last I wrote to you
but do not know that it reached you. At any rate I hope and
believe a second letter may not be distasteful to you—from my
humble self—from past assurances of friendship of "Col. Mar-
tin". I am willing to incur the risk—although the only charms
about my letter, will be the evidence of "memory" which will
ever be a most willing offering or tribute to the shrine of worth—
do not condemn me as a flatterer—I speak truly—when I tell
you my respect for many I met while at Camp S.E. [Letterman],
no limit. Nor do I think they could be capable of an act, that
would forfeit their claim to that respect—but enough. I know
you will be both glad and sorry to hear "our Tisha" left for her
home on Thursday last. Proximity to a loved one can but af-
ford us happiness and distance regret—but when we know the
latter will benefit the object of our affections we can not mur-
mur at such an occurrence—I know very well—there will be a
pang in Col. M's heart when he hears she who made prison life
endurable with her sympathy has indeed gone so far away—
but remember "although she cannot come to you, you may soon
go to her" and I'm sure this thought will modify the regret. On
Sunday evening last "Miss Sinclair" Mary's Aunt came around
to see me and said that morning she had received a letter for
"our Tisha" in your handwriting, which she had opened and
found there were several little things you needed. Cannot I fill
Sister Mamie's place in just this one respect? I send you what

Miss S. said you wanted—which please accept without think [thinking] me officious. I am sure you would not—do so—if you could but understand, what a pleasure it is to do anything in my power for those I love to call my friends. I often think and fear my enthusiasm be, by some misunderstood—but surely not by yourself, I believe you understand me, and know I have the misfortune to be a visionary body—and have sometimes fallen from a dizzy height—to find unworthiness (but not in my Rebel friends) I am free to admit, but this has not often occurred. I am generally alive to circumstances as they occur—I have my share of penetration[6] for which I am very thankful— Miss S. also told me you had been sick—nothing very serious. I hope and trust you have found Fort McHenry a good place for a sick man. I cannot conclude my letter without scolding you just a little but you are not to have written me a line in all the 10 long days, since last I had the pleasure of hearing from you— but I suppose you have some reason for not writing—do you see any probable chance of exchange? Some days ago, we heard all were about to be sent to Lok Point [Point Lookout prison camp][7]—but the hope has proved as delusive as "Will O the Wisp"—by the way I heard something of you day before yesterday that surprised me very much, though I do not know why I should have been—I heard "Col. Martin" was to be married as soon as he arrived at home, do you know if the report is true? I cannot believe it—for I think him in love with his "Angel Manse and darling sister" and we do know, two objects can not occupy the same place at the same time—I have not yet received your "Vignette", I am beginning to fear, I shall not receive it atall [sic]—I wish I knew of something that would interest you, but all life and gaiety for which our home was noted has taken the "Wings of the morning", and left us gloomy indeed. I can scarcely realize I am the same as before this unholy crusade against liberty—justice and constitutional rights—do you know I thank those who participate in this great struggle for independence and we who mourn the causalities therein are alike made prematurely old. I expect you will laugh when I tell you, since my return from Gettysburg I feel as if I was just 100 years old. to you who are accustomed to sights and sounds of suffering — does not seem half so horrible I suppose (you know my opinion of Dr's.) but I cannot bring myself to think with, or feel any kind of compassion when I remember how death, and desolation, are being sown broadcast over our suffering, bleeding country, since my return home I often find myself wondering if it *can be more than a fearful dream—Earth is as fair, the sun shines brightly now as ever leaving no evidence but hundreds and thousands of clay-colored wounds, to remind us of the deadly struggle, that was almost at our doors—but still the heart is <u>sad</u> and memory will go wandering back to these red wounds offering to each [three blanks noted here] of sorrow and regret, but unless I change the subject, you will soon be as gloomy as myself—which I do not wish to be the cause of, captivity is quite enough for you to endure—Col. I wish you would let me know by the returning bearer of this letter if I shall, or can send you the package in, to the son of "Col. Porter"[8] with any kind of surety it will reach you or if I should send it under-ground, the last of the week—please remember me most kindly to Maj. [blank] Capt. Houston—and Lts. Warren and Bean, Lee's [Dr's]— Parker, Minor — Richardson, Southall and Hays[9]—is there a Dr. Southall from "Norfolk" at the Fort—if so my respects to him also—I met him at the College Hospital, and with his address he gave me a dear little rebel flag—which I hold sacred to his memory. Did Lt. Warren receive a note of thanks from me, for his "carte do Visti" [carte de visite]. Hoping you are all comfortable and to hear from you very soon—believe me always you very true friend; with most solicitude for returning health and speedy exchange....*

[no signature transcription]

Appendix 7

The following narrative is included as almost all the men in it were Pheme's friends and mentioned in her diary.

Reminiscence of Reconstruction
by Capt. Robert M'Colloch, St. Louis

It was never too hot, too cold, too wet, too dry, or any other adverse condition to hinder the assemblage on fifty-two Sundays of the year at "Falling Springs" Church of those who loved to listen to dear Mr. Junkin as, with eloquence and kindly persuasion, he taught the right.

"Falling Spring" was the church founded by the Scotch Presbyterians, who were the pioneers on the Southern border of Rockbridge County, in old Virginia. A large part of Mr. Junkin's flock came from the beautiful valley that skirted the James and North Rivers, hemmed in by splendid mountains on either side. The roads to this valley to the church wound across the mountain, one side being high ground and the other, in many instances, an abrupt precipice. One Sunday in the early summer of 1865, just at the close of the war, the carriage of Dr. Watson, occupied by Mrs. Watson and two of her daughters and driven by a negro boy, was returning homeward from Falling Spring; at a narrow point in the mountain road the carriage of a neighbor, also driven by a negro, was hurried past the Watson carriage in such a manner as to force it to the extreme side of the roadway, greatly endangering the lives of its helpless occupants. Mrs. Watson and her daughters reached free from physical injury, but their nervous condition made the attempted concealment of the occurrence from the Doctor impossible. Dr. Watson was kind-hearted, generous, greatly beloved by all who knew him, and devoted to his family. His indignation toward the driver of the other carriage was very great, but he was prevented by the importunities of his family from going in search of the miscreant who had imperiled their lives. However, the next day, while traveling in the discharge of his professional duties, he was passing a field in which the negro who had driven the neighbor's carriage was plowing, and, hitching his horse to the fence, he went over to the plowman and reproached him for his reckless driving the previous day. A quarrel ensued, hot words and perhaps blows; the negro ran and the Doctor fired in his direction to stop him, wounding him in the leg. The Doctor took him home, dressed the wound, and, leaving him in the care of Dr. McChesney, went to a magistrate, stated what had occurred, surrendered himself as a prisoner, and was released under bond and abundant security. Having a pistol was no evidence of wrong intentions, as we were then citizens of District No. I. Gen. Schofield was military governor, and the custom of going armed had not been discounted. It must also be said to the credit of the negroes that they were well-behaved up to that time, their newly acquired freedom having not changed their respectful manner toward their former owners.

The shooting was unpremeditated, unforeseen, and unfortunate. In spite of skillful treatment, the negro died. Dr. Watson was tried and acquitted. Maj. Carse, who was provost marshal at Lexington, the county seat, took great interest in the trial, and he and the Doctor became friends. When the Doctor was released, he bade Maj. Carse good-by and extended him a cordial invitation to make his house a stopping place should either business or pleasure bring the Major down the beautiful valley on the James.

It was a beautiful September day when a number of us had assembled in the Highbridge churchyard to pay the last sad tribute of love and respect to one of our dead comrades, Harry Arnold. The funeral ceremonies over, we mounted our horses and turned homeward, one and another dropping out of the procession as his home was reached. There were five of us still left, one of whom was Dr. Watson, and we were nearing the point where he would leave us for his home, when we observed a solitary horseman approaching us. When he came within greeting distance we recognized him as Major Carse, the provost marshal, with headquarters at Lexington. There was a pleasant exchange of courtesies, and the Major reminded Dr. Watson of his previously proffered hospitality, and expressed a desire to enjoy it if the option on its acceptance remained open. The Doctor was very hearty in renewing his offer of a night's shelter, and in a few minutes more a cheery good night rang out as the Doctor and the Major turned away to the north and we continued east.

We separated as each reached his home. Supper was soon over and sound sleep came without wooing. A pebble came against my window, and in an instant I was inquiring of Charles, a faithful old servant who stood just under me, as to what was wrong. He replied: "The Yankees have just gone down the towpath with Dr. Watson. They are taking him to Richmond to hang him." There was just one thought with me, and that was that "we must reach him." Charles was told to saddle my horse quickly. I dressed in haste, and, directing Charles to do down to Dave Mohler, who lived half a mile away, and tell him to mount his best horse and with his pistols to go to the "Point" and wait for me, I rode hurriedly in the other directions for more help.

A mile up the river and across it were the two Paxton families and the Obenchains, and I knew there was one boy in each household who would go with me on any mission. The boat was on their side. Fortunately I made them hear me, they ferried me over, the story was told them, and we soon recrossed the river. A ride of two miles brought us to the "Point", where Dave Mohler was awaiting us. It was already midnight, and we had no time to hunt for others; so our little band consisted of Joe Paxton, Mac Paxton, Dave Mohler, Frank Obenchain, and myself. We were well-mounted and well-armed.

The party having Dr. Watson prisoner was variously estimated by those who had seen them at from twenty to forty, armed and mounted men, none of whom were in uniform. It was thirty-five miles to Lynchburg, and they had three hours the start of us; but we had planned that by hard riding we could overtake them while it was yet dark; and, by the surprise and fierceness of attack, and our thorough knowledge of the country, we could rescue the Doctor and get away into the hills before they realized the smallness of our numbers. They would not venture to follow us where could so readily lose them. Our good horses bore us swiftly down the towpath, the towering mountains on our left and the roar of the beautiful river as it dashed through the long falls on the right.

Five miles down was the rope ferry, where we must cross the river. Very soon we had covered the distance, and the Ridgeway house at the ferry loomed before us; but it was lighted, and we saw that there were men apparently on duty. We halted and held a council of war, our surmise being that we had overtaken our party, that, the river being very much swollen, the Ridgeway boys had refused to ferry over so large a party in the darkness of the night, and they were waiting for the morning. It was arranged that I should go down to the house, find Dr. Watson, tell him that I had a rescuing party, and bring him away with me, without a fight if possible; otherwise, a pistol shot was to bring the four boys to my help, and we were to do our best. But we were full of confidence, even with the odds so large against us. The approach to the house was made as quietly as possible, my four companions remaining about two hundred feet away, the darkness concealing them. The house was in full view, and they could reach it very quickly when necessary. The sound of my horse's feet brought one of the young Ridgeways to the porch. He recognized me and seemed to guess my mission.

"Have you got Dr. Watson here?" I asked.

"Yes, and he has a large escort; they came after nine o'clock. The river is very high, the crossing is dangerous in the dark, and we refused to risk it until morning."

I dismounted and threw my rein over a hook on the porch as he spoke.

"Where are they, and what is their number?" I inquired.

"There are about thirty of them. The Doctor and eight of his escort are in a large room upstairs, and the others out in the hayloft. They are heavily armed and evidently soldiers, though not in uniform."

"Where is their sentinel?" I asked.

"They have no one on guard. We told them that one of us would be up all night."

"Show me the way to the room where the Doctor is," I requested.

He went with me to the foot of the stairway and said: "The door is immediately at the head of this stairway."

I went up hurriedly, turned the bolt, and, pushing open the door, stepped into the room, which was entirely without light, calling to Dr. Watson as I stepped in. There was immediate springing from bed with the clicking of pistols, and the cry: "Who is there?" I closed the door behind me and asked the Doctor if he didn't recognize my voice. His reply was the query, "Is that you, Capt. Bob?" "Yes," I said, "and we have come to take you back home."

During all this the officer in charge had called for a light, which was quickly brought from below by those who were listening eagerly for developments. I allowed the door to open behind me, and the light made me the focus of nine pairs of anxious eyes. Eight of the men were standing in various conditions of dress and undress and each with a pistol in his hand, the Doctor was in a sitting posture on a cot, I with my back to the door, which I had closed, and young Ridgeway holding a lamp which lighted the scene. The situation was dramatic and intense, and was relieved by my saying: "Doctor, we heard of your arrest and have come to your rescue. We are going to take you back home. Come with us; we have no time to lose." The Doctor hesitated, and interest now centered on him, but the pistols all pointed my way. I was well armed, but with nothing in sight. I had the advantage of being the least excited of any one in the room, and felt that I could, if necessary, fire several effectual shots before I could be hurt. However, diplomacy and nerve were the weapons for me to use, and not bullets.

The Doctor broke the silence by saying: "If I go with you, the whole United States army would be sent to rearrest me, and you, my good friends, would be answerable for more than I am held for. I will not go." His answer was a disappointment to me and a relief to all the others in the room. Their pistols were involuntarily lowered and the intense nervous strain yielded in a long, deep breath. Then followed an hour of persuasion and argument. I represented to the Doctor that his trial would only be a farce, ending speedily at the gallows. The officer in charge became much interested, promising his personal efforts as to the Doctor's rights. I told the Doctor that we had an abundant force of his friends in waiting outside, and that, while there would necessarily be some sacrifice of life by reason of the resistance of our rescue, we were going to take him back with us; but persuasion was in vain. Actuated by his concern for his rescuing friends, he positively refused to go with me. I returned to our little band and sadly we rode homeward, the dawn just revealing the beautiful mountains and river as said good-by and separated.

The news of the attempted rescue spread over the country from Lexington to Richmond; but the secret of our small number and identity rested entirely with our own party of five, and for a year my identity was the only one discovered to the public.

When Dr. Watson and Maj. Carse left us they proceeded on the road to the Doctor's house, which was half a mile up the mountain gorge from the river, thick woods being on either side of the road. When they were within a few hundred feet of the house the Major suddenly reined up his horse, which seemed to be a signal, as they were immediately surrounded by a body of mounted and armed men coming from the woods. The Major informed the Doctor that he had been directed to arrest him and bring him to Richmond to answer before a military tribunal for the shooting of the negro. They had a horse for the Doctor, who was allowed to pack his saddlebags with a change of clothing, to bid his family a hasty farewell, and then the cavalcade started on its hard night ride of thirty-five miles to Lynchburg.

The Ridgeway boys ferried the party across the river the next morning. They rode in all possible haste to Lynchburg, took the train there, and soon turned their prisoner over to the provost marshal of Richmond.

Friends of Dr. Watson went to Washington and brought back to Richmond a peremptory order from President Andrew Johnson for the release of the Doctor, having convinced the President that the Doctor had been properly acquitted by the civil authorities at Lexington.

The Doctor, being restored to liberty, was concerned for myself. He sought a personal audience with Gen. Schofield, which was promptly accorded him, and he asked the General if I was to be arrested on the charge of interference with soldiers in the performance of duty. He replied: "I respect your young friend for his conduct, and he shall not be arrested while I am in command of District No. I."

The Doctor lost no time in returning to his home and friends, and the little episode was closed forever.[1]

Endnotes

Front matter

1. Excerpt from a letter to Colonel Rawley White Martin on November 23, 1863, the day Pheme was arrested.

The Times

1. Bariziza, Decimus et Ultimus, *The Adventures of a Prisoner of War* (Austin, TX: University of Austin Press, 1964), 58.
2. Scharf, J. Thomas, *The History Of Maryland*, Vol III (Hatboro, PA: Tradition Press, 1967), 319. Originally published in 1879, this work was written by a man who lived through the times. Through Scharf's meticulously researched and detailed account, his feelings of indignation are obvious. His views and reactions would have been similar to those of all Baltimore Southerners. All quotes in this section are from Scharf, unless otherwise noted.
3. *Ibid.*, 321.
4. *Ibid.*, 331.
5. *Ibid.*, 332, 336.
6. *Ibid.*, 263.
7. *Ibid.*, 264.
8. *Ibid.*, 263.
9. *Ibid.*, 265, 266.
10. *Ibid.*, 282.
11. *Ibid.*, 399.
12. *Ibid.*, 433.
13. *Ibid.*, 415.
14. *Ibid.*, 443.
15. *Confederate Veteran*, Vol. 12, 333.
16. *Confederate Veteran*, Vol. 28, 336.
17. *Ibid.*, 335.
18. "Created 22 March '62 to consist of N. J., Pa., Del., and Eastern Shore of Md. and Va., and the counties of Cecil, Harford, Baltimore, and Ann Arundel, Md." [Boatner, 549] West Virginia was added in March 1863.
19. Scharf, 489.
20. *Ibid.*, 522.
21. *Ibid.*, 526.
22. *Ibid.*, 547.
23. *Ibid.*, 548.
24. *Ibid.*, 550.
25. *Ibid.*
26. *Ibid.*, 551.
27. *Ibid.*
28. *Ibid.*, 568.

The Life

1. An excerpt from Pheme's poem, "I Am So Cold" in Provost Marshal file.
2. The quoted excerpts written by Mona McCormick, Pheme's sister, are from her unpublished manuscripts, *The Banishment of Miss Euphemia Goldsborough* and *The Obituary of Mrs. Euphemia Goldsborough Willson,* in possession of the descendants. Both manuscripts are transcribed in their entirety in the appendices.
3. Pember, Phoebe Yates, *A Southern Woman's Story* (St. Simon's Island, GA: Mockingbird Books Inc., 1959), 43.
4. *Confederate Veteran*, Vol. 28, 334
5. McCormick.
6. From an unnamed periodical in the GNMP files by an unidentified prisoner entitled "College Hospital in Gettysburg," dated February 1867.
7. McCormick.
8. *Confederate Veteran*, Vol. 22, 546.
9. Coco, Gregory, *A Vast Sea of Misery* (Gettysburg, PA: Thomas Publications, 1988), 142.
10. *Confederate Veteran*, Vol. 30, 355.
11. "College Hospital in Gettysburg."

12. McCormick.

13. Bariziza, 58. Bariziza went on to comment on the vast difference between the North and the South. "Whilst at Gettysburg, I could not but remark the difference between the conduct of our army and that of the enemy in invading our country. Here stood the town, after three days of hard fighting around and in it, almost entirely untouched. No wanton destruction of property of any description could be seen, no women and children complained that they were homeless and beggars. Then I called to mind the scenes around the city of Fredericksburg the winter previous; private homes sacked and burned, books, furniture,and every thing perishable utterly destroyed, women flying from burning houses with children in their arms, and insult and outrage at full license. I thought as I made the contrast in my own mind, of the utter uncongeniality of the two people, and thanked God we were forever divided."

14. Coco, 32.

15. McCormick.

16. "College Hospital at Gettysburg."

17. Narrative by Mrs. Jacob A. Clutz, "The Battle of Gettysburg," *Pennsylvania History*, Vol. 5, No. 3, (Philadelphia, PA: University of Pennsylvania Press, 1938).

18. McCormick.

19. Coco, 167, 168.

20. Bucklin, Sophronia, *In Hospital and Camp* (Philadelphia, PA: John E. Potter, 1869), 171, 172.

21. *Ibid.*, 154.

22. As Sam Watson died on the 13th and was presumably buried on or near that date, Mona's recollection of the date of Pheme's arrival must have been off a day or two. It would have taken at least a day to travel that distance.

23. McCormick.

24. *Ibid.*

25. *Ibid.*

26. *Ibid.*

27. *Ibid.*

28. Whatever the state of Pheme's finances, she made an extravagant purchase at this time. She paid $1200 in Confederate money for a dress. The dress was part of the wedding trousseau of Mrs. Brig. Gen. Archibald Gracie who had requested her aunt, Mrs. (Union) Lt. Gen. Winfield Scott, who had spent the war in Europe, to send her some new clothes from Paris through the blockade. Mrs. Scott complied and the items, including this black and white silk purchased for $100 gold, were received in Richmond. A few days after their arrival, Gen. Gracie was killed at Petersburg, and Mrs. Gracie, then in mourning, sold all the clothes. The dress was passed down through Pheme's descendants and in 1993 was donated by Mrs. Crim to the museum at the Gettysburg Visitor Center.

29. Woodward, C. Vann, ed., *Mary Chesnut's Civil War* (Binghamton, NY: Vail-Ballou Press, 1981), 830.

30. Dawson, Captain Francis W., "Our Women in the War," an address delivered on February 22, 1887, at the Fifth Annual Re-Union of the Association of the Maryland Line (Charleston, SC: Walker, Evans, & Coswell Co.), 4.

31. McCormick.

32. *Ibid.*

33. *Ibid.*

The Hospital Books

1. Excerpt from letter to Lieutenant Anderson J. Peeler from Pheme, dated September 3, 1863. [See Provost Marshal file]

2. Brockett & Vaughn, *Women's Work in the Civil War* (Boston, MA: R.H. Curran, 1867), 451.

3. Houston Letters, Leyburn Library, Washington & Lee University

4. Southern Historical Society Papers, Vol. 1, 248.

5. Shepherd, Henry E., *Narrative of Prisoner Life at Baltimore and*

Johnson's Island, Ohio (Baltimore, MD: Commercial Ptg. & Sta. Co., 1917), 5.

6. *Ibid.*, 5-7.
7. *Ibid.*, 10.
8. *Ibid.*, 7.
9. *Ibid.*, 8, 9.
10. *Ibid.*, 9.
11. *Ibid.*, 7, 8.
12. *Ibid.*, 10, 11.
13. *Ibid.*, 11, 12.
14. *Ibid.*, 13-18.
15. *Confederate Veteran*, Vol. 15, 400.
16. *Ibid.*, 212-214.
17. Southern Historical Society Papers, Vol. 1, 143, 144.

The Diaries

1. Fort Monroe stands on the tip of Old Point Comfort, Virginia, about 80 miles southeast of Richmond. It was one of the most powerful fortifications in the country. Controlled by Union forces during the entire war, it severely affected traffic in the Confederate ports of Norfolk, Portsmouth, Suffolk, Petersburg, and Richmond. For hundreds of runaway slaves it was "the freedom fort" as they were afforded protection as "contraband of war." Three units of black Union soldiers were formed there. During the war it was visited by both Lincoln and Grant. Political prisoners were incarcerated at Fort Monroe as early as 1862 and for a time it held Confederate prisoners of war. Some of the more famous prisoners were William "Rooney" Lee, son of Robert E. Lee, Sidney Lanier, and, after the war, Jefferson Davis.

2. Maj. Gen. Benjamin Franklin Butler commanded Fort Monroe for a short time in 1861 [succeeded by Wool, Dix, and Foster] and returned in that capacity in November 1863. It was then known as the Department of Virginia and North Carolina. Butler was infamous throughout the South, especially for his abuse of women. Pheme detested him. [See Provost Marshal file]

3. Belle Boyd, another exile, was a participant in the same event and wrote about it in her book, *Belle Boyd in Camp and Prison*. She had been arrested in the summer of 1863 and incarcerated at Carroll Prison in Washington, DC, while her "trial by court-martial" progressed. She was sentenced to prison for the remainder of the war, but her father was successful in having the sentence commuted to banishment to the South for the duration of the war. Belle arrived at Fort Monroe on Wednesday, December 2, 1863.

    December 2 was Pheme's fourth day at the fort. Pheme's sister, Mona, states that she was in a "cold, damp cell" before influence was brought on the authorities to have her removed from it. How long she was in a cell is unknown, but by December 2 she was housed at the Hygeia Hotel right outside the walls of the fort with other female prisoners.

    Belle Boyd joined the prisoners at the hotel. "Here I found the Misses Lomax, sisters of Confederate [Brigadier] General [Lunsford Lindsay] Lomax, and a Miss Goldsborough, of Baltimore, who were to be sent South. These ladies, however, were not the only sympathizers in the hotel; there were others whose names I dare not mention...On Wednesday evening the order came for Miss Goldsborough and myself to be in readiness to start that same night for Richmond." [164-165]

    Miss Boyd's narrative echoes Miss Goldsborough's. "We were then conducted to the wharf, placed on board a tug, and sent off to the exchange boat, the *City of New York*, which lay at anchor in the stream...Here we remained all night..." [166]

4. Belle Boyd wrote of her luggage being searched and many items confiscated. She wrote that during the search, "Miss Goldsborough sat by meanwhile, a quiet spectator of the

whole affair, she having undergone the ordeal of a search in the morning." [166] Belle continued, "I was informed that I must undergo a personal search...I earnestly appealed to their forbearance..." [165] and after giving up some letters and money, was allowed to proceed without a personal search. Why the two women were treated differently can only be guessed. Perhaps because it was late in the day and the tug was waiting for them. It should be noted, however, that Belle Boyd's story was written with publication in mind while Pheme confided her humiliation in a private diary. Another consideration is the fact that Belle knew how to handle the Union military. She had already shot and killed a Union soldier, engaged in successful spy work for the Confederacy, and been arrested a number of times. Belle was not a docile prisoner and knew how to cause trouble for those who wished to trouble her.

5. Belle Boyd also commented favorably on the Exchange Officer. "Upon our arrival on board we were kindly received by Major Mulford, who conducted us to the saloon and introduced us to his wife, a very charming lady-like woman..." [166]

6. Belle wrote: "...next morning, about seven o'clock, got under way. Shortly afterwards we ran aground, and it was not until eight a.m. that we succeeded in getting the vessel off again. Then, under a full head of steam, we steered for City Point." [166] "At the mouth of the James River we passed the Federal blockading fleet, and were here boarded by a boat from the flag-ship *Minnesota*, commanded by Admiral Lee. In a few moments we had entered the James...As we wended our way up the river we could see the signal-officers at the different stations busily announcing our approach, and occasionally we observed Confederate soldiers on picket duty." [167]

7. On March 8, 1862, the *Virginia*, which was the old *Merrimac*, that the Confederates had raised and refitted as an ironclad, entered the Hampton Roads with two small gunboats. She engaged in battle with the 50-gun *Congress*, which she rammed, and the 30-gun *Cumberland*, which was forced aground. The *Cumberland* sank and the *Congress* surrendered. Three Federal steam frigates approached the battle scene and ran aground, one being the *Minnesota*. The tide ebbed and the *Minnesota* was saved from destruction.

8. Belle Boyd wrote: "We arrived at City Point late on Friday evening. This place which could hardly be correctly dignified with the name of a village, is situate in a bend of the river. It was used as a depot by the Confederates, for the purpose of forwarding stores to those of their unfortunate countrymen who were prisoners in the North. Whilst the *City of New York* was coming to an anchor, Major Mulford, his wife, Miss Goldsborough, and myself stood conversing on the hurricane-deck." [168]. By June 1864, City Point became General Grant's headquarters, supply base, and a large general hospital.

9. Belle wrote: "A French corvette, which had been up the river to Richmond, lay at anchor near us. This evening, in acceptance of an invitation from Major Mulford, the French captain and his lieutenant came on board to spend the evening with us; and we enjoyed their visit heartily." [169]

10. Miss Boyd wrote: "The next morning, when I awoke, I found that the flag-of-truce boat had arrived during the night. Captain Hatch, the Confederate exchange officer, presently came on board. We were introduced to him, and very soon afterwards were, with our luggage, safely ensconced in the snug little

cabin of the _____ [*Schultz*]. Here, under my own country's flag, I felt free and comparatively happy.

"On our way up the river to Richmond we had to pass the obstructions situated between Chaping's and Drury's Bluffs. These places take their names from the bold appearance that the shore here presents. The obstructions designed to impede a hostile squadron became accidentally hurtful to our Confederate vessel. She ran foul of them, and it was found utterly impossible to continue the voyage. [The CSS *Schultz* was replaced by the CSS *Roanoke* on December 9, 1863.]

"At Drury's Bluff, therefore, we went on board a tug, in which we proceeded to Richmond. When we arrived, at eight p.m., I went immediately to the Spottswood [sic] House..." [169]

Pheme was not the first person Belle Boyd rubbed the wrong way, nevertheless, Miss Boyd served and suffered for the Confederate cause to the best of her ability.

11. The most likely identification of Pheme's escort is Maj. Gen. William Smith who had fought at Gettysburg. He had been elected governor of Virginia and was waiting to take office on January 1, 1864.

The Spotswood Hotel was on Main Street in Richmond. The Spotswood was to Richmond what the Willard Hotel was to Washington. The famous and infamous stayed there and it was filled with all people Confederate; politicians, dignitaries, officers, profiteers, spies, visitors, refugees, and exiles. Although it survived the Evacuation Fire, the building burned down on Christmas Day, 1870, with many of its guests perishing in the fire.

Mary Chesnut described it in her diary on June 22, 1861:"The Spottswood [sic] is built around a hollow square, and our rooms overlooked the billiard room &c &c on the opposite side of the inner yard. These public rooms were all on the lower story, and we looked into them...well—freely." [106]

12. William Gill, from Baltimore, was in Co. C, 1st Maryland Cavalry. He was left sick in Williamsport, Maryland, on July 14, 1863 during the Confederate retreat after Gettysburg. He was captured the following day and sent to West's Buildings in Baltimore, paroled, and transported to City Point. He would eventually return to his regiment and surrender under General Joseph E. Johnston in April 1865.

13. Levin Lake, Jr., Co. C, 1st Maryland Cavalry, also noted as Aide de Camp, Jubal Early's staff.

14. Reverend Mr. Wilmer, assumably from Maryland, was possibly Chaplain George T. Wilmer, who had been appointed Chaplain to the 6th Virginia Cavalry in 1861 but never reported for duty. He was also listed in the 32nd Virginia but resigned on July 26, 1862.

Lamar Hollyday, Co. A, 1st Maryland Battalion, was a former patient at Gettysburg. [See Hospital Books] Private Hollyday was "permanently disabled for service."

John Craig Lake, Co. A, 2nd Maryland Battalion, suffered a severe wound in the right leg at Gettysburg. He retreated with the army but was left at Hagerstown, Maryland, where he was captured, sent to West's Buildings, and paroled in September 1863. His records list him in three different Richmond area hospitals from October 1863 to March 1864. According to one source, while recuperating from his wounds, he contracted smallpox and died March 9, 1864, but this was not noted in his war records.

There were two possible Tom Pratts. Thomas G. Pratt (governor of Maryland 1845-1848) who was arrested along with his private secretary and held at Fort Monroe, eventually being sent South for refusing to take the oath. He was at Fort Monroe the same time Pheme was and may have been one of the people in Belle Boyd's mind when she wrote about the other sympathizers at the Hygeia whose names she "dare not mention." The other Tom Pratt, Thomas St. George Pratt, Co. A, 2nd Battalion Maryland Infantry, was the former governor's son and served with the Provost Marshal in Richmond. He was on leave from November 12, 1863 to December 12, 1863, dropped from the rolls of the 2nd in early 1864. He was promoted to 2nd lieutenant in the Marine Corps. The latter seems more likely as Pheme refers to the man without a prefix which would have befitted both an elder and a former governor.

Mr. Elder, if he had served in a Confederate Maryland unit, could have been: George Howard Elder, Jr., Co. C, 1st Maryland Cavalry, Philip Laurence Elder, Co. C, 1st Maryland Cavalry (also noted in Co. B, 21st Virginia), or Henry Elder, 3rd Maryland Light Artillery.

Charles Steele, Co. A, 2nd Maryland, was wounded in the left leg at Gettysburg on July 3. He was captured at Hagerstown, Maryland on July 12, sent to the Cotton Factory Hospital in Harrisburg, Pennsylvania in August 1863, then to the U.S. General Hospital at Chester, Pennsylvania. He wrote that he was "detained until about the 15th of Sept. when I was paroled and returned to the Confederate lines. Since that time being cut off from home (as were most Maryland Confederates), I have remained in hospital or with friends in Richmond."

15. Mr. Garnett and Cousin Em are Edgar Malcolm Garnett and Emily Dennis Hayward Garnett. Emily was born in Cambridge, Maryland and was the sister of Dr. Richard Hayward. The Hayward family moved to Tallahassee, Florida about 1835 and Dr. Hayward served as mayor of that city and treasurer of the state. He was also a trustee of the Leon Female Academy which is thought to have been the boarding school Pheme attended in the 1850's. Pheme referred to him as Uncle Hayward [see 1867 diary entry]. Mr. Garnett had been the Clerk of the U.S. Court of Claims in Washington, DC when the war broke out and his family moved to Richmond, where he assisted his brother, Dr. A.Y.P. Garnett in the military hospitals.

Major Elias Griswold, A.A.G., was formerly a lawyer in Cambridge, Maryland, whose war records include letters to the local lawyers with the surname Goldsborough. He probably had known Pheme from civilian life. He was with the Provost Marshal in Richmond under Brig. Gen. John Henry Winder (another son of Maryland). Later Maj. Griswold was assigned to special duty at Andersonville, Georgia, and Columbia, South Carolina, until November 1864, then at Greensborough, North Carolina, and was back in Richmond by March 1865.

McGill, a name often spelled in a variety of ways; i.e., Magill and Macgill, could be one of two Dr. Magills. Dr. Charles H. Magill, formerly from Baltimore, had a practice in Hagerstown, Maryland when the war broke out. In September 1861 he was arrested and confined in a number of forts. He was released in November 1862 and returned home. When the Confederates came through Hagerstown during the Gettysburg Campaign, he set up a hospital for Confederate sick and wounded. Knowing he was no longer safe in Maryland, he left with Lee's army when they returned to Virginia. Jefferson Davis appointed Dr. Magill a full surgeon. Serving through the remainder of the war, he was paroled in Lynchburg in 1865. During his absence from home, his family was constantly harassed and abused by the Union military. After the war the family moved to Richmond. The other Dr. Magill was his son, Dr. Charles G.W. Magill, who left for the South with his father and became a surgeon in the 2nd Virginia. Two other sons, David James and William, served in Co. C, 1st Maryland Cavalry.

Dr. Boyd was possibly Dr. William B. Boyd, assistant surgeon, who was the only doctor with that surname in the Compiled Service Records serving in a military capacity in Richmond at that time.

Lieutenant Charles W. Hodges, Co. C, 2nd Maryland would be killed near Hatcher's Run on February 5, 1865.

16. Jervis Spencer, Co. C, 1st Maryland Cavalry, whose records show he would be captured in August 1864, sent to Camp Chase, then Point Lookout where he was released in March 1865.

Willie Hollyday, Co. A, 2nd Maryland, was captured at Monocacy, Maryland, March 8, 1863. He was imprisoned at Ft. McHenry and sent to Ft. Monroe for exchange on March 13. [See Provost Marshal file] He was killed at Gaines Farm, June 3, 1864. He and his brother, Lamar (a patient of Pheme's at Gettysburg) were from Washington County, Maryland.

17. Major William M. Owen, Field and Staff, Battalion Washington Artillery, Louisiana.

18. Dr. Alexander Yelverton Peyton Garnett directed and inspected some of the Richmond hospitals and attended officers in their private quarters. He was also the private physician to the Davis family. He was the brother of Edgar Garnett who was married to Pheme's "Cousin Em." Their other brother,

Robert Payne Waring Garnett, served with General J.E.B. Stuart and later with the Essex Cavalry, 9th Virginia Regiment. Although most likely related, Dr. Garnett was not in the direct line of Gettysburg's Brig. Gen. Richard Brooke Garnett who was killed in Pickett's Charge, or Brig. Gen. Robert Seldon Garnett whose death was lamented in Pheme's moving poem, "I Am So Cold." [See Provost Marshal file]

19. Captain Andrew Matthew Houston, Co. K, 11th Virginia, was wounded in the arm at Gettysburg and was one of Pheme's patients. [See Hospital Books] He had retired to the Invalid Corps. The Houston family of Rockbridge County would host Pheme over the next few years, all of which was recorded in the diary. The effects of the war exacted a heavy toll on the family. Dr. David Gardiner Houston and Nancy Dix Houston had thirteen children, seven of whom reached adulthood. They were the following:

William Hale Houston: b. 10/29/31, d. 10/18/63; mustered into Co. B, 5th Virginia April 1861, in June promoted to QM Sergeant, and in September promoted to Commissary Officer. His company was transferred to the 27th Virginia Infantry where he was dropped from the rolls in August 1862. He re-enlisted in Co. H, 14th Virginia Cavalry and died in Rockbridge County of disease October 1863.

James Rutherford Houston: b. 4/19/34, d. 3/3/69; served in Captain Archibald Graham's Co. of the Rockbridge Artillery, Virginia Light Artillery; enlisted in July 1861 and given a certificate of discharge October 1862 for disease of the lungs (TB).

Mary "Mollie" Sophia Houston, b. 4/1/36, d. 2/7/14; married Captain Charles B. "Jack" Trevillian, Co. F, 4th Virginia Cavalry. Captain Trevillian was captured at

Greencastle, Pennsylvania on July 5, 1863. He was sent to Harrisburg, Philadelphia, Fort Delaware and then to Johnson's Island. Transferred to Fort Monroe January 1865. Thomas Houston mentioned him in his letters.

Captain David Gardiner Houston, b. 3/31/38, d. 7/4/63; served in Co. D, 11th Virginia and was killed at Gettysburg.

Captain Andrew Matthew Houston, b. 6/5/40, d. 7/21/69; served in Co. K, 11th Virginia, died from the effects of the wound received at Gettysburg.

Lieutenant, later Captain, Thomas Dix Houston, b. 8/18/42, d.4/3/00; was wounded several times during the war and imprisoned at Johnson's Island. By 1871 he was the only surviving son. [See biography endnote 24]

Edward Miller Houston, b. 3/7/45, d. 3/8/71; enlisted in Co. K, 11th Virginia in April 1863. He was acting as courier at the time of Appomattox and was on the list of prisoners.

20. Lieutenant Colonel Rawley White Martin, 53rd Virginia, was wounded in Pickett's Charge and was a former patient of Pheme's. [See Hospital Books, Provost Marshal file, and Appendix 6] She visited his home both during her exile and after the war. Rawley White Martin was born September 30, 1835 in Chatham, Pittsylvania County, Virginia. He was educated at the University of Virginia and the University of New York. He graduated in 1858 and began practicing medicine in Chatham in 1860. In 1861 he enlisted as a private in the 53rd, was present at all their battles rising through the ranks, and when the 53rd's colonel [William Aylett] was wounded at Gettysburg, the command devolved upon Martin. After scaling the wall with Brig. Gen. Lewis A. Armistead at the Angle on Cemetery Ridge during Pickett's Charge, he was immediately felled with four wounds, crippling him for life. From Gettysburg, he was taken to Ft. McHenry and then to Point Lookout where he was exchanged in June 1864. His records show he retired from service in October 1864, but he did some duty in Charleston, South Carolina and along the Rappahannock.

After the war he resumed his medical practice in Pittsylvania County and married Ellen Johnson from that county in 1867. They had five children; Rawley, James, Chasley, Nellie, and Douglas. It later became a tradition for the United Daughters of the Confederacy to hold a celebration on Dr. Martin's birthday which included speeches and a dinner, always attended by the veterans and civilians who had great admiration for Colonel Martin. Rawley White Martin died April 20, 1912 and is buried in Chatham.

21. Major D.H. Wood (later Captain), Quartermaster in charge of transportation.

22. The Tunstall House hotel was five blocks away from the Richmond and Danville Railroad.

23. Possibly this is a reference to the day Commissary Gen. Lucius B. Northrop was sacked and replaced by Brig. Gen. Isaac St. John. Judgements expressed regarding Nothrop's handling of his position ran from inept to insane.

24. Captain Thomas Dix Houston, Co. K, 11th Virginia, a former patient at Gettysburg, was one of the men recently released from Johnson's Island. He and his family play a prominent part in Pheme's diary. Thomas Houston was born August 8, 1842 in Rockbridge County, Virginia. At age fourteen he went to Washington College (now Washington & Lee). He had been there for three years, when after greasing all the blackboards with turkey grease,

he was asked to leave. In 1859 he traveled to Alabama, became an editor of a newspaper and was there when the war broke out. He enlisted in Co. G, 4th Alabama and fought with that unit at First Manassas where he was slightly wounded. When the 4th reorganized, he left it to enlist in the 11th Virginia with his brothers. He participated in all the 11th's battles and suffered a severe chest wound at Second Manassas. At Gettysburg he was wounded during Pickett's Charge and taken to the Confederate College Hospital where he came under Pheme's care. He was sent to Johnson's Island and then released in March 1865.

Shortly after the war he went to Texas and taught school. By the fall of 1866 he was attending law school in Lexington and graduated in 1867. He moved to Fincastle, Virginia where he edited a newspaper and was elected county judge. He married Emma Hoffman of Baltimore and they had two children, Maude and Henry Kemp. In 1881 they moved to Wheeling and then Charleston, West Virginia. Thomas Dix Houston died from a stroke on April 3, 1900. He is buried in the Houston family plot at High Bridge Church in Rockbridge County.

25. Captain Robert McCulloch, Co. B, 18th Virginia, was a former patient at Gettysburg and one of the men recently released from Johnson's Island. Pheme consistently misspells his name. She also refers to him as Mc or Mac. Thomas Houston and Robert McCulloch shared a room as wounded prisoners at the College Hospital in Gettysburg and were messmates at Johnson's Island. Houston described McCulloch as "young, gay, gallant, and brave, tall in statue—open but irregular features, warm hearted, he is ever at some mischief or other. He is my favorite, my gayest, my noblest

friend." [Houston Letters] Obvious through the diary is the special bond between Pheme and both McCulloch and Houston.

Robert McCulloch was born in Osceola, Missouri September 15, 1841 of parents who had recently moved to that state from Virginia. He and his two sisters were orphaned at an early age and returned to live with cousins in Rockbridge County. He was a second year cadet at Virginia Military Institute when the war broke out. Leaving immediately for Richmond where, as a VMI cadet, he served briefly as a drillmaster, he then fell in for short periods of time with both the 11th Georgia and the 4th Virginia. He finally attached himself to the 18th Virginia and remained with that unit where he rose from private to captain. He was wounded at First Manassas, Seven Days, Second Manassas, and twice at Gettysburg during Pickett's Charge where, it was said, every member of his company was hit with a bullet. He was sent to Johnson's Island and was released March 1865.

In 1868 McCulloch married Emma Paxton of Rockbridge County. They had three children, Richard, Robert, and Grace. Shortly afterwards they moved to Missouri. He worked for various street railway syndicates rising to high positions. He was president of the United Railway Company of St. Louis when he died on September 28, 1914.

26. Colonel George Proctor Kane was formerly the Marshal of Police in Baltimore. [See Provost Marshal file] He had been arrested in June 1861 and held until the latter part of 1862. He then became part of the Maryland Line and served as inspector and on the staff of Brig. Gen. Bradley T. Johnson.

27. The canal system along the James River was constructed to connect the inland to the sea, opening the west-

ern trade to the eastern ports. The canal system extended along the North (now Maury) River up through Lexington. Pheme used the canal system extensively in her travels.

28. Dr. David Gardiner Houston, patriarch of the Houston family, had died on September 18, 1864, four days after Pheme's departure on her first visit to the family home.

29. Lieutenant James W. Whitehead, Co. I, 53rd Virginia was from that area. He was wounded in the left leg at Gettysburg, transferred to West's Buildings in Baltimore, then to Johnson's Island where he was released in March 1865. Since Pheme appeared to be familiar with him, he may have been a former patient.

30. Possibly Maj. William H. Quincy of Brig. Gen. Micah Jenkins' staff. Quincy served as Jenkins' Quartermaster.

31. Rockbridge Alum Springs was a popular health spa in the western section of the county. It provided cottages, recreation, and arrangements for taking the waters. Stonewall Jackson was said to have visited there.

32. The Norvell House Hotel in Lynchburg.

33. Colonel Robert Enoch Withers commanded the 18th Virginia (McCulloch's former regiment) from May 1861 to July 1864. Though a physician, he became a newspaper editor after the war, Lt. Governor of Virginia, U. S. Senator, and U.S. Consul at Hong Kong.

34. Balcony Falls was a stop on the James River and Kanawha Company's canal route. It is near Glasgow, Virginia.

35. When the McCulloch children were orphaned in Missouri and returned to Virginia to live with cousins in Rockbridge County, they had two households which, according to census records, they were living at different times. The household of

Hobson and Elisa Johns and the household of Nancy Glasgow, both well-to-do and both in the same area of the county near Salling Mountain and the James River. Which household they were living in at the time of Pheme's visit is unknown.

36. Mary, the middle child of the McCulloch siblings, was 22 in 1866.

37. Magadalene "Mag" Mohler, who would have been 26 at this time, and her sister, Frances "Fannie" Jane Mohler, age 25, and their brother Maj. Elisha Grigsby Mohler, age 27, and presumably his wife. Major Elisha Grigsby Mohler was a VMI graduate. At the beginning of the war he was commissioned lieutenant in the Confederate Army and sent to Richmond to drill troops. In 1862 he reported to Maj. Gen. Earl Van Dorn then stationed in Arkansas. He was promoted to Brigade Quartermaster and later Division Quartermaster of Maj. Gen. Dabney Herdon Maury's command with rank of major. Major Mohler lived in Mississippi and was presumably visiting his father, Col. Jacob Mohler, stepmother Aurelia Paxton Salling Mohler, and his sisters. The Mohlers probably lived south of Salling Mountain near the confluence of the James and North (Maury) Rivers.

38. Captain Thomas Houston had spent some time in Texas, teaching and raising money for a Soldier's Orphans Association. He came back in 1866 to attend the Brockenbrough Law School, now the Washington and Lee Law School from which he graduated in June 1867.

39. Jane Elizabeth "Bettie" Paxton, age 25, was the daughter of William Paxton whose household was south of the James River in Rockbridge County. Captain Obenchain was most likely Frances G. Obenchain formerly of Douthat's Company (Botetourt County) of the Virginia Light Artillery.

40. Colonel Jacob Mohler, father of Mag, Fannie, and Maj. Elisha Grigsby Mohler.

41. Dr. William Finney Junkin was the preacher at Falling Springs Church in Rockbridge County. Falling Springs Presbyterian Church was attended by many of the people in the diary. It was built during the war, financed by the people pledging payment in bushels of corn. It still stands today.

42. Nancy Dix Houston, matriarch of the Houston family. The family home was called Sunny Knoll which was very near the Natural Bridge in Rockbridge County. They were active in nearby High Bridge Church, right up the road from their home, where their family plot holds all the Houstons with the exception of David [see Appendix 2 for the removal of his body from the Gettysburg battlefield] and Mollie who is buried in Williamsburg.

43. John Rowland Echols was at VMI during the war and fought at New Market. The Knight of the Seven Stars won the tournament and crowned Pheme queen. On October 2, 1873 John Rowland Echols married Bettie McCulloch.

John Campbell may have been from the J.C. Campbell household outside of Lexington.

McPaxton was Joseph McClung "Mac" Paxton, age 22, son of Thomas Paxton (brother and neighbor of William Paxton) and cousin to Bettie Paxton. He served in Co. I, 4th Virginia. He was wounded and captured at Gettysburg, paroled and released at City Point August 1863, given a certificate of disability, and served in the Quartermaster Department in Lynchburg.

Horace Houston was the son of John Houston, a relative and neighbor of the David Houstons. He was Thomas' cousin. Horace Houston, Co. F, 34th Tennessee (aka 4th Confederate Regiment, Tennessee Infantry). He enlisted in August 1861 at Knoxville, was captured at Chickamauga September 19, 1863, transferred to Louisville, Kentucky, and then to Johnson's Island, from where he was released June 11, 1865 upon taking the oath.

Edward Miller Houston, Thomas' brother.

Jake Arnold was most likely attached to the Arnold household down the road from Dr. Houston's home.

Thomas Goolsby Burks, Jr. was most likely the 22 year old son in the T.G. Burks household along the James River near Salling Mountain. He served in Co. I, 12th Virginia Cavalry. In November 1886 he was shot and killed near Gilmore Mills.

Francis L. Jordan, age 19, of the Samuel Jordan household in Rockbridge County, served in Co. C, 1st Virginia Cavalry.

44. Emma Paxton, age 19, was a daughter of Thomas Paxton, sister to "Mac" Paxton. She would eventually marry Robert McCulloch.

Bettie McCulloch, younger sister to Robert and Mary, was 19.

Miss Annie Weaver was most likely attached to the William Weaver household along Buffalo Creek.

Cassandra "Cassie" Burks, age 19, was a daughter in the Samuel Burks household in Rockbridge County that was situated almost into the Blue Ridge Mountains.

45. Mr. Preston Cabell was a state senator from Rockbridge County.

46. Mr. Garth is almost certainly a relative of the Houstons. The Garths and the Houstons enjoyed complicated family ties both blood and marital.

47. Martin Trevillian was probably T. J. M. Trevillian who served in Co. B, 1st Virginia Cavalry.

48. James Rutherford Houston, age 32, brother to Thomas.

49. Mrs. Elisa Johns, wife of Hobson Johns, whose household was between Sallings Mountain and the James River and who sheltered the McCulloch orphans at least part of their lives.

50. William Nelson Pendleton was an Episcopal minister and served in the Confederate artillery, first as Captain of the Rockbridge Artillery and eventually as Gen. Lee's Chief of Artillery. His son was Col. "Sandie" Pendleton of Jackson's staff.

51. Virginia "Jennie" Houston, age 16, was a daughter of John Houston, and sister to Horace.

52. Elizabeth "Bettie" Houston, age 24, was a daughter of John Houston, and sister to Jennie and Horace.

53. The Thomas Preston Paxton household rested on the James River between Salling Mountain and the Blue Ridge. He was the father of Mac and Emma Paxton.

54. Edward W. Douglass, age 27, lived with his mother, Lucy, along the North (Maury) River. He had attended Washington College in 1858-59 and was exempt from military service for chronic diarrhea in May 1864. He died January 10, 1892.

55. The William Paxton home is along the James River close to the home of Thomas Preston Paxton.

56. David Guin Mohler, whom Pheme consistently referred to as Davis, was born in 1846, the son of Col. Jacob Mohler, and brother to Fannie, Mag, and Maj. Elisha Mohler. At age 15 he attached himself to the 3rd Virginia and served with that unit until December 1863. He then entered Virginia Military Institute and fought with Company A of the Cadet Corps at New Market. He served on the Richmond front until February 1865 when he resigned to join Col. John S. Mosby's partisan rangers. He was captured on April 12, 1865, held a prisoner until May 15 when he refused to take the oath, was re-arrested and held at Elmira until July 13, 1865.

57. Martha McNutt Glasgow had her own household near Salling Mountain and across the river from the Paxton homes. She was a neighbor of Mrs. Johns.

58. Probably Lt. J. C. Warren, Co. C, 52nd North Carolina, a former Gettysburg patient and originally from Lynchburg. [See Hospital Books]

59. The Honorable Thomas S. Bocock, the only Speaker of the Confederate Congress.

60. Mrs. Thomas Bocock, wife of the former Speaker, was the daughter of Charles James Faulkner and Mary Boyd. They lived at Boydville, a house in Martinsburg, West Virginia, which still stands today. Charles Faulkner had been a United States Congressman and Consul to France. While in the latter position, he was arrested as a Southern sympathizer and imprisoned when he returned to the United States. He later served for a short time on Lt. Gen. Stonewall Jackson's staff.

61. Fenton, who was not mentioned elsewhere, was most likely a relative of Emily Garnett's by marriage. The name Fenton passed through generations of female Garnetts. Pheme was boarding with the Garnetts in March 1865. March 25, the date Pheme gives as their last meeting, was the night before Pheme left to visit Rockbridge County. Because of the surrender, she did not return to Richmond.

62. The Moffits lived down the road from the Houston households. The Miss Moffit referred to could have been any of three Misses in that household; Mary, age 35, Jane, age 24, or Helen, age 23. Mr. Moffit is most likely William, age 25, but possibly John, age 19. William was closer to Mary McCulloch's age, to whom he appeared to have been at-

tracted. E. Frances "Fannie" Echols, age 15, was sister to John Echols.

63. Dr. Abner E. Arnold who had served in the 1st Rockbridge Artillery until appointed Assistant Surgeon.

64. Possibly Mr. James P. Bryant who lived in the area.

65. Dr. James Watson's household was at the edge of Salling Mountain near a bend in the James River. The story of his arrest and attempted rescue is in Appendix 7.

66. Probably Lt. Col. William Thomas Poague of Rockbridge County who served in the Rockbridge Artillery and later McIntosh's Battalion. After the war he was in the Virginia legislature and later treasurer of VMI.

67. Probably Lt. Col. Henry Fitzhugh, Jr., who served with the 8th Virginia Cavalry and later as A.A.G. to Maj. Gen. William Wing Loring.

68. Alex Paxton, age 27, son of Thomas Preston Paxton, was brother to Mac and Emma Paxton. Sergeant Alexander S. Paxton served in Co. I, 4th Virginia. He enlisted in June 1861 and was wounded at Chancellorsville. His last dated muster was January 1865.

69. Mrs. Frances A. McChesney, head of her own household, lived in Rockbridge County.

70. Captain George Baxter McCorkle, Co. H, 4th Virginia (Rockbridge Grays), was captured at Gettysburg, sent to Ft. Delaware, then to Johnson's Island in July 1863. He was released with Captains McCulloch and Houston in March 1865. He would marry Mary McCulloch on Christmas Eve, 1867.

71. Mr. Endes lived over by Falling Springs Church.

72. Dr. Chandler, another neighbor, lived on one of the roads between High Bridge Church and Falling Springs Church.

73. Mr. Franklin McClintic was another neighbor in the area.

74. Possibly Maj. Asher Waterman Garber, formerly of the Staunton Artillery. Joseph Baldwin, age 20, was a member of the Cornelius Baldwin household along the North (Maury) River.

75. Mary "Mollie" Paxton, age 22, was the daughter of William Paxton and sister to Bettie Paxton.

76. Dr. Alexander Gallatin McChesney served as Captain of Co. F, 11th Virginia Cavalry. [See Appendix 7]

77. Frances "Fannie" Watson, age 24, and "her brother" who could have been either John, age 27, or Gus, age 19, or Joseph, age 15, all of whom were children of Dr. James Watson.

78. The Lusters Hotel by the Natural Bridge was run by John Lusters.

79. William Houston was probably Tom's cousin. Tom's father, David Gardiner Houston had a brother Matthew Hale Houston, whose first son was William Wilson Houston, born 1839 in Wheeling, West Virginia. In 1867 he was a pastor at Beth County, Virginia.

80. As there was no Dora in the immediate Goldsborough family, this may have been Dora Hoffman, another Baltimore woman who served as a nurse at Gettysburg.

81. Martha "Mattie" Houston, age 14, was the daughter of John Houston and sister to Horace and Jennie.

82. The Peaks of Otter, located in Bedford County, Virginia, are part of the Blue Ridge Mountains. Long famous for their beauty, they are visited today with the same enthusiasm. At present there are excellent accommodations and hiking trails at the Peaks.

83. Gus Watson, age 19, son of Dr. Watson. Joe Paxton, age 25, was a son of William Paxton, and brother to Bettie and Mollie Paxton. Ella Paxton, age 19, was a daughter of William Paxton, and sister to Bettie, Mollie, and Joe Paxton.

Probably Thomas Canoday who served in Co. C, 35th Battalion Virginia Cavalry.

84. The Peaks of Otter Hotel owned by Benjamin Wilkes.

85. Pheme and her friends had climbed Sharp Top. Adventurous travelers, including Robert E. Lee and daughter Mildred who also climbed that peak in 1867, described the same dangerous and difficult ascent and the beauty and grandeur afforded by the view.

86. Probably Capt. Lewis Harman who had served in Co. C, 52nd Virginia Infantry and as Captain, Co. I, 12th Virginia Cavalry. Captain William Kable, Co. F, 10th Virginia Cavalry.

87. The landlord at that time was probably still Lyburn Wilkes, son of the owner. The Peaks of Otters Hotel could accommodate thirty people. It boasted a number of outbuildings before the war and the hand of Maj. Gen. David "Black Dave" Hunter fell upon it.

88. This was a little rock house, or shelter to which it was sometimes referred. After looting and burning the hotel, Hunter's men took the time to smash in the roof of the structure, leaving the "ruin" seen by Pheme.

89. Sunny Knoll was the name of the Houston home.

90. Probably a neighbor; there were several Thompson households in the area outside of Lexington.

91. The "Point" in Lexington was where the Jordan Flour Mills and warehouses stood and where the bridge crossed the North (Maury) River.

92. Possibly Elisa "Lizzie" Gilmore, age 25, daughter of Joseph Gilmore who lived in the area.

93. Possibly Jackson or Lucian Grigsby, residents of Rockbridge County.

94. Captain George "Baxter" McCorkle.

95. Mr. Jno. G. Hamilton owned Fancy Hill which stands today. The family included his wife, Frances, and, in 1860, five children ages ranging from one to ten.

96. Probably the elderly Mr. Rev. Ewing who lived near Falling Springs Church and Fancy Hill.

97. The household of a Mr. Frank Anderson was in the neighborhood.

98. Apparently this is Robert McCulloch and Emma Paxton's wedding day.

99. Possibly the home of Isaac P. St. Johns.

100. Lucy Douglass, Edward's mother.

101. There were several Poague households in Rockbridge County.

Provost Marshal File

1. Lieutenant Colonel Alexander Bliss began his career in Baltimore as Quartermaster in the Middle Department, VIII Army Corps in April 1863 and continued until June 1865.

2. Marshal George P. Kane was arrested on June 27, 1861 and held as a political prisoner until late 1862. He later served in the Confederate army and Pheme met him in Richmond. [See Diaries]

3. Scimitar being a curved sword used by the Turks and Arabs. Timur the lame (1336?-1405) was a Mongol warrior whose conquest extended from the Black Sea to the Upper Ganges.

4. Bigots: a derogatory term applied by the French to the Normans, meaning one obstinately and irrationally, often intolerantly, devoted to his own church, party, belief, or opinion.

5. Casmir Pulaski (1748-1779) was a Polish general who fought for the colonies in the American Revolution.

6. dazzling.

7. Indra was the chief god of the early Hindu religion, associated with rain and thunderbolts.

8. For the story of the pond of Bethsaida, where healing miracles were wrought, see Book of Job, Chapter 5.

9. General Order No. 28, the "Woman Order," was issued by Gen. Benjamin Butler on May 15, 1862 in New Orleans. Butler was notorious for his abuse of the women of the

South. The gist was "when any female shall, by word, gesture, or movement, insult or show contempt for any officer or soldier of the United States, she shall be regarded and held liable to be treated as a woman of the town plying her avocation." The order provoked outrage from every quarter. When Mayor Monroe of that city protested, he was arrested. The "Daughters of New Orleans" wrote that "it would have been better for New Orleans to have been laid in ruins and buried beneath the moss that we should be subject to such untold suffering." [Simkins & Patton, 57] Butler's order branded him as "Beast." "New England's Butler, best known to us as Beast Butler, is famous and infamous now. His amazing order to his soldiers and comments on it are in every mouth. We hardly expected from Massachusetts behavior to shame a Comanche," Mary Chesnut wrote on June 12, 1862. [Woodward, 378-79] Both President Davis and the people of the North protested. In London a newspaper demanded intervention in the "tryanny of victor over vanquished."

10. Haman, the wicked prime minister from the Book of Esther, persuaded the king to issue an order condemning all Jews to death.
11. vice scuse: a wicked or immoral excuse
12. neth from nether, meaning nest
13. Anat was a Phoenician goddess of various things acting in various ways depending on the translation or interpretation. It is impossible to know what version with which Pheme was familiar. This century's mythology translations agree on one thing about her. When her brother is killed by Mot (Death) she seeks revenge against the murderer. "With her sickle she cleaves him. With her flail she beats him. With fire she grills him. With her mill she grinds him. In the fields she scatters him." [Addington & Ames, 78]

14. The Sepoy Rebellion in India 1857-59, between the Indians and British, brought about mainly because of the lack of understanding and respect of a different culture.
15. The story of Uzzah touching the Ark of the Covenant is in the Second Book of Kings, Chapter 6.
16. The story of Benjamin and the woman wronged is in the Book of Judges, Chapters 19 to 21.
17. Derived from lustrum which is five years, eight lustres meaning forty years.
18. William Hollyday, Co. A, 2nd Maryland, was captured at Monocacy, Maryland, on March 8, 1863. He was imprisoned at Ft. McHenry and sent to Ft. Monroe for exchange on March 13. He did not survive the war. William's brother, Lamar, would be one of Pheme's patients at Gettysburg. [See Hosptial Books] Both men would visit Pheme during her exile. [See Diaries]
19. Lieutenant Anderson J. Peeler, Co. I, 5th Florida [See Hospital Books]
20. Captains B & G are most likely Capt. William J. Bailey, Jr., Co. G, 5h Florida and Capt. Richmond N. Gardner, Co. K, 5th Florida. Col. L is Lt. Col. James W. Lockert, 14th Tennessee. Lieutenant G. may be Lt. Thomas Wilkes Givens, Co. K, 8th Florida [See Hospital Books for all above]
21. Almost certainly Alice Long, another Baltimore nurse at Gettysburg, who seemed to have made quite an impression on the men.
22. Sergeant Major William J. T. Ross, Co. C, 2nd Georgia Battalion. He had already been exchanged by the time she wrote this. [See Hospital Books]
23. Sergeant Julian Betton, Co. M, 2nd Florida [See Hosptial Books]
24. Captain George S. Jones, Co. B, 2nd Georgia Battalion, was wounded on July 2, 1863, transferred to West's Buildings, then to Johnson's Island in September 1863, and paroled

March 1864 from Point Lookout. Captain George H. Jones, Co. B, 22nd Georgia. [See Hospital Books]

25. Sergeant Columbus H. Woolley, Co. A, 4th Alabama. [See Hosptial Books]

26. If the "to do" was the dedication of the National Cemetery, one would assume this question was in jest.

27. He may have been referring to the treatment of the citizens of Baltimore, in particular something recently done to Pheme, which may have been a prelude to her arrest on November 23.

28. Sergeant W. W. Smith, Co. G, 5th Texas, was wounded and captured at Gettysburg, the wound listed as "Ball chest dangerous," transferred to City Point for exchange in November 1863. He was back with his regiment in May 1864 and surrendered at Appomattox. J. H. Brown, Co. F, 5th Texas and Sgt. Columbus H. Woolley, Co. A, 3rd Alabama. [See Hospital Books]

29. Callie was Tom Sneed's sister.

30. Miss Addie was probably a lady of Baltimore who communicated with the prisoners at West's Buildings. She may have been one of the women who nursed at Gettysburg; most of those ladies remain unidentified.

31. S. J. Bouknight, Co. M, 7th South Carolina was left at Gettysburg to serve as a nurse. [See Hospital Books]

32. The most likely candidate for this Col. Gibson is Lt. Col. John H. Gibson, 14th Virginia Cavalry. He was not captured at Gettysburg. He was, however, captured in November 1864 and was released from Ft. Delaware in July 1865.

33. Major William W. Goldsborough, Field and Staff, 1st Maryland Battalion was not related to Pheme. [See Hospital Books]

34. Dr. Charles Edward Goldsborough, residing in Hunterstown, Pennyslvania before the war, was the assistant surgeon of the Union 5th Maryland. He was captured

June 15, 1863 at Winchester and released November 12, 1863 from Libby Prison in Richmond. He visited his brother, William, at West's Buildings. Charles would later go to Ft. Delaware to nurse William again when he returned from South Carolina as one of the Immortal Six Hundred, and also another brother, Eugene, who fought under Confederate Lt. Col. Harry Gilmor. William would live; Eugene died at Ft. Delaware.

35. Probably Pheme's sister Gertrude.

36. Tobias Duvall, Co. C, 2nd Maryland, was wounded at Gettysburg. He was shot in the left arm, shoulder, leg, and thigh, one bullet passing though his privates. He was transferred to West's Buildings on November 10, 1863 and was released after taking the oath on November 19.

37. Thomas J. Sneed, Co. A, 7th Tennessee [See Hospital Books]

38. Though this date is clearly written, it must have either been a mistake or had been predated since on November 24th Pheme was under house arrest. It is very doubtful she would have been allowed writing materials, but even so, she surely would have mentioned her situation. This letter is in answer to one Col. Herbert wrote her from Johnson's Island which was dated November 11. [See Personal Collection] She states it was received "a week ago today." She mentioned Dr. Charles Goldsborough's arrival "two weeks ago" which is also referred to in Thomas Sneed's letter dated November 20. A reasonable guess would be that the letter was written immediately prior to her arrest.

39. Major William W. Goldsborough, 1st Maryland, was shot in the left lung. His brother, Dr. Charles Goldsborough, of the Union 5th Maryland, was released from Libby prison and arrived at West's Buildings shortly thereafter.

40. At midnight on this date the Goldsborough house was searched and Pheme was arrested.
41. Lieutenant Colonel Rawley White Martin, 53rd Virginia. [See Hospital Books, Diaries, and Appendix 6]
42. This may be a reference to the fact that some of the Confederate prisoners took the Oath of Allegiance.
43. Colobles is Pheme's spelling for the word kolobos (French derived from colobium) meaning sleeveless or short sleeved tunic.
44. Lieutenant John D. Perkins, Co. M, 2nd Florida, Lt. J. C. Warren, Co. C, 2nd North Carolina, and Maj. Archibald D. Crudup, Field and Staff, 47th North Carolina. [See Hospital Books]

Personal Collection

1. Major William W. Goldsborough, Field and Staff, 1st Maryland was shot in the left lung and was still at West's Buildings. His brother, whom Herbert mentions later, was Dr. Charles Goldsborough, of the Union 5th Maryland, who had been captured at Winchester, sent to Libby Prison in Richmond, and released on November 12. He was at West's Buildings with William. [See Thomas Sneed's letter, Provost Marshal file]
2. Lieutenant Robert R. Ferguson, Co. K, 53rd Virginia was gunshot in the left thigh which "united with great deformity." He was at West's Buildings for a considerable time. In his records is a letter dated August 5, 1864 written from West's Buildings. The text is as follows: "I have the honor respectfully to submit my case for your humane consideration. I was wounded at the battle of Gettysburg July 3 1863 causing a compound [illegible] fracture of thigh bone. My leg at this time is very much enlarged at the seat of injury and presents a honey [illegible] appearance. It continues to supperate [sic] freely, discharging a large amount of Pus Each day. My general health is quite feeble. I am confined to the bed all the time. I now think that I will not recover. As I would like to spend the remnant of my days with my family, I beg that I be paroled and sent South as soon as possible or a Special Exchange Effected for me that I may return to the heart of my family and Enjoy their kind ministry in my last hours hoping that this application may meet with your approval and Early attention..." By October 1864 he was in a Richmond hospital and was still there in January 1865.

3. 2nd Lieutenant R. Chew Jones was appointed August 1862 to the Conscript Bureau and was an inspector for the 12th Congressional District at the post of Christiansburg, VA.
4. Captain Richmond N. Garnder, Co. K, 5th Florida, Lieutenant Anderson J. Peeler, Co. K, 5th Florida and Lt. Minor who is unidentified.
5. When the 59th was organized in June of 1862, Jack Barnes was elected colonel. He was wounded "slightly" in both legs at Gettysburg, was at Camp Letterman by August 20, presumably where he met Pheme, transferred to West's Buildings by the 22nd and arrived at Johnson's Island on the 24th. Sent to Baltimore in February 1864, he was exchanged the following month. He returned to the field and was wounded severely outside of Petersburg in August 1864. Back in action by early 1865, he was paroled at Appomattox.
6. Colonel William S. Hawkins of Wheeler's Scouts, C.S.A., (aka Hawkins Scouts), 1st Tennessee Mounted Scouts, was captured January 1, 1864 in Hickman County, Tennessee. He was sent to Camp Chase and remained there until June 16, 1865 when he was transferred to Johnson's Island from where he was paroled.

7. General Winfield Scott was Commander in Chief of the Union army until November of 1861 when he was succeeded by Maj. Gen. George McClellan. "He retired to write his memoirs and to make a European trip in 1864." [Boatner]

8. Brigadier General Archibald Gracie, rising through the ranks of Alabama regiments, was killed on December 2, 1864 by a sharpshooter during the siege of Petersburg.

Appendix 2

1. Dawson, 38, 4.

Appendix 6

1. Lieutenant John Day Perkins, Co. M, 2nd Florida [See Hospital Books]

2. Miss Matilda Saunders, an active player in Confederate Baltimore, who was also a nurse at Gettysburg.

3. Lieutenant William M. McGallaird, Co. E, 8th Louisiana, Lt. John Day Perkins, Co. M, 2nd Florida, and Maj. Archilbald D. Crudup, Field and Staff, 47th North Carolina. [See Hospital Books]

4. Lieutenant John Crittenden Warren, Co. C, 52nd North Carolina. [See Hospital Books]

5. Wearing the colors of red and white were grounds for arrest in Baltimore.

6. Penentration: the capacity to penetrate, esp. with the mind; acutemess; insight, sharp discernment.

7. Pheme most likely believed Point Lookout would be the stopping point before exchange. Martin would be there about six months.

8. Confederate surgeon Simon Baruch, one of a group of 110 surgeons and 10 chaplains taken at Gettysburg, was also at Ft. McHenry at this time. In Baruch's narrative, "Surgeon's Story of Battle and Capture," he wrote: "Colonel Porter, who was in command of the 5th United States Artillery (I believe) at the fort, proved a courteous and kindly host within his line of duty." [*Confederate Veteran*, Vol. 22, 547]

9. Captain Andrew Matthew Houston, Co. K, 11th Virginia, Lt. John C. Warren, Co. C, 52nd North Carolina, Lt. Ellwood M. Bean, Co. C, 5th Texas, Assistant Surgeon Daniel Parker, Cos. A & D, 8th Alabama, Surgeon Henry Austine Minor, 9th Alabama, Assistant Surgeon Richard G. Southall, Co. I, 6th Alabama, and Surgeon J. M. Hayes, Field and Staff, 26th Alabama. [See Hospital Books]

Appendix 7

1. *Confederate Veteran*, Vol. 12, 427, 428.

Bibliography

Records:
RG94; Record of the Adjutant General's Office,
Compiled Service Records for Union Troops
RG109; The War Department Collection of Confederate Records,
Compiled Service Records for Confederate Troops
Papers Relating to Confederates in Union Hospitals 1861-1865
Reference Files Relating to Medical Officers for the Period 1861-1865
Johnson Island Prison Registers
Provost Marshal Files
RG153; Record of the Office of the Judge Advocate General, file
    MM1356, Colonel William Fish's court-martial
RG393; Records of the U.S. Army Continental Commands, Part IV,
Register of the Cases and Decisions of the Provost Court at Fort
    Monroe, vol. 272, entry 1653

Unpublished Papers
Houston letters, Leyburn Library, Washington & Lee University
McCormick manuscripts, *Obituary* and *The Banishment of Miss
    Euphemia Goldsborough* written for the 1898 Confederate Re-
    lief Bazaar in Baltimore, both in possession of the Goldsborough
    descendants
Martin papers, Manuscripts Department, Duke University
Mohler papers, Leyburn Library, Washington and Lee University

Newspapers
The Baltimore *American* & *Commercial Advertiser*
The Baltimore *Sun*
The Lexington *Gazette*
The *Valley Star*

Published sources
Addington, Richard, & Delano Ames, translators, *New Larousse En-
    cyclopedia of Mythology*, New York: The Hamlyn Publishing
    Group Ltd., 1959.

Bariziza, Decimus et Ultimus, *The Adventures of a Prisoner of War*, Auston, TX: University of Austin Press, 1964.

Boatner, Mark M. III, *The Civil War Dictionary*, New York: Vintage Books, 1991.

Boyd, Belle, *Belle Boyd in Camp and Prison*, reprinted by the Berkeley County Historical Society, Martinsburg, WV, n.d.

Brockett and Vaughn, *Women's Work in the Civil War*, Boston: R.H. Curran, 1867.

Bucklin, Sophronia, *In Hospital and Camp*, Philadelphia: John E. Porter, 1869.

Civil War Centennial Commission, *Tennesseans in the Civil War*, Nashville, TN: University of Tennessee Press, 1964.

Coco, Gregory A., *A Vast Sea of Misery*, Gettysburg, PA:Thomas Publications, 1988.

"College Hospital in Gettysburg," untitled periodical in the GNMP files, dated February 1867.

Dawson, Capt. Francis W., *Our Women in the War*, an address delivered at the Fifth Annual Re-Union of the Association of the Maryland Line on February 22, 1887, Charleston, SC: Walker, Evans, & Coswell Co.

Goldsborough, W. W., *The Maryland Line in the Confederate Army 1861-1865*, Baltimore, MD: Guggenheimer West & Co., 1900.

Grimal, Piere, ed., *Larousse World Mythology*, New York: G.P. Putnam's Sons, 1963.

Hadsel, Winifred, *Roads of Rockbridge County*, Lexington, VA: Rockbridge Historical Society, 1993.

Hartzler, Daniel D., *Marylanders in the Confederacy*, Silver Spring, MD: Family Line Publications, 1986.

Hartzler, Daniel D., *A Band of Brothers*, Bookcrafters, 1992.

Hartzler, Daniel D., *Medical Doctors of Maryland in the CSA*, Gaithersburg, MD: Olde Soldier's Books, Inc., 1988.

Pember, Phoebe Yates, *A Southern Woman's Story*, St. Simons Island, GA: Mockingbird Books, Inc., 1959.

Scharf, J.Thomas, *The History of Maryland*, Hatboro, PA: Tradition Press, 1967.

Shepherd, Henry E., MA, LL.D, *Narrative of Prison Life at Baltimore and Johnson's Island, Ohio*, Comercial Ptg. & Sta. Co, Baltimore, 1917.

Sheads, Scott Sumpter, & Toomey, Daniel Carroll, *Baltimore During the Civil War*, Toomey Press, Linthicum, Maryland, 1997.

Simkins, Frances Butler, and Patton, James Welch, *The Women of the Confederacy*, Garrett & Massie, Inc., Richmond, 1936.

Trout, W. E. III, *The Maury River Atlas*, Virginia Canals & Navigations Society, Lexington, Virginia, 1992.

Turner, Charles W., editor, *Captain Thomas D. Houston Prisoner of War Letters*, McClure Printing Co. Inc., Verona, Virginia, 1980.

Viemeister, Peter, *The Peaks of Otter; Life and Times*, Hamilton's, Bedford, Virginia, 1992.

War Department, *List of Staff Officers of the Confederate States Army*, Washington, Government Printing Office, 1891.

War Department, *List of Field Officers, Regiments, and Battalions in the Confederate States Army 1861-1865*, Washington, Government Printing Office, no date.

Woodward, C. Vann, editor, *Mary Chesnut's Civil War*, Yale University Press, New Haven, 1981.

Wright, Marcus Joseph, *General Officers of the Confederate Army, Officiers of the Executive Departments of the Confederate States, Members of the Confederate Congress by States*, Neale Publishing Co., New York, 1911.

Series
Confederate Veteran
Southern Historical Society Papers
The Virginia Regimental Histories series
Georgia Regimental series
North Carolina Regimental series
Genealogies of Virginia Families series

Index

Elam, Sgt. William Robert, 57, 143
Elder, Mr., 88, 176n #14
Endes, Mr., 99, 100, 183n #71
Ewing, Rev., 106, 184n #96

F

Ferguson, Lt. Robert R., 132, 187n #2
Fish, Col. William S., 9, 27, 29, 108, 110,
    126, 132, 150, 151, 154-157
Fitzhugh, Lt. Col. Henry, 98, 101, 104,
    105, 183n #67
Ford, J. F., 60, 142
Fort Delaware, 53-56
Fort Monroe, 5, 29, 30, 31, 86, 119, 132,
    152, 159, 173n #1, 176n #14
Frederick, Maryland, 8, 17, 38, 47
French, E., 120
Fulkerson, Col. Abram, 56

G

Gaillard, Cpl. T. E., 63, 142
Gales, T. L., 59, 141
Ganey, Jacob, 60, 140
Garber, Maj. Asher Waterman, 100,
    183n #74
Gardner, Capt. Richmond N., 66, 69,
    120, 121, 134, 140
Garnett, Dr. Alexander Yelverton
    Payton, 88, 89, 176n #15, 177n #18
Garnett, Edgar Malcolm, 88, 176n #15,
    177n #18
Garnett, Emily Dennis Hayward, 88,
    89, 91, 176n #15, 182n #61
Garnett, Brig. Gen. Robert Seldon, 111-
    113, 114, 177n #18
Gaskins, Sgt. William H., 57, 143
Gaulding, John R., 63, 143
Gibson, Lt. Col. John H., 124, 186n #32
Gill, William, 88, 175n #12
Gilmore, Elisa, 105, 184n #92
Givens, Lt. Thomas Wilkes, 72, 121, 140
Glasgow, Martha McNutt, 96, 182n #57
Glasgow, Nancy, 180n #35
Goldsborough, Ann Hayward, 13, 26, 40,
    88
Goldsborough, Dr. Charles Edward,
    124, 125, 131, 186n #34, #39
Goldsborough, Gertrude, 124, 129
Goldsborough, Martin, 13, 37, 40, 91,
    101, 151

Goldsborough, Mona, 13, 26, 129, 147-
    153, 158-159, 171n #2
Goldsborough, Maj. William Worthington,
    81, 124, 125, 131, 141, 186n #33, #39
Gomer, Capt. Azra P., 81, 143
Gracie, Brig. Gen. Archibald, 139, 172n
    #28, 188n #8
Gracie, Mrs. Gen., 139, 172n #28
Grant, Alexander D., 63, 142
Graves, Capt. G. A., 74, 141
Green Hill Cemetery, 40, 42
Greenmount Cemetery, 6, 46, 145, 146
Griffith, John J., 66, 140
Griffith, Josiah H., 59, 141
Griswold, Maj. Elias, 88, 176n #15

H

Hall, Lt. John W., 120, 121
Haltiwanger, J. L., 61, 142
Haltiwanger, Sgt. J. S., 61, 142
Hamilton, Jno. G., 105, 184n #95
Hamilton, Sgt. John H., 58, 142
Hancock, John, 60, 141
Hanson, Joseph, 63, 142
Harman, Capt. Lewis, 102, 184n #86
Harman, Sgt. N. F., 52
Harper, Lt. R. Thomas, 74, 142
Hawkins, Col. W. S., 134, 187n #6
Hayes, Surg. J. M., 82, 140, 165
Hayward, Maj. [Dr.] Richard, 13, 97,
    176n #15
Herbert, Lt. Col. James R., 79, 124, 131-
    132, 141
Hillhouse, Barton N., 120
Hodges, Lt. Charles W., 88, 177n #15
Hoffman, Dora, 19
Hollingsworth, Robert L. T., 65, 142
Hollyday, Lamar, 80, 88, 141, 175n #14,
    185n #18
Hollyday, Mrs. William, 119
Hollyday, William, 88, 119, 177n #16,
    185n #18
Houston, Capt., 99, 100, 101, 102
Houston, Capt. Andrew Matthew, 33,
    34, 77, 81, 89, 104, 105, 143, 165,
    178n #19
Houston, Capt. David Gardiner, 77, 144,
    178n #19, 181n #42
Houston, Dr. David Gardiner, 91, 177n
    #19, 180n #28

Mohler, Maj. Elisha Grigsby, 93, 94, 180n #37
Mohler, Frances Jane, 93, 104, 105, 106, 180n #37
Mohler, Col. Jacob, 93, 98, 104, 107, 180n #37
Mohler, Magadalene, 93, 180n #37
Mohler, Mary, 93, 96
Montgomery, D. C., 74, 141
Moon, W. H., 53
Moore, Robert W., 65, 141
Mulford, Maj. John Elmer, 87, 97, 174n #5, #8, #9

N

Nicholas, Mrs. Judge, 89
Nobers, Horatio G., 78, 140
Northrope, Gen. Lucius B., 33, 153, 178n #23

O

Obenchain, Capt. Frances G., 93, 96, 168, 180n #39
Owen, Chap. William Burton, 80, 141
Owen, Maj. William M., 88

P

Paine, Lewis [Powell], 145
Parker, Britton, 60, 62, 142
Parker, Cpl. Calvin Lee, 57, 64, 143
Parker, Asst. Surg. Daniel, 82, 140, 165
Patton, Col. Waller Tazewell, 21, 22, 33, 148
Paxton, Sgt. Alexander S., 99, 183n #68
Paxton, Ella, 101, 106
Paxton, Emma, 93, 106, 179n #25, 181n #44, 184n #98
Paxton, Jane Elizabeth, 93, 100, 180n #39
Paxton, Joseph, 101, 168, 183n #83
Paxton, Joseph McClung, 93, 96, 99, 100, 104, 105, 107, 168, 181n#43
Paxton, Mary, 100, 101, 106, 183n #75
Paxton, Thomas Preston, 96, 99, 107, 182n #53
Paxton, William, 96, 105, 106, 180n #39, 182n #55
Peaks of Otter, 101-104, 106, 107, 183n #82, 184n #84, #85, #87, #88
Peeler, Lt. Anderson J., 25, 68, 120, 121, 134, 140

Peeler, William D. C., 65, 142
Pendleton, Brig. Gen. William Nelson, 94, 182n #50
Perkins, Lt. John Day, 79, 126, 140, 160, 162
Pittman, B. F., 59, 142
Plank Farm, 18, 19
Poague, Lt. Col. William Thomas, 98, 183n #66
Point Lookout, 52-53
Pratt, Tom, 88, 175n #14

Q

Quincy, Maj. William H., 91, 180n #30

R

Rankin, Lt. Col. Will S., 79, 142
Reddick, Robert H., 60, 141
Reynolds, Samuel T., 57, 143
Robinson, Lt. James H., 72, 143
Ross, A. A., 57, 142
Ross, Sgt. Maj. William J. F., 73, 120, 121, 122, 141, 185n #22
Rouse, T. B., 59, 142

S

Saunders, Matilda, 19, 188n #2
Scharf, J. Thomas, 171n #2
Schenck, Maj. Gen. Robert E., 9, 10, 11, 12, 108
Schlandt, Lt. J. J., 74, 141
Scott, Mrs. Lt. Gen. Winfield, 139, 172n #28
Seavers, Henry J., 64, 142
Seldon, Mrs., 89, 97
Sharpe, W. G., 65, 141
Shekill, Dr. A. D., 80, 140
Shepherd, Henry, 47
Shine, Thomas W., 74, 140
Smith, John J., 64, 141
Smith, Sgt. W. W., 123, 124, 186n #28
Smith, Maj. Gen. William, 88, 175n #11
Sneed, Thomas J., 75, 78, 122-24, 130, 142
Southall, Asst. Surg. Robert G., 82, 140, 165
Southalls, Mrs. M. T., 88, 89
Sparrow, Thomas A., 59, 142
Spencer, Jervis, 88, 177n #16
Spotswood Hotel, 33, 88, 175n #10, #11
Stagner, Betsy, 42

About the Author

*E*ileen *Conklin* is a former Licensed Battlefield Guide at GNMP who has been researching women in the War Between the States since 1980. She has lectured on women's war service to audiences at battlefields, colleges, museums, and libraries and has addressed historical, military, and women's groups.

Ms. Conklin is the director and co-founder of the Conference on Women and the Civil War which is an annual event that recognizes women's efforts and achievements during the war years. The Conference is nationally known and attended and serves as a forum to share original research.

Her articles have appeared in *Military Images*, *The Gettysburg Magazine*, and *The Journal of Confederate History*. *Women at Gettysburg-1863*, her first book published in 1993, contains the war experiences of forty women who served on that field before, during, and after the battle. The Civil War community's reaction to this research was remarkable. Some of the women included in this volume have since been honored in various ways. Four nurses from the Philadelphia area, Emily Bliss Souder, Annie Bell, Mary Brady, and Mary Lee who were buried in unmarked graves now have headstones. The gravesites of both Isabella Fogg of Maine and Arabella Barlow of New Jersey now have bronze plaques commemorating their war service. In 1995 Euphemia Mary Goldsborough was inducted into the Maryland Hall of Fame.

Exile to Sweet Dixie is based on the research of the Goldsborough collection. It is the story of the life and war service of Euphemia Goldsborough, Confederate nurse and smuggler. Ms. Conklin is currently writing a screenplay based on Goldsborough's experiences.

THOMAS PUBLICATIONS publishes books about the American Colonial era, the Revolutionary War, the Civil War, and other important topics. For a complete list of titles, please write to:

THOMAS PUBLICATIONS
P.O. Box 3031
Gettysburg, PA 17325

Or see our on-line catalog at:
http://civilwarreader.com/thomas